***Textures* by Hernan Vera**

The Audience as Actor and Character

The Modern Theater of Beckett, Brecht, Genet, Ionesco, Pinter, Stoppard, and Williams

SIDNEY HOMAN

Lewisburg
Bucknell University Press
London and Toronto: Associated University Presses

Associated University Presses
440 Forsgate Drive
Cranbury, NJ 08512

Associated University Presses
25 Sicilian Avenue
London WC1A 2QH, England

Associated University Presses
P.O. Box 488, Port Credit
Mississauga, Ontario
Canada L5G 4M2

The paper used in this publication meets the requirements of the American National Standard for Permanence of Paper for Printed Library Materials Z39.48-1984.

Library of Congress Cataloging-in-Publication Data

Homan, Sidney, 1938–
The audience as actor and character.

Bibliography: p.
Includes index.
1. Drama—20th century—History and criticism. 2. Theater audiences in literature. 3. Theater audiences. I. Title.
PN1861.H59 1989 809.2′04 87-46440
ISBN 0-8387-5153-9 (alk. paper)

PRINTED IN THE UNITED STATES OF AMERICA

For John Cech, David Chalmers, John Gebhardt, and Hernan Vera—who, for me, embrace and define that inestimable word friend.

And, as always, for Norma, whom I love this side of idolatry and—I can't help it!—beyond.

Also by Sidney Homan

When the Theater Turns to Itself: The Aesthetic Metaphor in Shakespeare (1981)

Beckett's Theaters: Interpretations for Performance (1984)

Shakespeare's Theater of Presence: Language, Spectacle, and the Audience (1986)

Edited by Sidney Homan

A Midsummer Night's Dream. Blackfriars Shakespeare Series (1970)

Shakespeare's "More Than Words Can Witness": Essays on Visual and Nonverbal Enactment in the Plays (1980)

Shakespeare and the Triple Play: From Study to Stage to Classroom (1988)

Contents

Preface

1

Until I started thinking seriously about the concept of an audience, or of the spectator's "role" during a performance, I, an actor of modest means since the age of five, had always been uneasy in my seat, wishing I were onstage rather than in the house. Is the audience little more than a passive, appreciative—one hopes—receptor of the actor's energy, of his impersonation? Is it the actor—and the playwright behind him—who is alone deserving of the adjective "creative"?

Much recent critical theory, of course, would see such questions as reductive. In learning to deconstruct a work, readers in effect become collaborators with the writer, filling in the "white spaces" of the text, or expanding that text into the larger context of our culture, and thereby continuing a creative process initiated by the author. My colleague (and the "father" of reader-response theory) Norman Holland argues—and rightly, I believe—that the reader or audience is a central component in the work, that instead of ascribing, for example, human status to the end of *King Lear* by saying that its words "move me," we should, properly, focus on ourselves as both the stimulus and recipient of such an effect: "I feel such and such about the play's closing tableau," or "Here is how I, given my background, bring the text to life in the theater of my own mind."

When the Hollywood "star" thanks "all those little people, my fans" at the awards banquet, the remark, while condescending, holds a truth, for actors know just how dependent they are upon spectators to ratify a performance; a formality, the curtain-call bow is also a sign of appreciation. In the People's Republic of China actors and audience applaud each other. "How's the house tonight?," the actor asks the theater's manager, and the question seeks something more than the number of people in attendance. Playing before a matinee crowd is a different experience, *produces* a different experience, for actor *and* for audience, than playing later that evening. The cliché that no two performances are ever the same refers, in part, to the importance of the audience. If scholars sometimes tend not to think much about the audience, directors think continually about the play's effect on the spectator. When the play moves from the rehearsal room to the main stage, usually a week or so before opening night, directors typically wander among the seats, viewing the rehearsal from various angles, to assess the "look" of the production and, no less, its potential "feel" from the position of the audience. Performance criticism acknowledges the simple fact that plays constitute a transaction between actors and audience.

In this study I am concerned, then, with the concept of *audience*—in three senses. First is the "role" of the offstage audience, the way a play is calculated to invoke, even to manipulate audience response, how our "presence" is a factor in performance, whether it takes the form of actors playing directly to the audience, of bringing the audience onstage (as was the style in the 1960s), or of the playwright's designing an open ending that invites the spectator to interpret or assess a dramatic world that deliberately avoids closure. In his classic study, *Shakespearean Comedy,* Bertrand Evans demonstrates convincingly, I believe, how during a given scene the disparity between the audience's knowledge of the facts and the (usually) lesser knowledge of the characters is a central principle of Shakespeare's art. In Beckett's "dramaticule" *Come and Go,* because the play's most important line is whispered by one of the characters to another, the audience must fill in the vacuum by imagining what forces the character, hearing the whispered line, to respond *"Appalled"* (I cite here Beckett's stage direction).

The second sense of the term, the playwright's use of onstage audiences, reveals the play's metadramatic dimension—the material or ground of the stage's fictive world is here self-reflexive. Except in a soliloquy, one actor is in a speaking or an acting position, the other in a listening or an audiencelike position. But the issue of audience is no less symbolic than practical. During *Hamlet*'s "The Murder of Gonzago," after we watch Hamlet watch Claudius watch the dumb show, the same play with dialogue is aborted when Claudius, now a reluctant and self-incriminating spectator, bolts from his seat. In Beckett's *Krapp's Last Tape* the play's sole character, age sixty, plays audience to his voice on the tape recorder, where at age thirty-nine he comments on his life a decade earlier. Of the play's three audiences, we form only one.

This use of the onstage audience, whether literal or symbolic, is inseparable from the existentialist's notion that our human distinction and, no less, the cause of our anguish is that we alone, of all the earth's creatures, can play audience to our own actor. Our self-consciousness, that ability to extrapolate general principles from our witness of our selves, elevates human actions above being merely random or instinctive, even as this metacritical stance, if carried to extreme, would sacrifice life to thought. Thus, the three senses of this term *audience* embrace the practical (a play is designed for an audience to see, hear, and respond to), the symbolic (*audience* becomes another image upon which the stage's fictive world is constructed), and the philosophical.

Although the audience thus defined has surely been an issue as long as there has been theater, I focus here on our modern stage by considering a single play each (or in Beckett's case four short recent plays) of seven playwrights: Beckett, Brecht, Genet, Ionesco, Pinter, Stoppard, and Williams. How does each play "work" with its immediate audience? And if each play is a unique text, then the audience it both requires and stimulates should be no less so. To a degree, these seven playwrights constitute a fairly broad spectrum of "modern theater," although I realize that my representative list will not be everybody's. However, my concern here is not to produce a statistical survey but rather a gamut.

2

When in Ionesco's *The Chairs* the recorded sounds of the so-far silent onstage audience, making its exit after the Orator's disastrous performance, duplicate our own as we, too, leave the theater, the spectator realizes that all along he or she was represented onstage by those invisible guests in the set's empty chairs. Our imaginative effort in going along with the conventions of mime parallels the skill of the two actors playing the old couple. I open, therefore, in chapter 1 with *The Chairs* since I believe it celebrates the copresence of actor and audience. Indeed, for me Ionesco surrounds this *modern* play, one concerned with the interdependent roles of actor and audience, with an *old-style* play, the Orator's performance that the Old Man and Old Woman wrongly hope will produce some absolute, some *truth* about existence—a pedagogical theater, in effect, relegating the audience to mere recipient of a sermon. *The Chairs* thus embraces productive and reductive notions of the spectator's role.

That productive role expands in Pinter's *The Birthday Party* (chap. 2) beyond the copresence of actor and audience, obligating us to interpret, however idiosyncratically, the play itself. For if he gives us a plethora of competing facts in his later plays, Pinter offers too few facts in this early work. Like Goldberg and McCann, we, too, *invade* the stage and, in turn, invade Stanley, who has so far avoided seeing into himself. If Ionesco's is a theater of *presence*, then Pinter's is one of *exposure;* in both plays, and with both playwrights, the audience cannot remain passive. In Pinter our interpretive ability *makes* the play, for we may see Goldberg and McCann, those visitors resembling us, either as forces of the outside world who come to save or destroy Stanley or, conversely, as projections of an inner self that Stanley's public posture tries to conceal.

Genet's *The Balcony* and Brecht's *Galileo*—chapters 3 and 4, respectively—constitute a polarity. In *The Balcony* there is a tension between actor and audience, existence and essence, and life and the theater, even as the theater itself grants meaning or essence but at the cost of life—or the "fixity" of death—as Genet defines it. In Irma's "house of illusions," as the French phrase for *brothel* is translated, clients and staff resemble ourselves in our common eagerness to achieve certainty or meaning through the conscious assumption of a role. Yet that role, once assumed, drains us of life, however random or meaningless life may seem. Genet recognizes both sides as validating the other: without criminals, there would be no police; as actors in life we also need to be audience to ourselves. Here the revolutionaries and the establishment need and grow to resemble each other, and as Genet questions the boundaries between off- and onstage, between audience and actor, the synthesis is at once exhilarating and threatening.

A major rewriting of an earlier version, the chapter on Brecht's *Galileo* recounts my own recent experience as a director of that play. Of all the playwrights considered here, Brecht, of course, has spoken most directly about his notion of the audience's role in the "epic" theater and, no less, of the actors' own audiencelike perspective on characters who, as their playwright insisted, should be social, even political, rather than just psychological types. My production of *Galileo* offered, therefore, a chance to enact, indeed to test Brecht's theories, to see for myself how much his concept of an audience differs from the less consciously stated theories of the other playwrights considered here, and to what degree he abides by—perhaps even against his will—more *conventional,* timeless laws of the theater. Written in a style more personal (at times anecdotal) than that of the other chapters, chapter 4 traces my own initial difficulty with Brecht, the circumstances that led to my involvment with *Galileo,* and, at length, the period in which I hammered out my director's concept and took the play through rehearsals. Even after opening night, aided by my actors and our audiences, I found myself adjusting, trying to refine a production in which the actors performed on three islandlike stages surrounded by an oceanlike audience, in a theater where there was no "offstage." When an actor finished a particular scene, he or she took a seat with fellow spectators. If the synthesis in Genet between actor and audience is a tense, uneasy one, in Brecht it is a planned, inevitable, "natural" and—as I observed in my own production—"physical."

Stoppard's *Rosencrantz and Guildenstern Are Dead* (chap. 5) and Williams's *A Streetcar Named Desire* (chap. 6) are paired for a different reason. The messengers from Shakespeare's *Hamlet* try to remain uninvolved spectators in Stoppard's first act, only to be drawn into the play (act 2), and then to become incipient playwrights in act 3 when they discover first Hamlet's name and later their own on the letter they carry to England. Stoppard's play on the "trinity" of audience, actor, and author parallels the three essential components of every production. As an audience to *Hamlet,* Stoppard reacts to that play by authoring his own, in a sense moving from spectator to participant—"to observe is to participate," as his own Player tells the pair.

My interest in *A Streetcar Named Desire* lies not so much in its sociological or psychological dimensions as in the tremendous burden that Williams places on his audience to weigh the competing claims of Stanley and Blanche: her imaginative but dead world against his physical but alternately shallow and violent one. Incompatible with each other, rivals embodying the conflict of mind and body, not to mention gender, they, or the actors behind them, appeal, or *play,* to us. As she exits on the arm of her gentleman caller, that romantically transformed Doctor, Blanche's line, "Whoever you are—I have always depended on the kindness of strangers," seems directed not just to her escort but to us, her offstage witnesses. In Stoppard it is Rosencrantz and Guildenstern; in Williams it is we who are drawn into the play.

I turn in chapter 7 to four of Beckett's plays that have recently appeared, here commenting on an artist who, perhaps more than any other, is conscious of and involves his audience, indeed, makes the spectator a character in his plays. In Beckett's *Nacht und Träume* the dreamer, A, is audience to his dreamt self, B, while in *Catastrophe* a tyrannical director, D, plots how to manipulate the audience's response to his Protagonist, P. In *What Where* V plays audience to himself through the characters Bam, Bem, Bim, and Bom, as he searches for some ratifying purpose in life. The four figures entering the stage from the darkness in the ballet *Quad* manifest our own need to see ourselves onstage, yet also our concomitant fear of such self- and public exposure. Before turning to these four recent plays, I survey Beckett's canon as a way of summarizing and reflecting on the threefold definition of audience informing the previous chapters.

In the Afterword, "'My' Theater and Its Audiences," I play the observer of myself, as audience, actor, and director. After recounting some personal experiences in the house, I discuss my own director's concept of audience with reference to three recent productions of Shakespeare. I end on this personal, anecdotal note to show some of the influences on my thinking. I can only hope that the reader will see my efforts here as a way of keeping myself honest, of seeing myself.

Acknowledgments

I thank these publishers for their kind permission to quote from the following plays: Grove Press, Inc., for Beckett's *Catastrophe, What Where, Quad,* and *Nacht und Träume;* for Genet's *The Balcony;* for Ionesco's *The Chairs;* and for Stoppard's *Rosencrantz and Guildenstern Are Dead;* Judy Daish Associates Ltd., for Pinter's *The Birthday Party* as published by Grove Press; New Directions Publishing Corporation, for Williams's *A Streetcar Named Desire;* and Suhrkamp Verlag, for Brecht's *Galileo* as published in the Charles Laughton translation by Grove Press.

The cast and the crew of the two theaters I serve as stage director, The Hippodrome State Theater and the Acrosstown Repertory Theater, allow this would-be scholar to put into form, into flesh and blood, what he thinks and dreams about in his study. They *teach* me, with patience and understanding, and for this I am deeply grateful.

On a lovely April evening in New Orleans, before an audience of English professors, I had the pleasure of directing my friends, Bob Egan and Dennis Huston, in scenes from Stoppard's *Rosencrantz and Guildenstern Are Dead*. Nor will I forget our unorthodox rehearsal earlier that afternoon in Franklin Park, on the banks of the Mississippi, before an impromptu audience of bemused and, I hope, intrigued tourists. Some of that experience is in chapter 5.

I relied on the technical skill, the good advice, of Don Loftus when I recently made television films of Beckett's five works for that medium. What I say here about *Quad* and *Nacht and Träume* made its way into that project, for which Don was, properly, not an assistant but rather my collaborator.

I first tested these chapters on my colleagues, students, and actors at Jilin University in Changchun City, in the People's Republic of China. I will always remember that thrilling opportunity to "play" before an audience, now dear friends, representing a culture and a theatrical tradition in many ways different, and certainly much older than my own.

Two good friends here supplied skills I lack—and I am in their debt. Hernan Vera did the illustration "Textures" for the book jacket and frontispiece. Wendy Latimer's drawing of the relation between stage and audience for a production of *Galileo* that I directed graces chapter 4.

Once again I record here my unabashed pleasure in working with Mills Edgerton, Director of the Bucknell University Press, Julien Yoseloff, Director of Associated University Presses, and his managing editor, Lauren Lepow. With special thanks to that model copy editor, Leslie Foley.

Such errors as might remain are entirely my own. And in one instance I decided to disobey that model copy editor: since I have tried at all times to make clear just where I am in a particular play, I give page references, but not act or act and scene references for the work in question.

1

Ionesco, *The Chairs:* "Hurry Up! . . . You're Making Our Guests Wait"

Ionesco's own commentary on his work, and on the theater generally, may well equal in volume the combined texts of his plays. In this regard he is surely Beckett's opposite. His *Fragments of a Journal, Notes and Counter Notes,* or *Present/Past/Past/Present* demonstrate how central for him the audience is to the production: both offstage and on- the spectator is at once the source and recipient of the play. The playwright's ideal audience member is a "free man," one "detached from all obsessions."[1] Ionesco casts himself in this same role: he is a self-professed comic writer because of his "detachment" and his powers of "observation."[2] His personal ideal, one duplicated by his audience, is "not to be onstage":

> To see and hear everything from the audience. As if one were outside the universe. If we are onstage, if we are part of the orchestra, we hear only the tumult, we are aware of only the dissonances.[3]

This distinction between the house and the stage explains why Ionesco has little patience with the Brechtian theater, where "actors [can] address the audience" and thereby disturb such Olympian detachment.[4] It is the laugh, that badge of the comic or free man, that disengages the spectator from the character—at least, I think, on the thematic or psychological level.[5]

This audience, ideal or not, is a leitmotif in his plays. There are, most obviously, the onstage audiences—the characters in *The Bald Soprano* in attendance for the Maid's recitation of her fire poem or, in the same play, the parodic recognition scene between the Joneses, where husband and wife alternate as startled audience to each other. In *The Lesson* the Professor, at first modestly, and the Student, at length hysterically, switch roles as audience and performer. The parents are audience to the newlyweds in *Jack, or The Submission,* as are the court attendants to the dying monarch in *Exit the King,* or Madeleine and the Detective to Choubert in *Victims of Duty.*[6] This onstage audience is often satirized, as is the gullible onstage crowd in *The Leader* or, conversely, the indifferent soldiers in *Amedee*. Berrenger's opponent in the final scene of *The Killer* is a sinister, practically mute audience of one, and when Berrenger resurfaces in *Rhinoceros* he is clearly the outsider, the helpless audience to his fellow humans transformed into beasts. At times the audience literally becomes part of the set: in *The New Tenant* living portraits of the Gentleman's ancestors "*observe*" the central character from picture frames upstage, while in *The Future Is In Eggs* the Grandfather is at first an inanimate portrait located upstage of the former newlyweds of *Jack, or The Submission,* before stepping out of the frame to become another live onstage observer.

Our own detachment championed by Ionesco is a central issue in *The Killing Game,* where by a variety of dramatic techniques the playwright so distances us from the onstage tableau of plague deaths that the disease's victims seem rather comic instead. Yet in *Improvisations* Ionesco as a character addresses the audience directly at the end, thereby elevating the spectator to participant. Indeed, such involved audiences, heroic or comic, concerned or cynical, are so pervasive that the playwright only once uses the more conventional device of having an audience onstage watch a play-within-a-play. In a scene in *Hunger and Thirst* Jean attends a performance involving two prisoners. In *Maid to Marry* a boring middle-aged couple anticipates, like an audience, the arrival of the Lady's daughter, and then to underscore the fact that their expectation rather than the character's actual appearance is the issue, the action reveals to both audiences that the Daughter so praised by her mother is actually a man in a gray suit with a bushy black moustache. In *What a Hell of a Mess* Character, essentially mute for most of the performance, portrays a silent audience to a variety of actors delivering self-revealing monologues for his benefit. His pose as an indifferent spectator is challenged only when the people he has spent a lifetime observing come back to haunt him. As Character tries to dismiss the spectacle as a bad joke, Ionesco, violating his usual distinction between onstage and off-, has him turn laughing toward us, as in his closing lines Character and audience merge: "What a joke, my friends . . . the laugh's on us . . . What a hell of a mess."[7]

1

In *The Chairs,* however, such variations on the notion of the theatrical audience are the entire play. Indeed, here those variations suggest a single, although complex phenomenology of "audience." Ionesco's inspiration was, appropriately, the most physical, and hence graphic "prop" associated with the audience. In his conversations with Claude Bonnefoy he reveals that he "first had the image of chairs, then that of a person bringing chairs as fast as possible onto an empty stage," and thus "it was the chairs themselves, and what the chairs meant" that was both the source and the essence of the work, that in fact gave it its title.[8] Occupied by their invisible guests, the onstage chairs ironically reflect those offstage filled with real people.

As Ionesco's detached, comic spectator, we watch the onstage tragedy of the old couple, whose attempt to find meaning in life hangs precariously on the appearance of a hired Orator. Yet we are also imaged in those two characters since the house, properly and figuratively, includes both the stage and that building containing it. Our own imaginative effort in "seeing" the invisible guests occupying those onstage chairs only further cements the play's two audiences into a single, paradoxical entity.[9] Even with the absence of a proscenium, let alone the more intimate thrust stage of Shakespeare's day, the modern theater's customary division between on- and offstage areas is dissolved by the half-circle of *The Chairs*'s set: the audience forms the second horseshoe that, combined with the one onstage, completes a perfect full-circle of involvement. That the onstage half-circle is rendered slightly imperfect by what Ionesco labels doors 9 and 10, facing each other in a hidden recess, creates at best a tenuous distinction between the otherwise perfect curve onstage and its offstage match. In a brilliant article on *The Chairs,* David Mendelson observes that if the stage were turned 180 degrees, we would find it "absorbing the audience."[10] Even the "common" circle we inhabit with the characters is in the center of an island that is in turn bounded by the earth's sphere. Before the first line of dialogue, therefore, the play physically, *graphically* includes us or, rather, expands the locale normally designated as "onstage" to include that normally designated "offstage."

But this same circle of involvement is "closed" in a way that underscores Ionesco's sense of theatrical presence and its significance for us. We see the Old Man, a mirror of ourselves, leaning out the left window, looking beyond the immediate stage set to the water surrounding the island. However, the Old Woman quickly brings him, and us, back to the present stage with "Come my darling, close the window," and then asks him to do just what we ourselves would ask an unsophisticated spectator to do if he were blocking our vision: "Come, come, my darling, come sit down" (p. 113).[11] Outside this dual presence of audiences witnessing a present and anticipated happening, or play, it is dark, without "sunlight"; there one cannot "see the water" (p. 113). If the phrase "hemmed in by the crowd" seems ironic, given that until the Orator's appearance *The Chairs* is a two-character play, it is an accurate description of the play's combined, omnipresent, and inclusive semicircles of audiences.

Thus, we are all Ionesco's generic man, "at once and the same time being spectacle and spectator,"[12] and nowhere is this fact more graphic than at the end where, in the playwright's stage directions, the sounds are both "*of the* [*onstage*] *world,* [*and*] *of us, the audience.*"[13] In Ionesco's more compressed equation, each spectator is, like the playwright himself, both "myself and another self both at once."[14] His goal, and our destination in *The Chairs,* is to "be face to face with myself."[15] Surely no actor onstage is ever ignorant of the spectator offstage; that legendary fourth wall is, more properly, a two-way and imaginary mirror. Although Ionesco abhors having actors stare out as spectators or audience, in *The Chairs* Hamlet's one-way "mirror . . . up to nature" sometimes admits a literal two-way vision and identification. At one moment the old couple almost acknowledges us as they "*advance, downstage, facing the audience* [*but*] *speaking to the invisible Lady, who walks between them*" (SD, p. 123). Just as Hamlet's own "You that look pale, and tremble at this chance, / That are but mutes or audience to this act" (5.2. 334–335) threatens to forge a metadramatic union between us and the characters onstage, here the Old Man, in a tone that is ironic for the invisible onstage audience but less so for the real offstage audience, asks, "Who are all these people, my darling? What are they doing here?" (p. 143).

This acknowledgment of the audience occurs most often when we share with the actors the imaginative task of creating the onstage audience out of the stage's own void, those empty chairs. During one conversation with the Invisible Lady, for example, the old couple appear to us in profile as they converse with their onstage guest and then are seen full-face as they "turn their heads toward the audience," only to return to half-profile when their guest smiles at them (p. 125). At this moment we are aided in imagining that she smiles by a sort of domino theory of reactions: the Invisible Lady "smiles" at them, they acknowledge her smile with actual full-face smiles seen by us, and, once we have been cued into this return to conversation with the guest, they can then return to those initial half-profiles. As the onstage audience swells uncontrollably, this adjustment in the play's level of illusion is figured in the old couple's turning their backs to the audience—that is, moving from being figures in the fictive onstage world, to being intermediary half-profile figures between that world and the house, and, at length, to being a literal extension of ourselves, facing in the same upstage direction. The first row in the house now becomes, technically, the second row, or whatever row follows the number of rows of chairs onstage. Ionesco's marginal comment here is important: as the couple turn their backs to us, "*The chairs, turned toward the dias, . . . form regular rows, each one longer as in the theater*" (p. 139). We thereby have something resembling two trapezoids, one onstage above the other offstage. One can imagine how doubly effective this moment must have been—albeit unintentionally so—at the premier performance when, as Alan Lewis recalls, only "eight rather uncomfortable people" were in attendance.[16] In Ionesco's own revealing trinity, the stage, the invisible onstage audience, and the offstage crowd are one.[17]

Because of this link between actor and audience, every reference to the audience or to the evening's entertainment has a second, unreserved literal meaning.[18] As the Old Woman stops to complain about her rumpled dress, her husband's complaint, "Hurry up! . . . You're making our guests wait" (p. 123), describes our own situation as we also wait for them to usher in the first guest. Seconds before, we have heard the sound of a boat gliding through the water, followed by the Old Man's "Yes, they're coming!" (p. 122). And there is a literal truth in his comforting words to his guests, "You can't all know each other . . . you're seeing each other for the first time" (p. 139), for we all know that feeling of being part of an audience, a single body fronting the stage, acting as one, yet otherwise unfamiliar with the spectators to our own right and left, before and behind us—we are the "lonely crowd," to invoke David Riesman's sociological study of the 1950s. Technically, we are the first guests to appear, arriving even before our hosts; our presence thus contradicts the Old Man when, concerned with his wife's tears, he cautions her: "The guests are sure to come this evening and they mustn't see you this way" (p. 118). There is a similar contradiction that we supply to Hamlet's "Now I am alone" (2.2.449) after the actor impersonating Hecuba makes an exit. When the Old Lady mistakes the sounds of the first guests arriving for that of the Orator, we can supply the corrective: her error is doubled since we have preceded the first invisible onstage arrivals. The Orator, properly, is pushed further back in the sequence, and the play thus literally begins before the Old Man's opening line: we, not the onstage actors, "activate" the evening. Ionesco's equation of himself with every other man, or of the spectator with the spectacle, parallels the line "I am not myself. I am another. I am the one in the other" (p. 145), even as it parodies Breton's surrealistic game "the one in the other"—and surely it may do both.[19] It also conceptualizes the present enactment of the theater, those two live bodies on its stage accompanied by however many live bodies are in attendance offstage.

The only perfectly identical objects offstage and on- are, of course, the chairs: there are real chairs all over the *stage*, as that term now embraces the house as well. It will be the old couple's neurotic investiture of the chairs with a significance beyond this literal and pervasive status, as well as our own parallel investiture, that "allows for" *The Chairs,* that affords the evening its meaning. Ionesco cites this complement of the physical and the imaginative: The play is "the chairs themselves" and "what the chairs mean."[20] Appropriately, the couple "address [their] warmest thanks to the cabinet-makers who have made these chairs," and then to "the master carpenter" (Ionesco himself?) responsible for the ultimate chair, "the armchair," in which the most significant member of the onstage audience, "Your Majesty," is "sinking so softly" (p. 156).

In what is, arguably, the most perceptive commentary on the play Richard Schechner suggests that it is the "projected consciousness" of the old couple that makes the evening significant, that, however deluded by fantasy or their own psychic needs, they manage to fill the chairs with imaginary guests and hence with meaning. In one sense we find them pathetic, rather than tragic victims of their own bad faith; for them—to use Schechner's phrases—"what is not is," while for us "what is, is not." Yet when we connect the tangible chairs with intangible guests, we suspend our disbelief and give in to the onstage convention established by the characters and their playwright; our imagination has harmonized with theirs as we are drawn "relentlessly into the world of the Not." In effect, we have created these guests within ourselves, and when the old couple depart we are left holding the bag. Our anguish is for both this unsought responsibility and the suspicion that our participation, even more than theirs or that of their onstage audience, has been the real issue.[21]

This increasing attention to the seating of the audience, following as it does that opening section given to the Old Man's recitation of his squandered life and the Old Woman's attempts to mother him, is a double ruse. As the doors open and shut "*all together ceaselessly,*" as the old couple glide as if on roller skates in their frenzy to accommodate the evening's guests, as the play is taken over by "*the rhythm*" of bringing in more chairs and as the couple's dialogue changes from a recitation of the past to very present, pressing concerns, we are fooled if we think that these others, rather than ourselves, constitute the real audience, and fooled again if we distinguish offstage audience from onstage performers.[22]

In one sense it is difficult to identify with the plight of the old couple: their narration is incomplete, sporadic, while the tone of Ionesco's "tragic farce" itself complicates our response. Nor can we be sure of the facts we do have: are the couple victims of their own delusions? Do they lie to each other and hence to us as well? Yet their pasts, their failures, actual or imagined, *are* relevant when connected with the play's major concern, the seating of the guests. For what we do observe, or rather overhear, is their interaction with the guests as it has been colored by, is stimulated by, the imaginary link forged between that past and their present, literal task of welcoming an audience onstage. As characters, they create themselves no less than they create an audience to fill the imaginary void before us. Such creation is three-fold: the couple recreate their personalities to justify their presence as they await the Orator; by their craft the two actors justify their presence before us; offstage we silently and inwardly ratify these two creations, one psychological, the other artistic and technical.

Thus redefined as creative acts rather than as psychologically relevant actions, whether reported or witnessed by us, the "events" of *The Chairs*, stretching from the arrival of the Invisible Lady to that of the Emperor, demonstrate the seamless link between an imaginary past—or personality or character—and a present that is, pardoxically, at once a literal and an imaginative collaboration among character, actor, and audience. Hence, conventional greetings to the Invisible Lady and the Colonel lead to the old couple's distraction at what they take as a budding romance between these first two guests. The Old Man's recitation of his military record to distract the Colonel and his confession of a past romance with "La Belle" are followed by the Old Lady's grotesque flirtation with the photo-engraver whom she at first confuses with a physician. A retreat to trivial conversation, such as the recipe for "crepes de Chine," leads to revelations of mistreating both their child and the Old Man's mother. A second distraction, when the audience becomes unruly, coupled with the circuslike atmosphere as the hosts sell programs and refreshments, is juxtaposed with the Old Man's chilling confession of waking to "absolute silence." The pattern here is a complex one of growing intimacy with the guests, a series of intimate self-revelations, and a conflict between the couple's private, tortured selves and the etiquette of being good hosts. Because we are the play's ultimate audience, these intimacies with our onstage surrogates and their confessions, fictions for both actor and audience, are generated by the demands of the evening rather than the principles of *character* or *flashbacks*, as those latter terms are conventionally understood.

We are the "real and visible audience" (p. 160), the heart of the play; the couple exist for *us*, and when they exit they leave us to deal with what they optimistically but wrongly think is the performance's "featured attraction"—the Orator. In point of fact, we have no imaginative connection with him, nor could we: if the "*invisible people*" are made real by our effort, he himself is real, beyond our imagination, and therefore, in Ionesco's curiously reversed logic, "*unreal*" (p. 154). He is neither the play nor even the play's end, despite the old couple's wishes. While amplified by complementary recorded sounds from backstage, it is our voices, our sounds—the "*bursts of laughter, murmurs, shh's, ironical coughs*" (p. 160)—that we hear in the final moments of *The Chairs*. Ionesco asks that the closing tableau, that empty stage witnessed by the audience offstage, be held as long as theatrically practical: now that we are relieved of the effort spent earlier in peopling the stage with our mirror images, we hear and (can imaginatively) see ourselves. In Ionesco's terms, "This nothing that is on the stage is the crowd."[23] Mendelson observes that here the "real audience has the last word."[24]

Hence, the two audiences determining the structure of *The Chairs* dissolve to a single audience, ourselves. This pattern is echoed in numerous ways, from the most practical business of stage projection to the psychology of character. Most obviously, through the pairing of characters—the Old Man and the Invisible Lady, the Old Woman and the equally invisible Colonel—the imaginary counterpart becomes a projection of one's self. Less obvious is the relation between the physical onstage world and that invisible "world" admitting the imaginary presence of guests, or the co-presence in the Old Man and Old Woman of a gregarious, even appealing public and a tormented inner self. Even the two hosts, while each makes a "*complete turn around the stage*," reflect the other's movement (p. 143). The stage lighting itself manifests a similar deliberation, for *The Chairs* begins with half-light, moves in its center to a full, glaring lighting, and returns at the end to that opening half-light.[25] By acknowledging each other, binaries thus conflate to one, their single origin; the structure of the play, like the shape of the set when combined with the semicircle of the house, is circular.

2

Fashioning himself the director of an evening that is to climax with the Orator's enactment of his "message to . . . humanity" (p. 119), the Old Man is unaware of his status as a character in Ionesco's play. Still, at times he senses that he is not real, is a mere impersonation created to fill a void, as when he speaks of waking in the midst of an "absolute silence" so pervasive that it seems "the perfect circle," with "nothing lacking" (p. 145). Ionesco has a parallel comment in *Fragments of a Journal:* "Not to be, that there should be no being, is impossible and absurd; to be is equally absurd, though 'possible'. . . . Why is there what there is, why does what is there appear as it does, why isn't there something different, why are things as they are? Everything is there, all the time, and it's exhausting."[26] To rework Schechner's contrastive phrases cited earlier, "what is"—that is, what is real and therefore the "issue" of the play—is the audience, invisible onstage and visible but silent offstage. Theatrical presence thus embraces what is happening and is made to happen when the audience confronts the two actors who, for the bulk of the evening, alone constitute the play's official "cast." The present, not the past, and most surely not the future, here equals reality, and, by this equation, we are the presence of the play.[27] If *audience* implies an offstage, coequal (but not singular) presence in the other plays to be discussed, or thereby something more symbolic, such "extraneous" considerations are absent in *The Chairs*. The play is about how to fill up a room, both literally and imaginatively. The Old Man's "error" in looking out the window at the start, that is, in averting his eyes from the present stage set, is corrected when he later cries out, "We have to make do with what we have." I would observe that he refers here specifically to the chairs. (p. 138).

In numerous ways *The Chairs* eschews the past in the name of this presence. We never hear "what happened to Francois I," and all that predates the play is relegated to "history" or "shadows" (p. 113). The Old Man's "memory" fades (pp. 114–115) as the play itself moves from an attempt to understand the past to their present task of welcoming guests. That past actually threatens this theatrical presence, often in the form of the Old Man's regression to a child that in turn forces the Old Lady to play his mother (pp. 117–118).[28] When he imagines the Emperor arriving (that is, the successful figure he has most wanted to be), inevitably the Old Woman bursts out with "I love you, I'm your little mother" (p. 150).

Although he disdains symbolism in the conventional sense, as an instance where the artist does little more than borrow a preexisting equation (beauty is a flower, for example), Ionesco does allow for one old-style symbol, and it is fitting that water is equated with this discredited past. In *Fragments of a Journal* Ionesco notes that for him water "appears . . . as dirty, as an image of anguish. Water engulfs one, or at any rate soils one (to soil is to threaten with death)."[29] Appropriately, the room, the present stage set, is on an island surrounded by stagnant water, and the Old Lady worries that, by leaning out the window, her husband might fall in. But when the boats bear the audience over that same water, they glide effortlessly, making "blots in the sunlight" (p. 113). In *A Stroll in the Air* Berrenger, the artist, floats above the stage, while his audience on the ground struggles to comprehend his vision. The further the Old Man delves into the past with his "remarkable memory," the "deeper [he] sinks" (p. 114), forcing his wife to conclude that now "all that's gone down the drain, alas . . . down the old black drain" (p. 116). Her husband also speaks of having both "spoiled" and "spilled" his career, before turning to his wife with that regressive "Where are you, Mamma, Mamma" (p. 117). Their past is at one with an old-style theater against which Ionesco rebels. The Old Woman longs to hear "the story," an event prior to the present, or what I have called in *Beckett's Theaters* an earlier, discredited "story theater," that tale told by those old-fashioned playwrights who still saw existence as a logical and chronological entity.[30] It is significant that the tale, told fitfully here, begins with its characters "soaked through" and trying desperately to make their way "in the rain" to the "gate of the garden" (pp. 115–116). That account then dissolves, or sinks, into a second one. Transformed from characters in its predecessor to the present onstage audience, the couple now reads the account of the "pot-bellied idiot" as "idiotic," for in laughing at the actor lying with his belly on the ground, they themselves laugh "like idiots."

The past and its symbol water form a trinity with darkness and, as one, point to all that is rejected in Ionesco's theater of presence. Outside the single stage set it is "dark already" (p. 113); conversely, as *The Chairs* abandons its past, Ionesco's stage direction requires that "*the light grow stronger . . . and stronger as the invisible guests continue to arrive*" (p. 132). Again, the play begins and ends for the couple in half-light: as we remain in our seats during the final moments we see that "*the main door is wide open onto darkness,*" even as for us the house lights rise (p. 160). At the center of the play, when the stage lights are brightest, the Old Man indeed does not "have a mamma anymore" (p. 118); he later reveals that he "let [his] mother die all alone in a ditch" (p. 135). And the boy in the Old Woman's story, the fictive surrogate for the Old Man trying to retreat from the present, rejects his mother, despite her denial that she and her husband have killed birds (pp. 134–135). This loss of the past, symbolized by both water and darkness, is terrifying, a displacement, and the issue thus evolves onstage and off-: can we replace the discredited past, all that might have been, with what is? Can we "make do" with what we have?—some chairs and a quantity of imaginative effort?

This audience of presence, then, is an imaginative force in the play, one resolutely opposed to the past, a comic element (we will recall here Ionesco's own connection between comedy and the spectator) coexisting with that tragedy of wasted lives preceding the play. When their guard is down, or when they are simply distracted by the process of seating their guests, the old couple sense this same force, indeed, contribute to it by involving us in projecting guests onstage. "Let's amuse ourselves by making believe, the way you did the other evening" (p. 114), the Old Woman advises, and perhaps the most literal reference in "the other evening" is to last-night's performance of *The Chairs*. At one point the Old Man, parodying the technique of a Method School actor, imitates "the month of February," although when he does he only manages to impersonate Stan Laurel scratching his head (pp. 114–115). When the Old Woman gives herself to this force, however fitfully, she becomes alive, younger, although grotesquely so. The "*business*" of ushering in guests, of imagining them, transforms her into a physically robust, sexual creature, as she "*shows her thick red stocking, raises her many petticoats, revealing an underskirt full of holes, exposes her old breasts, and then, her hands on her hips, and throwing her head back, makes little erotic cries and projects her pelvis, with her legs spread apart*," like a "*prostitute*." The stage direction stresses that this character is "*entirely different from her manner heretofore*" (p. 132). Still, even this "inner life" ceases abruptly, as the couple fall back to confusing the Orator's coming with the main purpose of the evening.[31]

This imaginative presence is the goal of the audience's ratification and subsequent interpretations: it is what we make of it, how we read this present life theatrically enacted that is the issue. Ionesco announces in his *Notes* that he "solicits interpretations,"[32] and more than one critic has observed that the present play is open-ended, thereby encouraging such interpretation, valuing, in Robert Champigny's terms, social gesture over designated context.[33] In contrast, the Orator's own interpretation, the "message (p. 119) by which the couple hopes he will explain life's meaning, is dead, and horribly unimaginative, indeed, so garbled and inarticulate that we become fooled in trying to make sense of his oral and then—if the blackboard is used—written gibberish.[34]

That "old story" theater, the theater of message prefigured in the Orator and his anticipated role, cannot share the same stage with this presence wherein the audience becomes not only the receptor but also the fashioner of the stage world. Similarly, Beckett's *Waiting for Godot* announces that presence, waiting, (the more accurate translation of the original French title is *While Waiting for Godot*) is all we have. *The Chairs* at once celebrates such imaginative presence even as it recognizes that the force sustaining it is based on nothing, illusion, a void terrifying to those who prefer the conventional theater—act 1 in Mr.

Whimple's study in the morning; act 2, the study later that night where the "problem" of the play is enacted; act 3, the next morning, the garden where all is resolved. In hiring the Orator, the old couple thus work against the very middle section of *The Chairs*.

Ionesco's theater is a risky business. Solitary in the sense that it exists only to be undone and then risks being done again at the next performance,[35] and based on what is not, it relies on the imagination to inform—although only in a temporary sense—that blank sheet, on a stage empty of actual guests. In an art form offering only the illusion of real life, its mirror, an imitation, this theater always threatens to disturb its delicate balance and spill over into the void, a nothingness so deep that no imaginative effort can revive or refashion it. And there are moments in the play when this void, this unimaginative nothingness, seems to usurp the stage and, as a consequence, our participation as audience. I think here of the "*inaudible conversations*" that displease the old couple, a silent stage dialogue that would exclude us, or of the stage direction, or rather anti-stage-direction, "*Some embarrassing things take place, invisibly*" (p. 128). At one point the old couple sit on either side of the invisible Belle and the Photographer, with "*four empty chairs between them,*" and there follows what Ionesco's stage direction calls "*a long mute scene,*" punctuated at intervals with " 'no,' 'yes,' " that is with dialogue meaningless to us because we lack sufficient context (p. 134). The Old Man voices our concern when such a void or absence threatens to deny our participation in the evening: "Sometimes I awaken in the midst of absolute silence. It's a perfect circle. . . . But one must be careful, all the same. Its shape might disappear. There are holes through which it can escape" (p. 145). We may recall a similar and, I think, illustrative void in Pirandello's *Six Characters in Search of an Author* when members of the family insist that to be "real" a conversation whispered between two of its members must not be heard by the audience; or, if spoken by the actors, they demand that it be spoken so quietly that it falls outside a normal hearing range. However foolish a figure he may cut elsewhere in the play, Pirandello's Director insists that if the audience is to comprehend the tragedy, nothing onstage can go thus unheard; characters onstage may well not hear dialogue—as in the Elizabethan aside—but the audience must be privy to every word. Wordlessness is thus foreign to a medium that always exists simultaneously as a visual and a verbal entity. In Beckett's *Come and Go,* when the most important line goes unheard by us as one character whispers something of importance to her friend, the playwright still offers us a sufficient biographical context so that we can imagine the nature of that unheard line, if not its specific contents.

3

As the past gives way to the present, and as the *meaning* of *The Chairs*—a word that in any other context Ionesco abhors—is at once confined to and intensified by the presence imaginatively sustained by the audience, the distinction between actor and audience, performer and witness to that performance, loses its relevance. Simply, the audience becomes a simultaneous performer.[36] The invisible characters themselves, the Lady and the Colonel, are now given dialogue, although—again—unheard by us. Far from being indifferent spectators, both are drawn into the tortured lives of their hosts. With every member of the audience becoming an actor, it is little wonder that, given this multiplier of two, the stage soon overflows with people, in something of a quantum leap. In their new combined roles, the old couple's unity now parallels our own as the otherwise invisible guests take over the stage. Figuratively and literally there are "not enough chairs" (p. 139).

The Orator, in contrast, runs counter to such mergings: he is solely a performer, a sole performer, and, as we know, one who fails with his audience. In the final third of the play his appearance breaks the pattern of this middle section that earlier had broken the couple's futile attempt to relive the past, characterizing the play's opening. Nothing but a *spectacle*, in the most pejorative sense of that word, stripped of the complementary role of spectator, the Orator is an absurd figure, from that old story theater.[37] He parodies the conventional positive picture of the actor—an "*automaton*" (p. 155), signing autographs "*automatically*" (p. 155). When he arrives he violates the play's growing sense of a single energized audience; the Old Man "*freezes*" or, alternatively, "*lifts his eyes to heaven*" (p. 155), as if playing to some cosmic onlooker.

The Old Man's failure here does not repeat those of his past, those events prior to, and therefore irrelevant to, the present stage experience. Past failure is merely the impetus for the old couple to arrange this evening. Rather, the Old Man fails in this present; by inviting the Orator, he misconstrues his own role as audience. By believing that the theatrical experience is one-way, with the energy flowing from actor to audience, without reciprocity, the Old Man thereby asks the impossible in wanting the Orator to "speak in [his] name" (p. 153). The guest's theater is, correspondingly, a political one, a "message" (p. 119), an occasion where a spokesperson can be hired to deliver an exclusive interpretation, indeed, a "scientific lecture" (p. 138). Such theater reduces the audience to a mere recipient, an inferior. A precursor of the Orator, the Emperor, in the Old Man's own words, has "deigned to come" onto the stage, now seen as a "miserable home" (p. 152), and when the Old Man vows "to gaze" (p. 152) upon the ruler, we will perhaps think of the parody of such figures in Ionesco's *The Leader.* In a daring strategy the playwright thereby inserts the "enemy" or "the other" in the midst of *The Chairs* to create a countertheater violating his own theater of presence, one where the actor as God speaks of a "perfect" system (p. 146),[38] providing with "absolute certainty . . . one truth for all" (p. 147).

Bottom's wretched production of *Pyramus and Thisby* may parody Shakespeare's finer achievement in *A Midsummer Night's Dream,* but its tragedy, while rendered absurd or comic by the actors, is not without relevance to what the larger play promises to be, a tragic *Romeo and Juliet,* before the lovers escape to the forest.[39] But Ionesco does one better: his anti-play opposes everything the larger play has established or—to be more charitable—defines by its own bad example that larger play or presence. Such presence is even challenged physically when the Orator mounts the dias (p. 143) as a messiah who, in the old couple's optimistic prediction, will allow his host to save "his own soul by saving the world!" (p. 146). Once the Orator is onstage, the attending figures and the concept of audience itself degenerates; the Old Lady begins selling "*invisible programs*" along with "eskimo pies, caramels . . . fruit drops" (pp. 142–143). We are surely in Ionesco's despised boulevard theater.

Actually, the Old Man not only invites but creates this character, even anticipating the debacle once the Orator "speaks." For his own introduction (pp. 157–158) is a savage, although unintentional parody of what we would call the warm-up act in vaudeville. He first denigrates his own person and that of his wife, then gestures melodramatically toward the Orator who "*does not perceive it,*" distracted as he is with signing autographs. The Old Man, predictably, wanders from his own prepared text with lines like "but with such leftovers one can still make a very good soup," threatens to launch into another review of his own life and thereby to reintroduce the now discredited opening third of *The Chairs,* and at length falls back on a militaristic metaphor that, given the playwright's background, echoes the jingoism of history's own warmongers: "we have fought the good fight, nothing remains for us but to withdraw . . . immediately, in order to make the supreme sacrifice," and so on.[40] It is revealing that once he concludes this formal introduction, the Old Man observes that "at this supreme moment, the crowd pitilessly separates" him from his wife (p. 158). I also note that the water symbolism, associated earlier with the past and death, now reenters the dialogue: the couple joyously anticipate rotting together "in an aquatic solitude," a parody, surely, of Ionesco's own notion that the theater, at its best, unites us in our solitude.[41]

As opposed to our own exit from *The Chairs*, the old couple offer a grisly parody of a theatrical exit when they throw themselves out the window to their deaths. At the play's opening, that window had been singled out by the Old Woman as leading to death in the "stagnant water" below. Their final "line" is that of "*the sea-green noises of bodies falling into the water*" (p. 159).

4

I have suggested that, structurally, *The Chairs* has three parts: the futile attempt to account for the past, the imaginative middle section where "audience" literally and conceptually assumes the stage, and the anti-theater ushered in by the Orator. If this three-part division is useful, then we might think of the Orator's "speech" ending the play as something of a musical coda. It admits, I believe, both a negative and a positive reading, and I here resurrect Ionesco's own invitation: "I solicit interpretations."[42]

In one sense that final moment exposes a theater turning against itself. Already an actor working *against* audience, the Orator, once he gets to the dias and "*decides to speak,*" turns out to be a deaf mute capable of little beyond the "*gutteral sounds of a mute*" (p. 159). If the blackboard is used in production, his incapacity is extended to the written word itself, as the cryptic but still recognizable "ANGELFOOD" quickly degenerates to random letters parading as words—"NNAA NNN NWNWNW V." Even those words or nonwords are erased as, "*not satisfied*" (p. 160), the Orator tries to make an exit by first writing "Adieu," although the upside down "V" before that word distorts its would-be meaning. He then adds to the confusion by supplanting the "A" itself, before changing to two upside down "Vs" surrounding an inexplicable "P." Failing with his audience, the Orator desperately tries to place the blame on us, rather than himself, as he "*bows petulantly, brusquely*" (p. 160) before making an exit straight out of that old-style theater ("*bows ceremoniously,*" and to the Emperor at that). As a performance his is clearly a disaster, and while the Orator is at once "responsible" for what he does and yet a victim of his own physical limitations, he also performs before an onstage audience already ruined by the old couple, both by the tone the Old Man set in his introduction and, more generally, by the couple's own notion of the theater's function.

But the same Orator is, unawares, only a warmup act himself to the ultimate "scene"; the final moments of *The Chairs* concern not him but the stage itself. Those chairs now empty even of their invisible guests become a void that we must then fill, both with an imaginative effort, required from the opening moment, and, no less, by our own exit from the theater. Our participation becomes manifest, *literal*, as our exit sounds are duplicated by, and in turn duplicate, the sounds now coming from the stage; the audience literally ends the production. We may have questioned, even resisted participating in the evening, trying to distance ourselves from a play so unconventional that it assaults the understandable yet questionable demand that the theater be realistic, if by "realistic" we mean duplicating an attending world unrelated to theatrical presence. Nor has *The Chairs* avoided displaying such a notion of art's purpose; consider the examples of such realism introduced earlier in the guise of painters, photo-engravers, cameramen, and newspaper reporters. Still, as I have noted in my own experience with the play, when confronted by the onstage reproduction of their own offstage movements, the audience is *forced* to participate; they rise from their chairs, put on coats, gather belongings, and make their way up the aisles and out of the theater. One woman sitting beside me during a university production remarked: "I suddenly feel that I've been taken in, or maybe just taken!"[43]

An audience of critics and scholars has also spoken to the issue of how we can read this ending, or double ending, if we combine the Orator's exit with our own. The play, not to mention its playwright, has had its detractors, those who find Ionesco charming but shallow, a threat to what they see as the positive social obligations of the theater.[44] Some of these responses tend to stop with the Orator's exit, and there is no denying that his appearance is the most shocking event in *The Chairs*. But again, as Ionesco goes to great pains to remind us, his exit does not end the play. In letters and notes to the director of the premier performance of *The Chairs*, the playwright asks that the ending "be very long" so that the audience, otherwise "tempted into giving the easiest explanation of the play, the wrong one," will have time to reflect, to experience the empty stage. The real issue, for Ionesco, is not the suffering of the Old Man and Old Woman: "This may perhaps be true up to a point, but it has absolutely no importance," for "the interest lies elsewhere." That "elsewhere" is surely the audience, a body "quite independent of the old couple's madness." After the Orator's exit, the "tightly-packed crowd of non-existent beings should acquire an entirely objective existence of their own." By our witness to the empty stage, by our imaginative effort now at one and alone with the playwright's, suddenly "the chairs, the scenery, the void" will "inexplicably come to life." This is the "effect beyond reason, true in its improbability, that we are looking forward to and that we must obtain."[45]

Various critics, in individual ways, have echoed Ionesco's instructions. Arguing that the play values gesture over designated meaning (or what the Old Man seeks and the Orator fails to deliver), Robert Champigny sees *The Chairs* as affirmative communication, since the Old Man's "socioreligious project, which would turn us into fictional beings, is exposed by the play's theatrical presence."[46] In a parallel argument, J. S. Doubrovsky suggests that in devaluing language, the play actually pushes the otherwise absurd state of a languageless world so far that tragedy turns to farce, and tears to laughter.[47] Marian Toplin rephrases Ionesco's own claim that he is "inventing a new language" that everyone "speaks . . . already"[48] as his attempt through language to create a new reality to replace a world otherwise characterized by loss and expulsion from paradise.[49] For Rosette Lamont, it is the playwright, not the Orator, who communicates, and successfully so: Ionesco is "another human" who "reaches out to us, and shows us that he too is afraid, that he too is horrified, disgusted," and we, his audience, are thus "filled with the knowledge of our humanity, and thus of our freedom."[50]

The irony, then, is that the Orator's failure is actually a success, a failure that by its own sacrifice binds us together, for the old couple's hope that a god, an actor, or a playwright could define for them the significance of life only exposes our own longing for certitude, for an absolute. In Richard Schechner's words, "Our acceptance of their projection is proof of their ability to communicate with us."[51] We understand the old couple, even the Orator, through our willingness to "entertain" the play and then, further, through our human sympathy expressed at their failure. Still, in entertaining Ionesco's larger play, in remaining to the end, after all three visible onstage characters have exited, we communicate with ourselves, the "real and visible audience," leaving "with this ending firmly impressed on [our] minds." Then, and only then, can the curtain fall "*very slowly*" (p. 160), because we have taken the play into our own hearts, that stage where each of us enacts a solitary self and to *that* enactment plays audience.

2

Pinter, *The Birthday Party:* "Until a Few Minutes Ago, Ladies and Gentlemen, I, Like All of You, Was Asking the Same Question"

Nothing is hidden from the audience in Ionesco as we collaborate with the old couple in filling the stage's physical vacuum. In the final moments of *The Chairs* the stage literally expands to include us as the noises of the actual audience leaving the theater duplicate recorded sounds from backstage. Pinter, in contrast, hides much, as does Stanley, when he attempts to evade detection by Goldberg and McCann. This situation generates a very different role for the audience. This "ungenerous" playwright, as he has been labeled,[1] inevitably frustrates audiences who assume that their position should be one of omniscience in contrast to that of the characters,[2] especially with a situation that, at least in the play's opening moments, seems familiar, familial, even to the level of cliché.[3] John Russell Taylor also observes that the playwright's apparent reluctance to take the audience into his confidence achieves a symbolic status in his canon: we receive too few facts in early plays like *The Birthday Party* and *The Homecoming*, and too many in later plays such as *Old Times*.[4] I think the popular notion that beneath every line of Pinter's ordinary, seemingly *natural* dialogue lurks something sinister is reductive, if it assumes that only the erotic or exotic provides material for horror or for tragedy. More properly, that mysterious quality in the playwright is, I believe, at one with the uneasiness the audience experiences when an otherwise familiar situation is incomplete, missing an ingredient that would normally allow us to dismiss it out of hand. When our role as audience, thus made difficult, is shared onstage by characters no less intent on plucking out the heart of a mystery that remains incomplete, susceptible to interpretation, or is a "matter of perspective" in the best sense of that otherwise overused phrase—then *audience* itself becomes a component, perhaps *the* component in the play. To distort Robert Frost's cryptic poem: in Pinter we dance round a circle and suppose, / Vainly imagining there is a mystery in the center that knows.

1

If we are confronted in *The Birthday Party* with a single, unchanging set, that "*living room of a house in a seaside town,*" with two upstage exits and an upstage-center exit to a kitchen, only a small part of which can be glimpsed through the hatch (p. 9), we must also imagine just offstage an extension of the stage world. Meg speaks of "the front" where she wishes Stanley would take her for a walk, even asking Petey to urge him to accompany her there (p. 11). Beyond that walk, we learn much later, is the shopping district to which Petey himself suggests Meg go to "clear" her head (p. 69).

Stanley, in contrast, clings to the visible set. Lulu observes that the room is "stuffy," and, failing to get Stanley to go outside, asks that he at least open the back door. When the living room's foul smell is linked with himself, Stanley—revealingly—lies about two related issues: he claims to have disinfected the room with "Dettol this morning" and to have scrubbed himself by swimming "in the sea at half past six" (p. 26). We have been present, of course, since the start, during that conversation between Meg and Petey while Stanley sleeps upstairs, yet his lies, while hardly to be reversed as facts, somehow manage to flesh out the dimensions of a set we cannot see, yet cannot ignore. Although Meg's house is "on the list" (p. 13), it has never served as a tourist place; no boarder, Stanley is practically a member of the family of three. Still, the house will soon be invaded, from the "outside," in the form of this curious, ethnic, vaudeville team of the Jew and the Irishman.

Once that invasion occurs, this notion of an "implied" set radiates through the play. Goldberg enumerates on other seaside places where his Uncle Barney, a "cosmopolitan man," took him: "Brighton, Canvey Island, Rottingdean—Uncle Barney wasn't particular" (p. 29). By the final act this imaginary geography has expanded to the East when Goldberg offers an "Abdullah" to the provincial Petey, who promptly declines one (p. 74). Desperately trying to find out if he has known McCann, Stanley himself establishes a place, his hometown, with a host of specific locations: Maidenhead, Fuller's Teashop, Boots Library, High Street (p. 42). And his own justification for his present situation—if it is to be believed—is that he was hounded by critics at a concert in Lower Edmundton, and then, at his next engagement, was locked out of a deserted hall. His patent lie to Meg that he is "considering a job at the moment" itself invokes a worldwide tour, starting in Berlin and then moving to Constantinople, Zagreb, and Vladivostok (pp. 22–23). In her own version of Stanley's disgrace as a pianist, Meg conflates the two concerts: after the successful concert, she tells Goldberg, Stanley was locked inside the hall, was unable to get out until morning when the caretaker released him, and then came "down here" on a "fast train" to stay, permanently (p. 34). Stanley's room is thus taken over, *changed* by Goldberg and McCann. Likewise, the play's single, unchanging set, itself a parody of the generic set of a domestic comedy, becomes increasingly claustrophobic to Stanley, while what we see as audience—conversely—expands in its symbolism. The details of sets implied offstage, stretching from the beach to the town to Stanley's hometown to the world, grow at a staggering rate.

Trying to avoid, to *lock out* the large world, as if retaliating for being locked out of the concert hall, Stanley is locked into this set expanding before us, just as he was locked *inside* the concert hall in Meg's version of his aborted career. This confined, claustrophobic set, contradicted by our presence and, no less, by our knowledge of the surrounding world, now challenges the little room to which Stanley has retreated. And into that same room come two men, appearing by chance on a beach, then changing into potential but for a time anonymous boarders, who later acquire names, themselves suggestive of the Christian/Judaic axis of the Western world. This Goldberg and McCann in turn become hosts at a birthday party, sexual intimates of Lulu and Meg, and, at length, Stanley's persecutors, or saviors, or both.

Are Goldberg and McCann literal, external forces preying upon Stanley, or are they invoked by him, projections of his unconscious fears and guilt? Is his exclusive world ripe, by definition, for such scenic expansion, or is it Stanley's own psyche that here resists his conscious wish to be sealed in Meg's womblike living room? If the play's single set parodies one type of conventional theater, it no less challenges that theater, and challenges the audience as well to explore its fluid, psychological dimension. Like poetry, the set is at once itself and more. Given a paucity of facts, in a play where Goldberg and McCann—not to mention Stanley—try to conceal themselves from each other as well from us, as audience we are also adrift in conflicting possibilities generated by a set that *seems* solid, three-dimensional, yet refuses to remain so. The critics' quandary, then, in choosing among options for interpretation may be a calculated factor induced by Pinter rather than an interpretive dilemma, or sign of the playwright's own indeterminancy or "coyness."[5]

In a way, *we* are Goldberg and McCann, coming to the theater's "little room," as Bert States calls it,[6] at once abandoning the broader geography of the world outside the "house" yet simultaneously remaining incapable of doing so. At the interrogators' two trials of Stanley, or, conversely, at his self-induced trial, our own silence, demanded by theatrical convention, may implicate us in the action, making us passive, paradoxically noncommital participants, guests at this ambiguous birthday party. To not act or speak is here, at very least, a crime of omission; our own silent, wordless status is parodied by Stanley as audience in the final act where he murmurs inarticulately, yet falls short of actual dialogue. If *The Birthday Party* is unlike *The Chairs* in its suggestive, fluid sets, it does resemble Ionesco's "tragic farce" in that the stage, properly, expands beyond the apron to include the "characters" in the house.

Stanley himself is trapped between his visitors on- and offstage, and thus there is a literal irony in his line, "There's nowhere to go" (p. 27), or in Goldberg's advice on physical health, "Let yourself go." The self that Stanley tries to hide is discovered by us and, once discovered, will be changed by our own existential "stare." Like a mother—we learn that Stanley's own mother died in a sanitarium—Meg tries to force her "son" back into childhood by treating him like her little boy or promising Stanley that the new guests won't "wake [him] up" (p. 38). But the mission of Goldberg and McCann, of the audience, of the actor assigned the part of Stanley, and of the actors forming an ensemble with him, is just the opposite—to wake him up, through the medium of a birthday party, to confront him with his adulthood, to "bring him out of himself" (p. 36).[7]

The defrocked priest, McCann, demands that Lulu "confess" herself (p. 85), and in a larger sense *The Birthday Party* is a confessional overheard by audiences on- and offstage. To be literal, the "set" is not Meg's living room but, more accurately, that living room as surrounded by a theatrical house teaming with priestlike overseers, each coming to an individual *reading* of Stanley, yet all linked by their participation in this process of discovery. That process, this coming out, is inevitable and is prefigured in such seemingly disparate images as McCann's "gargle" (p. 33) or Goldberg's promise that he and McCann will form the "hub" of Stanley's "wheel" (p. 87).

Since viewer here assumes parity with object, the play itself is pervaded by the notion of audience, of the overlooker. Indeed, it begins in this fashion, with Meg and Petey devoting seven lines of dialogue to the issue of Stanley's entrance for breakfast (p. 10). At one point Stanley plays an upstage audience to the offstage conversation between Meg and Lulu. However, just as Goldberg and McCann are about to enter, he "*slips on his glasses, slides through the kitchen door and out the back door*" (p. 28), rejecting this role of audience, and not confronting them until the second act where, again, he tries—this time unsuccessfully—to exit from the microcosmic living room. In act 2 Stanley is forced into the role of a spectator sitting in a chair as the party guests stare at him, and in the game of blind man's bluff he plays the sightless audience in search of that game's actors. Before all this occurs, Petey exits to play chess, yet it will be Petey alone who is the audience to a transformed Stanley in his final entrance and stage appearance.[8]

There is a pattern in *The Birthday Party,* physical as well as psychological, wherein an onstage character, often seated, observes a character coming into the set, as an audience would. Even when Petey enters alone in the play's opening minutes, it is Meg, audiencelike but offstage, who asks, "Is that you Petey?," as the first eight lines of dialogue are occupied with determining just who is onstage (p. 9). Such literal entrances, witnessed by the onstage audience, are inseparable from the point raised earlier about Pinter's psychological expansion of the single onstage set. Those outside come in, bringing the world with them. Meg's otherwise innocent question about the weather, "Is it nice out?" (p. 10), will assume darker ironies with each step we ourselves take into the play.[9] For we move with Stanley from Meg's simplistic assurance, "You'll see when they come" (p. 21), to Goldberg's comically fatalistic "If we hadn't come today, we'd have come tomorrow" (p. 35), to the thrice repeated "Tonight." That "tonight" designates the coincidence of the visitors' arrival on Stanley's birthday and the irrefutable linking of actors and audience: we are present this evening for a production of *The Birthday Party.* Coincidence is here interwoven with theatrical presence.

Even objects *experience* this transformation to a simultaneous presence and significance. Stanley overhears the offstage conversation between Meg and Lulu, and the puzzling reference to the "it" that the offstage "*Voice*" has brought. Then, as Stanley "*quickly sits at the table*" (p. 25) to avoid being seen playing audience to the two women, Lulu enters with a "*solid round parcel*" and places it on the sideboard. Near the end of act 1, Meg unwraps the drum and offers it to Stanley as a modest replacement, even symbol, for his aborted career as a pianist. Then, prompted by her to play the drum, Stanley beats it so savagely that just before the act-1 curtain he transforms himself into some sort of beast, "*his face and the drumbeat now savage and possessed*" (p. 39).

This interaction between audience and set, audience and actor, and audience and props is concentrated in the major event of the second act, the birthday party itself giving the play its ironic title. The game, blind man's bluff, in essence a play-within-a-play, has been scripted by Goldberg and McCann, with Meg and Lulu its supporting players, and its ultimate object, Stanley himself, the birthday boy.[10] He is the unwilling actor to this audience, their subject, whose "attitude" determines the nature of the play, literal and philosophic, imposed on him. In fact, as she falters in making her congratulatory speech, Meg is advised by Goldberg to "look" at Stanley for inspiration (p. 57). However much that inane birthday oration may characterize Meg, it also seems to comment on Stanley's futile attempt to evade detection, to pass himself off as someone who causes "no trouble" (p. 43), a zero, an actor who cannot act, who will not serve as object for the stare of this audience oddly composed of friends and strangers.

The already narrowed set of the first act is reduced even as, paradoxically, its significance enlarges. The second time the torch is shown in Stanley's face, Pinter's stage direction calls for the light outside the living room, shining through the single window, to become "*fainter*" (p. 59). Then, after the house lights themselves fail, the outside lights go off and the torch itself becomes, in effect, a spotlight held by the onstage audience to illuminate the scene's single actor, surrounded by four spectators who are as invisible in the darkness onstage as is the audience in the house. All of us now stare at Stanley as he, audience-like, bends over Lulu, who is lying "*spread eagled on the table*" (p. 68) like some specimen to be examined by a physician. Actor and audience, Stanley thus plays all roles at his own party—subject and observer or, in modern critical terms, *sign* and *signifier.* Like the set in act 1, the birthday party initially seems innocent, nothing beyond itself, literal and thereby exclusive. It is the audience's role that invests the party with significance, converting the event to something terrifyingly *inclusive*.

We may or may not want to agree with Charles Carpenter when he reads that party as an allegory of Meg's and Goldberg's giving birth to a new Stanley, with the drum first punctured and then recovered paralleling sexual penetration, the emergence of the child from the womb, and the restoration of the mother after birth. Carpenter further sees Stanley's bending over Lulu not as an act of rape but rather as his examination of her as a replacement for Meg, his mother-figure now mated to Goldberg.[11] Still, we must supply *some* reading by the end of act 2. Mute like Ionesco's Orator, in the final scene Stanley cannot articulate the play for us. If by design he has concealed his life from the invaders, from Goldberg and McCann, if they themselves are little more than servants of the offstage and unseen Monty, messengers like Shakespeare's or Stoppard's Rosencrantz and Guildenstern unaware of their mission, then making sense of Stanley's hidden life as it is bisected by these cosmic interrogators becomes our responsibility. At the end, just two characters hold the stage. By his own admission, Petey "wasn't there" (p. 91) during the party. Meg, seemingly oblivious to what happened, reduces the momentous occasion to an instance of pathetically unconscious and ironic vanity: she was the "belle of the ball. . . . They all said [she] was" (p. 91). We remain as the only trustworthy witness to the birthday party.

The pervasiveness of *audience*, as both a concept dominating the play and a literal factor in stage blocking, resonates in specific lines, whose ultimate reference, I think, is to both sides of the stage. Stanley's question to McCann, "Do you know what you're here for?" (p. 45), thus bursts with possibilities. If McCann is a projection of Stanley's fear or guilt, then here Stanley checks McCann's understanding of his mission. But like Hamlet's "You . . . That are but mutes or audience to this act" (5.2.334–335), the line may also include us, at present struggling with the meager facts. In similar fashion, Goldberg's response, "Until a few minutes ago, ladies and gentlemen, I, like all of you, was asking the same question" (p. 59), seems in part directed to us, especially since it comes just at the start of the climactic birthday party, to which the third act, as most theater goers seem to agree, appears anticlimactic. The visitors onstage and we offstage constitute the play's "reception committee" (p. 72).

That offstage reception committee is not passive, but rather charged with assessing the "new" Stanley, born at the party appropriately designated as his birthday. The assessment from critics is predictably and, I think, properly divided. Stanley is seen as socially undeveloped, a manikin confronted by Goldberg and McCann, ambassadors of civilization. For others, the visitors represent a projection of Stanley's own base insecurities and self-doubts. He has also been described as Christlike but flawed, and hence a Christ of "complicity" in the world's sin, persecuted by the other characters inhabiting a meaningless world, a paranoid pseudo-community. Stanley has even been equated with the artist in conflict with his public.[12] Samar Attar justifies proposing "another explication" of the play because for him *The Birthday Party* seems to be some sort of black hole, devouring any and every bias or perception we bring to it.[13] In his *The Poetics of Silence* James Hollis expresses discontent with all three of his attempts at reading Pinter.[14] One critic suggests that *The Birthday Party* is so open-ended because personality is fashioned by, is at the mercy of, the language of the other characters.[15]

What is manifest here, I think, is not just a case of multiple meanings, or interpretive options. Thomas Van Laan observes that

Pinter seems to deviate from the normal relationship that playwrights establish with their audiences, that the disparity between the seemingly closed, understandable play and the fluctuating "life-context" outside the drama is at one with his "manipulation" of his audience, that process by which he keeps us "disoriented."[16] We are involved with *The Birthday Party* precisely because it *includes* us, bifurcating our onstage representative among Stanley who, like the audience, is a private self surrounded by an audience; McCann and Goldberg, visitors coming like us into the play, into its single set, and thereby activating the options for interpretation; Meg and Lulu, at once spectators and participants; and Petey, who in his role as a reluctant audience embodies our own semiconscious desire to avoid the active, somewhat atypical role demanded of us.

2

As Sartre says in his reconstruction of Genet's life, it is the "glare" of the other, the witness of the audience, that is society's most potent force, a force here bringing both Stanley and the actor playing him out of hiding. Like the birthday boy himself, Pinter confesses to a feeling of hostility toward his audience.[17] Stanley reacts defensively to this fashioning power of the other and the audience's dichotomous sense that the character is at once a fictive self and the actor behind the mask: "I'll be all right when I get back . . . but what I mean is, the way some people look at me you'd think I was a different person. I suppose I have changed, but I'm still the same man that I always was" (p. 43). As a character, Stanley is exposed, drawn out of himself, literally called down from his second-floor bedroom, and, what is more, exposed by the characters Goldberg and McCann, who operate by a script he cannot fathom. Furthermore, he is witnessed by an audience who, while seen by the actor impersonating Stanley, remains unseen by Stanley himself. However, in the game of blind man's bluff, even the onstage characters, our surrogate audience, become like us when they are no more seen by Stanley than we are.

The actor also draws from himself, uncovering in part his real-life person to enact the role; the superficial banality of Pinter's plots makes that process relatively easy; we have all had birthday parties, all experienced homecomings, all telephoned friends across the way. What Stanley as character fears to do, the actor therefore does as his "job." Goldberg uses this very word as he lays out for McCann their purpose in staying at Meg's place; indeed, he might almost be an actor speaking to a fellow actor about his latest role: "And then this job came up out of the blue. Naturally they approached me to take care of it" (p. 31).

Then, too, performance itself is an exposure to the view of an audience, and I think here of the tremendous gap between a play in rehearsal, even a dress rehearsal, where the audience is often little more than the technical crew going about their work, and the play as it exists on opening night and subsequently during its run. What had been private, confined to cast and crew, is now made public, *birthed*—and, as anybody who has worked in the theater knows, the process is full of anxiety and not a little pain. *The Birthday Party* itself mediates on these three interlocked concepts of our function as audience. In this sense, dreading exposure, Stanley tries to abort the play. We learn early that he "didn't sleep well" the night before (p. 15). His reluctance to come out is then reexpressed by the "stuffy" room (p. 26) and, later, by his own unwashed or "bad state" (p. 45). For this unwilling performer thrust before an audience, the set itself, even his own body, announces his presence, and, predictably, on this day, his birthday, Stanley wishes he were "back home" (p. 43), a return to the womb surely parodied by Meg once she is alone with "her" Stanley.[18] The microcosmic world he inhabits here is for him "someone else's house" (p. 43), and in a revealing use of the theatrical term, he informs the visitors that they will "have to find somewhere else" since Meg's tourist home is "booked out" (p. 47).

If the drama is internal, if, as some critics have suggested, we are inside Stanley's mind as he peoples his little world, like Beckett's character in *Eh Joe* with his "mental thugees," then Stanley's unconscious self complements the actor's conscious knowledge of his role and of the play as a whole. Thus, even the most physical things in *The Birthday Party*—props, such as Stanley's glasses, which he tries to hide behind and which are taken from him and partially destroyed, or the chair with which he tries to cover his head (p. 55)—are at once realistic psychological defense mechanisms and futile gestures only exposing Stanley's inability to deny the audience. Against his intentions, he hastens toward the very confrontation he so fears. The disclosure of this private self cannot be suppressed: the first two acts end with violent "coming outs" on Stanley's part—his savage beating of the drum in act 1, and his insane examination (some critics see it as a rape) of Lulu in the second act.

Coexisting with these efforts to evade the stare of his audience is Stanley's attempt to rewrite his character, to alter his past and hence invalidate Goldberg's and McCann's "job" as they perceive it. His lie to Lulu, that he bathed in the sea earlier in the morning, and his announcement to Meg of a pending world tour are comic overtures to this revisionist history. More serious is his effort to affirm his innocence before McCann, to establish his character as one that has never caused "trouble" (p. 43). Before the defrocked priest, Stanley offers a fairly detailed autobiography: he wanted to stay at home but was drawn away by business; having tried to give up that business, he exists at present on a small private income; he leads a quiet life, always has, doing little more than playing records in a home where "everything [is] delivered to the door." If things have now changed in this pseudo-home, then at least he appreciates what he has lost (p. 45). This "story"—no more true or false than any other story in *The Birthday Party*—is no more true or false than the play itself. Audiences onstage, for a variety of complex reasons, are thereby reading the action no less than audiences offstage. In a typically insightful essay on the play, Bert States argues that here the characters, as readers or as what he calls rival playwrights, are usurping the traditional function of the audience.[19] Other critics suggest that the past is seen as a malleable commodity, not fixed but, instead, ripe for reinterpretations.[20] In "Harold Pinter: The Metamorphosis of Memory," A. R. Braunmuller calls *The Birthday Party* a competition between Stanley and the audience, as he tries to replace a dangerous present with a personally revised past.[21]

Perhaps Stanley is not so much a revisionist playwright as one who, both consciously and unconsciously, invokes these visitors because of some need, which he cannot suppress, to face his corrupt self. If Goldberg and McCann represent Stanley's own deepest fears projecting into this consciousness, then Stanley is indeed a playwright, even if it be an unintentional one.[22] The play's set would then exist inside the head of the main character, who is not facing death, as Beckett's Hamm is, but facing himself, moving from the idyllic security of childhood, that presocial stage, to adulthood. Stanley's comment to McCann is doubly suggestive—"I've got a feeling we've met before" (p. 42)—as is Meg's confusion of Goldberg for Stanley in the final act (p. 72). [23] If Stanley finally meets head-on his darker self in the guise of the visitors, he experiences the tension, indeed the pain, when two worlds collide—his present, relatively private, stuporous life in the small "public" world of Meg's house, where his natural parents have been replaced by banal or indifferent surrogates, and a private world no less real, mired in sins committed in the past, or sins the "playwright" imagines he has committed. Or, like Sartre's "Saint Genet," Stanley may here be responding to the world's negative image of himself, most graphic in the examination sessions conducted by the visitors in act 2, by choosing to dredge up and then to live out that image, in effect usurping society's judgment by making it his own. In a curious twisting of the Pirandello theme, we make of ourselves what others would have made of us.

Is Stanley a victim or a villain? Are Goldberg and McCann saviors or persecutors? Is Stanley destroyed at the end or is he reborn? The either-or assumption behind much of the play's criticism might more profitably, I think, be replaced by the otherwise unsightly slash line: "and/or."[24] And to say that Stanley is the "object of other people's existence" is, I think, inadequate if those "other people" fail to include the people offstage.[25]

3

In the final act, Goldberg experiences a curious let-down, almost a nervous breakdown. Irritable with McCann, who has dared to call his friend "Nat" (p. 79), "*fatigue*[d]," as the stage direction indicates (p. 78), or "knocked out" (p. 79), as he confesses to his partner, Goldberg launches into an extraordinary speech filled with truisms and clichés, laced with neurotic self-justifications, and ending with an incomplete line twice repeated: "Because I believe that the world. . . ." Pinter asks that this be said with three distinct, progressively more serious tones: "*vacant*," "*desperate*," "*lost*" (p. 80). Physically as well as mentally, the character, otherwise so charming and commanding, even domineering, seems at low ebb; he wheezes (p. 81), submits to a physical examination from his partner, and at length requires McCann to blow in his mouth to restore his energy, not once but twice.

What should we think of this apparent setback? In terms of the issues just raised, I can, properly, offer only a plural answer or, for directors and their actors, some options. Perhaps as a self-induced persecutor, an invader bringing Stanley out of hiding, someone created by Stanley, Goldberg has now served his purpose. Existing only in terms of his function, or "job," he is now finished as a character. If he has been Stanley's opposite, a man honoring his parents, given to hard work, someone active in society, alive on the world's larger stage—as he boasts—he is so only to serve as foil to his creator, only to activate Stanley. Now, as Stanley is about to make his final stage appearance, that ambiguous entrance as either a saved or damned soul, as either reborn or dead, Goldberg becomes irrelevant. We see for the first time the servant's inner self; earlier relishing his position, he becomes ill after that position is rendered irrelevant when his task is completed.

In a sense, Goldberg now metamorphoses into the incipient subject for Pinter's next play. Stanley has served his painful time in the spotlight, before the glare of the audience; even as he examined Lulu on the table, he has been examined by us. This seemingly last-minute neurosis in Goldberg may suggest a play waiting in the wings, one where the former interrogator, so insistent on how physically and mentally sound his life has been, is forced like Stanley to confront his darker self in the form of two more visitors. Again, it is revealing that Meg, the protective mother of the first act, confuses Goldberg for Stanley in the final act:

> GOLDBERG: A reception committee!
> MEG: Oh, I thought it was Stanley.
> GOLDBERG: You find a resemblance?
> MEG: Oh no. You look quite different.
> GOLDBERG *(coming into the room):* Different build, of course.
>
> (p. 72)

The stage direction has both Meg and Petey gaze at the door as Goldberg enters, and thus her protest that he looks "different" is questionable. And Goldberg's "different build, of course" denies only a physical, not a psychological resemblance. Only by resurrecting his own past, the comforting nuclear family of his childhood, can Goldberg compose himself—and just in time—before Stanley's final entrance. McCann himself must browbeat Lulu, who has charged Goldberg with seducing her, and thus Goldberg contradicts his public image as a man honoring women, as someone never taking "liberties" (p. 46). Goldberg's response to Stanley is itself curious. He and McCann "*woo him, gently, and with relish*" (p. 86), and in the litany following this stage direction they promise him everything from ointments to prayer wheels, day-and-night service to high political positions (pp. 86–88). As a director, I would advise the two actors fawning over their silent subject to make their subtextual emotions here combine admiration for the tragic-comic soul before them, respect for his having faced his darker self even at the cost of a physical and emotional collapse, envy for Stanley, and yet also a hatred that in turn reveals a self-hatred, a fear, particularly on Goldberg's part, that his own turn to "play the game" will come someday, perhaps even soon. James Boulton speaks of Pinter's audience as experiencing a "Kafka-like uncertainty,"[26] and I am reminded of Kafka's "The Country Doctor," where the physician, here Goldberg, lies in bed with his patient, here Stanley, so as to transfer the client's disease to himself.

Does the infection, in turn, spread to the audience? Stanley suddenly demands of Meg, "Tell me, Mrs. Boles, when you address yourself to me, do you ever ask yourself who exactly you are talking to? Eh?" (p. 22). At the birthday party the various characters delve into memories of their own childhood. If both the audience offstage and its onstage surrogates activate a play involving everyone in the theater, we cannot remain the inactive "other" to the actors/characters onstage. Stanley's and then Goldberg's questions about identity, of either the person addressed or doing the addressing, are directed to us, for if we "bring out" the reluctant Stanley, he and the play bring us out as well. The theater, as I remind my own students, is a mutual coming together of actor and audience; both venture out, from reality, from themselves, to assume in a single room the fictive roles of either character or audience. Both presences, on- and offstage, are equally significant, indeed, vital to the play's enactment. We experience our own formative childhood during the course of the play, and even as we witness the onstage actors, Stanley in particular and Goldberg in the play's closing moments, we also become them. This is an act no more difficult, no less natural, no less inevitable than what the actor experiences in at once leaving his real-life self to become a character, even as he draws on himself, his own past, to become the other.

4

The presence of the audience, as a powerful factor in the play, is manifest in the symbol of the eye.[27] The first moment Stanley is alone onstage, as Meg busies herself in the kitchen, he "*rubs his eyes under his glasses*" before reading the paper, the same newspaper McCann later tears into strips as if, embodying Stanley's regressive fear, he were trying to erase the outside world. I note also that Petey is an avid newspaper reader (perhaps in part as a way of avoiding conversation with Meg), and that twice McCann shows his anger when Petey threatens to disturb his carefully torn strips of paper. Stanley also "*withdraws from the table*" when Lulu offers him her compact so that he can "have a look" at his face (p. 26).

In act 2 the eyes are alternately assaulted or rendered irrelevant when the lights fail. Seeing is itself displaced by the game of blind man's bluff, where the character applying the blindfold takes great pains to make sure that whoever is "it"—the blind seeker—cannot see out. But Goldberg and McCann play their own unofficial version of the game before the other guests enter, as they tear Stanley's glasses from his face prior to the first of their two interrogations (p. 52). The action, cruel on the surface, might also be taken as their forcing Stanley to look inside himself, to blot out the shallow comfortable world he has known before they arrived, and to journey into his past—

the murder of his wife, his mother's hospitalization, the betrayal of country and his church, and his ignorance of the basic laws of existence (pp. 52–55).

As the party starts, the glasses are returned, and, as a sort of parody to this motif of sight and seeing, the conversation turns to other glasses, that is, Meg's "very best glasses" (p. 56) to be brought out for the drinks. Still, just before Lulu's entrance, sight is again the issue when McCann, like a theater's lighting designer, produces a torch from his pocket, switches off the overhead lights, and spotlights Stanley's face, the action perhaps reminiscent of a police interrogation. Meg expresses her concern that the flashlight hurts Stanley's eyes, but, reassured by Goldberg, she begins her speech as her subject himself is highlighted by the spot. Once Lulu is onstage, the lights are turned off a second time, when the torch is directed at Stanley's face while toasts are being made in his honor. Pinter's puzzling stage direction requires that this second time the light outside the window be "*fainter*" (p. 59), as if man-made, rather than natural, lighting were the force here: as the visible "stage" shrinks to the dimensions of Stanley's face, the psychological geography expands by inverse proportion. The public image Stanley struggles to maintain in the first act, by keeping his eyes on the stage's little world and off himself, here meets a private, inner self. As with those psychological forest landscapes in the center of Shakespeare's comedies, the three-part structure of *The Birthday Party* moves from society to the self and, in the final act, back to a now altered society.

Stanley is essentially an audience to the sexual flirtations and grimy innuendoes of the couples, McCann and Meg, Goldberg and Lulu—literally so, for as they carry on he "*sits still*" (p. 62). However, if the onstage business enacts the inner fears of a man accused of "contaminat[ing] womankind" (p. 54), if Stanley in essence plays audience to four actors portraying his own sexual crimes, ranging from incest (implied in act 1 when the mother-figure Meg refers to the "lovely afternoons" [p. 19] she has enjoyed with Stanley in his bedroom) to seducing younger women, it is during the unplanned loss of light, the stage "*BLACKOUT*" (p. 66), that he plays simultaneously the actor seen by the onstage audience (when McCann manages to find the torch) and an audience of one examining the actor Lulu lying on the table. As the "*torch draws closer*" (p. 68), the onstage audience threatens him: "*His giggle rises and grows as he flattens himself against the wall. Their figures converge upon him.*" The second act thus represents a variation on the first, as the invasion from the outside and Stanley's increasingly futile efforts to deny his private self are displaced by a diminished "set," illuminated by a single torch, now defined as

Stanley's face, minus glasses (broken and not to be repaired until the following act). This is the most self-consciously theatrical of the three acts, with its play-within-a-play, the patent games of a birthday party, and this equation of an onstage prop, the torch, with the technical side of stage lighting. This second act is also the most revealing, literally penetrating, as we watch Stanley watch four characters/actors enact his own sexual fears and imagined crimes. Then, in a reversal signaled by the extinction of all stage lights (with the blackout, the light outside the window, which has already been reduced to a faint glow, is also extinguished), we watch this audience "*converge*" on Stanley, who himself plays an audience observing Lulu.

Literally, act 3, taking place "*the next morning,*" offers a restoration of sight, although the light here is a qualified one. In the first act, Petey notes that not all mornings are the same since "it gets light later in winter" (p. 11). Now Stanley's glasses have been returned, but the frames "are bust," as McCann says, and Stanley himself has absurdly tried to "fit the eyeholes into his eyes" (p. 76).

If Pinter's third act seems anticlimactic or close to the comforting final act of the well-made play (first act initiating the problem, second act given to that problem, final act providing a facile resolution), it also has that ambiguous tone of its predecessors. Although Stanley's glasses are restored, it is an ominous restoration. Petey volunteers to get some "Sellotape" as a temporary repair for the glassless frames, but Goldberg declines the offer, observing that without his glasses Stanley can be kept "quiet for the time being" (p. 76). Stanley enters holding the broken glasses in one hand; given all the previous discussion about the state of his glasses, we cannot fail to notice the incongruous figure he cuts. Yet, conversely, he is also well dressed, "*in striped trousers, black jacket, and white collar*" (p. 85), a marked contrast to his appearance in the first act. And if he is indeed "myopic," as Goldberg claims (p. 86), we must wonder if his loss of sight—even if we could discount the parallel with Oedipus[28]—is either a sign of degeneration or evidence that he now sees inwardly. Does his speechless state represent a movement from the old, shallow public self to this "child" reborn, reduced to babylike sounds? His one line in the final secne is "Uh-gug . . . ug-gug . . . eehh-gag . . . (*On the breath*) . . . Caahh . . . caahh . . ." (p. 89). Now, given a second chance, and on his way to the absent character Monty, is he to meet a god or divine force promising a new life, or at very least providing a cleansing and reindoctrination to life in a mental hospital? Stanley actually has two lines in this scene, for along with those childlike sounds, he responds to Goldberg's question "What do you think? Eh, boy?" by clenching and unclenching his eyes (p. 88). When McCann asks Stanley's opinion of "this prospect," Stanley's hands "*clutching his glasses begin to tremble.*"

5

Goldberg's exhaustion and neurosis in this final scene seem to grow in an obverse correlation to the quieting of Stanley, who had ended both previous acts with displays of savage energy. In the final scene, are Goldberg and McCann, having ruined Stanley, now taking him to some scrap heap disguised as a mental institution? Or, like midwives having assisted in the painful but necessary "rebirth" on Stanley's birthday, are they accompanying him on the first steps of his pilgrimage from this regressive self into the present, real world, with the promise that they will make him a "mensch" (p. 88) in the process? There can be, I think, no single answer to such questions of meaning. Each member of the audience provides an answer that is right only for the perceiver.

However, that coda does much more than just mark time, for if Meg alternately frustrates and amuses us with her chatter, Petey, the otherwise "absent" character in the play, the one who went off to play chess during Stanley's birthday, now emerges as a significant, complex spokesman, given to tantalizing suggestions rather than comforting but reductive pronouncements on what we have just seen. He is once again reading his newspaper, bringing in the outside world. Significantly, the strips fall to the floor as Petey opens the paper, yet this time there is no McCann to respond angrily when someone disturbs his hobby—or his revealing obsession. Petey's lie to Meg, that Stanley is still asleep, is followed by an intriguing line, "Let him . . . sleep." Does he imply that Stanley, who before the first act had slept fitfully, now enjoys restful sleep, although not where Meg has been led to believe he rests? Or is his comment a theatrical one? Stanley's role is now finished and the actor is disrobing in the dressing room; when he returns for a curtain call still in Stanley's costume and make-up, he has changed from his fictive to his real self.[29] Is Petey's puzzling line directed at us? The character Stanley now rests within us. What we make of him in this play, where our activist, interpretive role linked us with the onstage characters, establishes us as an "actor" or even a playwright during the performance.

There is a "*pause,*" and this time when Petey resumes the conversation with Meg, he is a loving, understanding husband, quite different from the grouchy soul we saw at the start; he assures her that he, too, would confirm, if he had been present at the party, what Meg says everyone else said, that she was the belle of the ball (p. 91). This nonaudience of one can imagine, even if his motive be just flattery, what it must have been like to have been an audience observing Meg as she entered the birthday party, in her declining years, to be sure, but still resplendent in her evening gown.

In her *Strategems to Uncover Nakedness: The Dramas of Harold Pinter,* Lois Gordon argues that to deny his relation with his natural mother—did Stanley himself commit her to that sanitarium? (p. 52)—Stanley fled to the present place, but while wanting to preserve the nuclear family, sinned in displacing Petey as Meg's sexual partner.[30] Such analysis, of course, depends in part on recreating a life for Stanley before the play, although I do not mean to imply that such "biographical" criticism is unwarranted: Pinter invites it with those facts, however bare or hurried, about Stanley's past, in this play where the central character dwells on that past even as he tries to escape it. Moreover, as a director used to providing actors with subtexts for their characters, I often recreate such "pasts" in the form of a letter to the actor, written as if I were the character he or she will later impersonate onstage. If one of Stanley's crimes *is* adultery and the threatened disruption of the marriage of Petey and Meg—and, again, Meg's flirtation with McCann at the birthday party then becomes an onstage enactment of what went on in Stanley's bedroom during those "lovely afternoons"—if this is a *fact* as much as anything can be called a fact in Pinter's dramatic worlds, then in this act of kindness to Meg, here in the final moments, we see a shakey marriage being healed, now that Stanley has finally left the set. In Freudian terms, the son, in leaving home and seeking his own identity, has now removed himself from a futile sexual competition with the father.

6

The union of actor or character and audience, which is also a dichotomy, is inseparable from the concept of theater itself. By definition, the medium is one of presence, the fictive onstage enactment occupying the same space and time occupied by the real spectators witnessing the production. We ourselves are at once engaged and disengaged—experiencing Aristotle's "fear" and "pity"—by what we both see and hear. Meg's house by the sea is a special place, as is the theater, removed from the town, isolated, occupied only by people who, like actor and actor, or actor and spectator, develop an intense and special relationship for a prescribed period of time. The beginning and ending of our evening in the theater also define the boundaries for Stanley's initial entrance and final exit offstage.

If both actor and audience are co-equal participants in this fictive venture, then, by a process of exclusion where two negatives (that is, illusions) make a positive, our mutual presence equals a reality, however temporary. The play's own metadramatic dimension, its self-reflexive nature, thus acknowledges "what is" or "what is happening" during the performance. The characters' reality becomes ours, by an act of will and of the imagination on our part that is conscious in direct proportion to the actors' own will and imagination. In this fashion, our own sense of the evening's coming to an end—we have read the playbill, we know there will be three acts and two intermissions—is acknowledged by McCann when he says, "I want to get it over" (p. 79). We, too, await Stanley's entrance; we too, are anxious to see his condition after the bizarre ending to the birthday party the night before. The argument so pervasive in Genet's work is relevant here: what distinguishes the theater from real life is that the former is always conscious, the latter most often unconscious of its fakery, of its role playing; and, thus, the more the theater underscores its artifice, the more *true* or *real* it becomes. Far from distancing the audience, the play's metadramatic dimension only reminds us of the common reality to which those off- and onstage contribute during the production.[31]

Still, Goldberg's "You're dead. You can't live" (p. 55), whatever its thematic implications, also recognizes a basic truth about all the characters: they are not real, have never been real; they offer only the illusions of a life for which we have been collaborators. Even as the theater serves as a window to the world outside its confines, it generates its own hall of mirrors, its own autonomous (however fleeting) rules, its own logic.[32] Perhaps this is why Goldberg can adopt so many names, or why McCann can suddenly be called "Dermot" in the final scene. Illogical, at very least confusing in life, such flexibility in names is no more illogical than the actor's abandoning his own name during his impersonation of a stage character.

Here the characters can function as playwrights offering us competing scenarios and the attendant competing interpretations of their world. For they do nothing less or more than Pinter, the playwright, the "Monty" waiting in the wings, has done. The three acts themselves are at once events in a seemingly realistic sequence—"*A morning in summer . . . Evening of the same day . . . The next morning*" (p. 8)—and critical commentaries. Act 3 parallels, varies from, and thereby comments on, act 1, and vice versa; and act 2 provides a context for the acts surrounding it. The surrounding acts frame act 2, which in turn provides a stage for its own play-within-a-play, the birthday party.

Pinter's theatrical world is in a sense inhospitable to anything outside its confines, demanding that any character, any prop or thing entering its set, be transformed into a component of its own presence, its present significance, although that significance dissolves into life itself when we leave the auditorium. Although it is a major event of his past and the stimulus for his present character, Stanley's career as a pianist must be aborted for the sake of the present demands of *The Birthday Party*, locked out just as Stanley himself was locked out before his second concert—or locked in, metamorphosed to the present demands of the play, as Stanley was locked inside the concert hall, at least in Meg's rewriting of the episode. Even the item in the newspaper about Lady Splatt's having a baby girl is converted to the source of tension between Meg and Petey. Although she does not know the fortunate mother, Meg is saddened that Lady Splatt did not have a boy, and there is an obvious connection between that wish and her motherly attitude toward Stanley. From Petey's reading of the newspaper we also learn that there is a new show at the Palace, but it is not a musical as Meg hopes (she reasons that if it is a musical, and is performed on the pier, then "Stanley could have been in it"). It is a "straight show," with "no dancing and singing," a show where the actors "just talk" (pp. 13–14). That is to say, "they" are performing something like *The Birthday Party*.

Petey himself is involved offstage in something dimly approaching theater: he sells tickets and arranges the deck chairs for tourists. But his dull job is parodied at the birthday party when Stanley and McCann circle each other, with chairs held menacingly over their heads. Even if Petey prefers some other stage, being audience or actor in that chess game during the birthday party, his outside *life* is irrelevant; when he is on the present set he must be involved in its action. We learn, after the fact, that he restored the lights after the breakup of the birthday party. And as Stanley is being led offstage in the final scene, Petey suddenly cries out ("*broken*"), "Stan, don't let them tell you what to do!" (p. 90), as if he has at last sensed the larger play, or seen himself in Stanley, as a younger man before the stultifying marriage to Meg. In the closing moments Petey is uncharacteristically active, assertive, offering that tantalizing lie to Meg that Stanley is asleep and then, in his solicitous agreement with Meg's image of herself at the party, allowing for the marriage, possibly disrupted by Meg's relation with Stanley, to continue. In effect, Petey allows for that boring domestic comedy to go on, a glimpse of which we see in the opening scene before Stanley's first entrance.

As the play opens, we wait like Meg and Petey to see the Stanley they have been talking about. At the end, we resemble Stanley, for his exit precedes ours by a matter of minutes; he exits upstage, we, downstage. Meg and Petey remain, figuratively, until the start of next day's performance of *The Birthday Party.* Even the sound of the car starting offstage and then driving away (p. 90) anticipates our own progress out of the theater, past the ticket window, and to the parking lot—to the very "home" for which Stanley longs. Meg's final word, "was"—"I know I was"—signals the end of this theatrical presence. The play is, has been, and now exists solely in our memory. *The Birthday Party* itself has forced the past into the present, in particular Stanley's past, yet also that of the other characters as they recount their childhoods during the birthday party. If this same presence did not end, then it would sever the future no less than the past.

To a degree, Goldberg's past—if we can believe him as well—bears on his present character, yet only to a degree; his biography offers no real justification for the demonic streak we witness in him. Nor can it supply any absolute subtext for the actor. Pinter is not given to flashbacks, to filling in gaps in characterization, or to providing a shorthand explanation for an existing personality trait. When he does use flashbacks, as in *Betrayal,* it is to show the deficiencies of memory. Here in *The Birthday Party* memory is at the mercy, the needs, of the one doing the remembering. Again, critics speak of the "menacing" or "threatening" element in Pinter, of something sinister waiting just below the apparently normal, even superficial, dialogue. Perhaps the reverse is no less true: his theatrical present threatens the characters and their audience precisely because it seems to float free of that otherwise orderly sequence of time from past through present to future. As in Kafka, with whom Pinter has been compared, we, like Kafka's K in *The Trial,* have a sense of being "arrested," caught in a present event for which the past ultimately provides no convincing explanation, and from which we can make no certain prediction of the future. In the imaginary "act 4" of *The Birthday Party,* will Stanley be ruined further or restored to health? We cannot say. The title of one of Pinter's more recent plays, *Old Times,* shows the devouring nature of this present. Stanley himself echoes this title when he asks Lulu if Meg had many guests before him in "the old days" (p. 28). Along with Pinter's characters, we are locked in *The* [*Theater's*] *Room,* one shutting out past and future, everything outside itself.

That room presently experienced by actor and audience may be even smaller than we think. For, as I have suggested, it is possible that despite the appearance in *The Birthday Party* of a society, of the various personality types that make up a community, we may actually be witnessing a drama that is taking place in Stanley's head. In the middle of his sparring with Meg, Stanley suddenly puts "*his head in his hands*" as he cries out, "Oh God, I'm tired" (p. 19). My director's notes ask for a large "beat" just before his action and the line coupled with it. It is as if the play changes gears here, as if this "insert," occurring in the midst of discussions about tea—Stanley's relation with Meg and his own father, and his criticisms of her housekeeping—suddenly plunges him, and us, into the ambiguous heart of the play. I note that Pinter asks for a "*silence*" after Stanley's outburst. Meg goes to the sideboard and begins to dust the room, all the while watching Stanley, before coming back to the table where he continues to sit head in hands. Only when she begins to dust the table is he drawn out of this posture; Stanley then resumes the former tone and subject of their conversation with "Not the bloody table" (p. 19).

Like Stanley, however, the theater cannot remain or be internal; it is a witnessed public event, and thus very unlike that time when we retire to the study, lock the door, and become absorbed in a good book. At this moment, when Stanley puts his head in his hands, hiding his eyes from us, blotting the world from his own sight, we see the very tension, the conflict, or source of power in the play—this tug between individual consciousness and society, between the solitary self and those visitors always waiting to enter. Alone, anything is possible. Still, the external world forces us to face necessities, demands, and scenarios not of our own making. As Goldberg explains, "The possibility can only be assumed after the proof of the necessity" (p. 53). Goldberg himself has given a successful lecture at the Ethical Hall on "The Possible and the Necessary."

At once like the real world, built from the desires and fears, the wishes, the private scenarios, of men and women, Pinter's plays, *The Birthday Party* in particular, also threaten—and pleasantly so—to become inner, theatrical, autonomous stage fictions, severing their ties with the real world offstage. We assist the actors and their playwright in this movement counter to the Necessary. In trying to shut out reality, his past, and those who come into the hitherto exclusive world of Meg's seaside home, whether the intruders be Goldberg or Lulu, would-be father or would-be lover, Stanley also tries to close down and shut out existence. Still, he cannot do so; he is not allowed to do so anymore than are we, who have for a brief time been collaborators with those onstage during the present performance of *The Birthday Party.* Like the characters now returned to their real-life roles as actors and fellow humans, we exit from the theater—although in opposite, yet complementary directions.

3

Genet, *The Balcony:* "You Must Now Go Home, Where Everything . . . Will Be Falser Than Here"

The theatrical dimension of *The Birthday Party,* in particular our role in interpreting the meager or conflicting facts that Pinter's characters provide, is perhaps not so evident at first, but rather grows on us, culminating in the birthday party of act 2. In *The Balcony,* however, Genet's inquiry into what *role* can mean both onstage and in the world offstage confronts us from the very start. To the side of a "Bishop," who is theatrically arrayed in a cleric's cope and the tragedian's cothurni, stands a rather ordinary young woman washing her hands, preparing for the role she must play to complement the role already assumed by the figure centerstage.[1] Near this woman, who is in transition from person to stage character, stands Irma, our audience surrogate, silent, confined like us to watching the little drama about to unfold. Genet's stage direction requires that "*throughout the scene she hardly moves*" (p. 8). Further, by "*standing very near the door*" Irma defines the boundaries of the stage itself. In the Elizabethan drama her role would be that of the Presenter.

As the play expands from this initial tableau, as characters hurry in from battle-torn streets seeking protection or solace, or both, as the rebels themselves approach the balcony that is first made visible in scene 8, Irma's perspective as onstage audience is expanded by that televisionlike apparatus multiplying the number of stages she can witness. She is thus the ideal audience, aware of the "plays" being enacted in many more rooms than the one we observe. Indeed, her superior vision is in direct contrast to the situation in Genet's *The Blacks* where, ironically, the several onstage audiences prove irrelevant since the ultimate action occurs offstage and is only reported to us much later by messenger.

Accused by Carmen of being someone without feelings who "observe[s] it all from a distance" (p. 30), Irma is also dependent on her own passionate, private theater. Just when she has decided to abandon her position as observer, or playwright-in-the-wings, to assume the role of the dead Queen, her lover, Arthur, reminds her that his walking through the corridors looking at himself in her mirrors is "also for [Irma] to see [him]" (p. 45). If anything, her paradoxical role as an onstage audience, at once disengaged and engaged, is similar to that of the central characters in Genet's *The Maids*. Like Irma, they observe the scenario they have devised and attempted to control, and yet the purpose behind their public play is inseparable from their passion both for each other and for the milkman, or from their conflicting passions for Madame. And in her final speech, whose central line is this chapter's subtitle, Irma reminds us that we, too, are both audience and actors.

If we see Carmen as Irma's reflection or counterpart—she is, literally, the assistant director in the brothel—then both their past and present relationships, as well as their separate "stories," further define this link, at once formal and psychological, between the audience and the actor. Carmen contends that although Irma's present "confidence" in her is a pale vestige of what must have been a former lesbian passion, both women are still "tied" together in their association with George, the Chief of Police (p. 29). The most immediate strain in their relationship, however, comes from Carmen's wanting "to see" her child (p. 30). Appropriately, as Irma charged her friend with (potential) betrayal she stands beside what Genet describes as "*a curious piece of furniture at the left, a kind of switchboard with a view-finder and earphone*." For Irma, Carmen threatens to substitute an open-ended, hence "unreal" theater, where Carmen becomes the "fairy godmother" observing Chantel who, in turn, sees ("pictures") her as a saint "in Heaven" (p. 31), for the brothel's theater, dominated by Irma as both director and audience. But in Irma's more circumscribed theater Carmen has already played a saint at whose sight a leper was miraculously healed (p. 30). In a way, then, the real threat to Irma's brothel does not come from the revolutionaries, who, as they approach an "establishment" both literal and social, only begin to resemble their opponents. Rather, the assault takes the form of Irma's other self, Carmen, who would substitute for her own assigned roles as actor, audience to Irma, and assistant manager a real role as a would-be mother, a role at variance with that of her childless mistress and her "sterile" women. As her former lover, now consigned to being a business partner, Carmen only mirrors the conflict in Irma.

Genet's own well-known preference for a theater of symbols, or for one resembling a Catholic mass, requires an audience at once separate from but also psychologically involved in the onstage action. Irma is that audience—like us. She comes to the present play with a history, tries to sever that former self from her role as director, yet later abandons such would-be neutrality when she takes on the role of Queen, itself a mirror to her real self: as she says, in "the center of the Palace is a woman like me" (p. 63). Having been both actor and audience, she at length frees herself from this duality only to remind us, the offstage audience, that if we have thought ourselves dispassionate spectators, then we now must become actors in life's theater where, she insists, "everything—you can be quite sure—will be falser than here" (p. 96).

1

Centered in Irma, this complex notion of audience replicates throughout the play.[2] Real men or characters, like actors, impersonating exalted public figures, the three clients of the opening scenes also observe themselves playing roles. The character-turned-actor playing the Judge argues that his "function" is not to pass an ethical sentence on the sinner, but simply to observe, since to do anything more would risk becoming a real judge. Possessing the title without having the attendant responsibilities implied in the term "judge" allows him, in effect, to avoid the existential dilemma of his single self's being bifurcated into a "real" character and an "unreal" actor. Since he has consciously assumed a role made even more false or theatrical by its absurdity when measured in terms of his impoverished life offstage, the "Judge" seeks a wished-for projection of his self. Irma's television is thus a physical expression of this "self" audience. The General even tries to extend his vision beyond the already existentially liberted stage when he bends down to peer through what he hopes is a crack in the wall (p. 22). But jealous of her dominant position as audience, Irma intervenes. Still, the larger stage represented by those other rooms is exposed when cries of pleasure or pain intrude from backstage into the present set, despite Irma's efforts at soundproofing and covering the windows with hangings. Can those divided cries be our own?

In trying to lose their socially insignificant selves in a noble role, these first three clients, driven by unconfessed psychological needs, destroy the balance between self and other, character and actor. As Richard Coe comments, the way to self-revelation in Genet is always one of indirection or humiliation, such as the base role chosen by Said in *The Screens:* one consciously assumes a part divested of social or financial gain.[3] Appropriately, it is the aristocrat, the nameless "man" of scene 4, who in dressing "*as a tramp though neatly combed*" (pp. 27–28) will survive as the ultimate audience to George's immolation. Indeed, as Walter Sohlich argues in a very perceptive article, the aristocrat-turned-tramp will be transformed to the beggar of scene 8, observing with us that moment when both clients and brothel mistress are "reduced" to real-life roles.[4] In the final scene, this same character watches the Police Chief's "simulation" or "impersonation" (p. 47) before escaping unharmed from the play to "sing" (p. 92) of what he has experienced. We might then think of this man as four times metamorphosed—aristocrat to tramp to beggar to slave to singer—as Genet's onstage surrogate, the ultimate audience to life's own play, dwarfing Irma's more limited efforts. At length a singer or poet like his playwright, he has purposely chosen humiliation in a theatrical world that, in its fakery, its unreality, its estrangement from life, is more true because it is conscious of its fraudulence, and because, by definition, it frustrates any attempt at selfhood. Or, to invoke Genet's equation directly, we play roles both on- and offstage, but since we are unconscious of such role playing in life, it is, correspondingly, less "true" than the theater.[5] Irma cannot control the rebellion outside the brothel, yet that counterforce offstage is as much Genet's creation as is the onstage play we observe. I reverse myself, then: *The Balcony,* like *The Blacks,* is a sham concealing the real action taking place offstage. And it is to this larger reality, now seen as unconscious "theater," that the singer escapes.

As the Judge "*gets up and moves towards the wall,*" he plaintively asks, "May I have a look?" (p. 16). His otherwise simple request admits, I think, multiple responses in this play constructed on our desire to see ourselves as we would have others see us or, for that matter, as others choose to see us. As Genet comments in "What Remained of Rembrandt Torn Up into Very Even Little Pieces and Chucked into the Crapper," those "others" are ourselves: "His gaze was not that of someone else: it was my own that I was meeting in a mirror."[6]

If Genet inherits from Pirandello and the existentialists the notion that individual validation comes from the perception of others, then, as Sartre observes, man also rebels against his personal inauthenticity by serving as an audience to the self.[7] As offstage audience, we identify with the characters, seeing ourselves in them, precisely because the ultimate object of their perception is the same as ours, the self. Still, the self thus seen, as well as this act of perception, is an ideal. In truth, the people who enter Irma's brothel are inadequate because they seek to portray only a wished-for self. The rigid figure of the Bishop, centerstage, sees not his real self in the mirror, nor even an actor costumed for the role of Bishop, but the platonic or historical concept of Bishop. "The majesty, the dignity that light me up come from a more mysterious brilliance: the fact that the bishop precedes me" (p.

12). We will recall what is perhaps the most compelling point in Sartre's portrait of Genet, that is, the playwright's assumption of that role (the orphan turned homosexual thief) thrust on him by the "look" of society.[8] In *The Balcony* the characters reverse that situation, taking on a role patently denied by the world outside the brothel.

Genet's theater, therefore, complements but does not duplicate life; in a way, it is at opposite poles from what passed as "naturalism" in the nineteenth century. If the playwright, as Sartre defines him, adopts a theatrical stance for self-preservation, here *in* Genet's theater the characters complement that stance with a role that is both creative (in the sense that they deny their literal selves) and dead. The artifice enacts an essence whose basis is inseparable from death or nonexistence: in Genet's binary terms, we construct a statue in our mind that would serve equally as "grave" or "pedestal" (p. 46). In theatrical terms, the "impersonation" and "simulation" (p. 47) are lifeless reflections of physical life, mere roles. Preferring the self-consuming artifice to reality, even if it be that of a potentate of the church, the Bishop abhors being a real bishop for then one "should have to be constantly aware of being one so as to perform [his] function" (p. 11). Even live actors onstage fall short of this "theatrical truth" that opposes life and has death as its goal; when the Bishop's eyes close for the last time, he will see not himself but rather the bishop's bonnet "behind [his] eyelids" (p. 8). If "costume drama" is a justly negative description for those nineteenth-century stage extravaganzas, Genet here rescues the term. That same opening tableau shows the "Bishop's" real-life black trousers, shirt, and jacket draped over the chair; like his two successors, he insists that such artifacts of a lifeless life be removed from the stage.

The mirror is here the "unifying agent,"[9] the intermediary between an offstage world that is fraudulent because it lacks essence and the onstage world whose essence is meaningful precisely because it lacks the ennervating "life" of what passes for reality offstage. In his ballet *'Adame Miroir* Genet gives that mirror a central position when the Sailor's reverse image, playing Domino, usurps his "reality," thereby forcing him into the mirror as the Image. Disastrously liberated from inside, from living behind the mirror, his theatrical "reality" robbed from him by the Sailor-turned-Image, the Domino longs for his former reflected self. At the end, seeing only his reflection as Domino in the mirror, he dances with that image until the mirror opens so that, in Richard Coe's wonderfully ambiguous phrase, "the Domino is admitted back into reality."[10] That last word itself, like the mirror, includes both its customary and—at least in Genet's theater—its theatrical meanings. The clichéd fourth wall of the stage, supposedly admitting only the audience's vision, is here a two-way mirror. In passing through that mirror, however, one cannot regain the self as misperceived offstage.

2

Still, this enacted "self" as perceived by both others and oneself has a "double," for there is always present an inner self beyond stage enactment, a self to which the owner alone serves as audience. This self is, properly, *a*theatrical, one for which the theater itself can only be a referent, an imperfect intermediary that, in translating this inner self to its stage, perforce loses something in the translation. Seemingly an indifferent audience to the wished-for selves enacted in her brothel, Irma also confesses that all the time she has been "probing" herself (p. 12), although she assiduously, however incompletely—as in her sexual and Platonic passion for Arthur and George, respectively—tries to subordinate that inner being to her (mostly) hidden role as director and playwright. However, Irma, too, will become "client" when she assumes the role of Queen.

If the history of the theater can be traced to the introduction of a second character, allowing for dialogue, and then a third character, allowing for plot, then Genet's characters long to reverse the process, to return to that inner stage beyond enactment. Although the Bishop wants to be by himself (p. 11), when he condescends in allowing Irma to "eavesdrop," his "you" (in "I know you do, anyway") expands to include us. Similarly, we recognize the irony in Hamlet's "Now I am alone" (2.2.549), said once the actor so effectively impersonating Hecuba exits from the stage. However superior to her clients, Irma, too, longs to be "alone, mistress and assistant mistress of this house and of myself" (p. 95). Her jealousy of Carmen betrays a recognition that the latter makes the more successful attempt to enact that inner self; the seemingly indifferent manager of the sterile prostitutes onstage also holds concealed within her a self that is correspondingly passionate and nurturing. And if the brothel allows the clients to stage a wished-for self, that both they onstage and we offstage can then perceive, once they exit from Irma's establishment there springs forth in them a "secret brothel, [a] precious pink cat-house, [a] soulful whore-house" (p. 31).

The entire onstage set, the world we witness, thus hides its opposite; conversely, when the men return to reality, to their wives, they "keep a tiny, small-scale version of their revels in [Irma's] brothel" (p. 34). Irma defines this inner theater as "a Chinese lantern left over from a carnival, and waiting for the next one"—that is, a nonpublic stage, known only to its owner, generated from a past performance, anticipating the next public staging, yet at present still a private "theater" challenging the stage's normal function. Beyond "enactment," as that term is usually defined, this same theater is, in Irma's more expansive phrase, "an imperceptible light in the imperceptible window of an imperceptible castle" totally at the command of its inhabitant. This imperceptible, individual reality coexists with the stage's perceptible but, for that very reason, less than fully true reality, even as the stage, in Genet's equation, is itself superior to what passes for reality outside. Appropriately, Irma's three "imperceptibles" are spoken against a background of machine gun fire from backstage. The audience of *The Balcony* therefore witnesses three theaters: one present both visually and orally; an inner one only implied; and reality, here manifest savagely and also comically in the sounds of warfare.

3

These three stages and their corresponding audiences are inseparable from the playwright's well-known argument that the coexistence of actor and audience, or the person in motion and the motionless person witnessing that motion, is the means by which we achieve essence. In Genet's terms, or rather the Judge's, the fake thief validates the function of the fake judge; and, of course, the converse is no less true (p. 15).

Thus, even his reversal of the theater's metamorphosis from one to three characters takes a parabolic curve. If one's enacted self is ultimately a poor translation of that inner self, since the public self alone is validated in being perceived by an audience, even if it be an audience of one, then this same audience also unwittingly validates the presence of our invisible inner self. In the preface to *The Blacks* Genet can reduce the demands for an offstage audience of whites from many to one to a fake audience composed of many blacks in white masks, even to an audience of one black impersonating a white. But if the blacks refuse those white masks, still an audience of one white is necessary: "*then let a dummy be used*" (p. 4). If we cannot be an audience to our social or racial opposites, or if the insignificant man never encounters a man of significance, then the former must impersonate the latter so as to confer meaning on himself. We perforce must "love" our opposite, even our persecutor, for without him or her we are inauthentic.

In this sense the impoverished client acting the Judge's part ultimately represents not only wishfulfillment, as I suggested earlier, but rather—to adjust the phrase—fulfillment through the "image" that its impersonator can "touch" and therefore can "love" (pp. 18–19). This desire for the opposite of one's self defines the erotic pleasure to be derived from Irma's brothel. One can understand, therefore, the playwright's displeasure with the first London production, where the actresses, rather than the three male clients, were dressed seductively.

That little man of scene 4, perhaps an image of Genet himself, is also the most fully developed example of this adoration of one's opposite. In the fourth scene the three panels from the first three scenes change to three mirrors reflecting this tramp, who is the first "real" man of high station we observe in the brothel. The three mirrors used here are "fake" mirrors—and therefore more real than real mirrors, in Genet's reverse metaphysics—since the stage direction calls for three actors to stand behind empty frames impersonating the little man as he impersonates a tramp (pp. 27–28). At this moment the concept of audience overwhelms the theater: we watch an actor watching a triple reflection of his wished-for self, even as those three reflections, to perform their parts well, must watch every motion of the character *and* the actor they reflect. The little man is clearly us; our fourth wall is framed by the glassless mirror. Genet's more conceptual term for this situation of actor-audience and audience-actor is *complements* (p. 19), and the erotic nature of such complementarity is best conveyed in Roger's expression of love for Chantal: "You envelop me and I contain you" (p. 59). This is not mere physical love; rather, the "real" revolutionary can only be validated by the brothel's "unreal" actors and actresses—and, again, the reverse is no less true.

This mutual interchange between audiences and actors is not only erotic but *creative,* heightening the imagination rather than purveying sexuality. Although his real-life function is that of a death bringer, once George is transformed into the idealized Chief of Police, then he himself becomes an artist or creator, fashioning a static image that, to use his perversely reductive variation on "grow," will then "go and *rot* in people's minds" (p. 84 [author's emphasis]). Here, even the word for *growth* must admit its opposite in *decay.*[11] Impersonated by Roger, George is or soon will be dead, while his image, or name, "reverberates to infinity" (p. 92). Carmen also argues that Roger, dismissed earlier as being, like all revolutionaries, "without imagination" (p. 39), now becomes the artist, prefiguring his opposite in the Chief of Police and giving him form. In becoming his opposite, in making the imaginative leap from enemy to lover, Roger avoids death or, rather, will now never cease to die: "you don't stop dying" (p. 92).

It is the slave alone, embodied earlier in the aristocrat impersonating a tramp, whose escape from the appropriately named Valley of the Fallen, from George's now eternal domain, and rise to the daylight above makes him the singer or poet of Roger's action. His song, like *The Balcony* itself, supplants a singular, unperceived, dead reality offstage with the stage's imaginative, perceived artifice, a mutually shared life where one encounters one's own validating opposite, where, like the Sailor in *'Adame Miroir* who denies Alice's crossing back through the mirror world to reality, one lives forever in the paradoxically dead world of the theater. Here, life is not the person who existed, who once breathed, but the *persona* created by the playwright, sung about even as the slave, like Genet himself, will sing of Roger's emasculation, which in turn assures George's elevation, itself enacted on a stage unseen but "sensed" by us. The playwright of *The Balcony* "reverberates to infinity" by creating his onstage surrogate in this composite character, aristocrat-tramp-beggar-singer-in-reality. At once himself and the other, the praised and the humiliated, he passes from "dying" into the state of "nothing" (p. 90)—that is, death's correlative—and then into life itself as he begins "*to crawl up the stairs*" (p. 91). Like his playwright, then, he will sing of others created from the perception of one's self.[12] We ourselves are the subject for this ultimate audience, and of this playwright. As Roger, earlier a man of action rather than of words, now realizes, his "history was lived so that a glorious page might be written and then read" (p. 91). Whatever his source in Genet's own public or private life, Roger now resonates in the playwright's imaginative creation and in our witness of his play. The process parallels, I think, Shakespeare's portrait of the young man in the sonnets: the historical man dies yet lives in the poet's line, just as the father dies only to live in his progeny. It is imagination here, not prostitution, that is the procreative act, and I cite again the frequent observation that the French phrase for brothel is *maison d'illusions*.

The imaginative life illuminated by the theater of playwright, actor, and audience is at once fraudulent and radical, calling into question that lifeless life, unconsciously pretending to be real and, here in this party political play,[13] trying to preserve its establishment of death. Roger exposes this radical fraudulence in his abrupt question to Chantal: "You know all the roles, don't you? Just now, you were reciting lines to me, weren't you?" (p. 59). The tramp-turned-singer finds his namesake in both Carmen and Chantal, and, appropriately, it is the latter's "cameo eyes" that will "comfort and enchant the rabble" (p. 57) since those eyes corrupt their practical mission with a symbol. Similarly, the revolutionaries corrupt themselves by transforming Chantal from a real person to a symbol to an abstract design on the revolutionary flag. The singer is the theatrical radical, or embodiment, of Genet's own radical theater, overthrowing the professed political radicals of life itself.

The "real" man, Roger, must be tutored in these radical acts of the imagination by becoming a regular client of the house of illusions. He starts, appropriately, in the Mausoleum Studio where, as Carmen observes, everything is prearranged for him so that, not having to "indulge [his] imagination," he will not make "many" errors there (pp. 88–89). His role as apprentice actor, one not yet ready to go before an audience, is underscored when his first imaginative act, the ill-timed and therefore theatrically nonproductive castration, is performed "*with his back to the audience*" (SD, p. 93), a stage position any accomplished actor would think unnatural. His amateur's status is satirized by Irma's comic "On my rugs! On the new carpet! He's a lunatic!" (p. 93). Note that Irma delivers this line not as the "real" Irma but as the Queen; her self-realized impersonation thus contrasts with Roger's beginner's effort. As the Chief moves to an inner theater, and the slave, having realized his opposite, is liberated to the daylight, Roger, the professed opponent of illusion and its house of illusions, begins his own journey into a world of fraudulent but comforting essence. Or, as Irma observes, "The more killing there is in the working-class districts, the more the men roll into my studios" (p. 31).

4

We are, of course, the only real audience present during the production of *The Balcony,* although even that assumption will be challenged by the play and, in particular, by Irma's closing remarks.[14] In Genet's words, the play and its audience constitute a "problematic meeting."[15] Our presence is acknowledged early, as in Irma's question to the Bishop's demand for privacy: "Won't anyone be able to witness it?" (p. 8). She also confesses to feeling "uneasy . . . professionally" if nobody but she and the woman are allowed to observe the opening scene (p. 9). If the play is concerned with imaginative rather than sexual union, still the characters would commit their actions in private, beyond enactment; like the Bishop, the Judge asks, "Are all the doors firmly shut? Can anyone see us, or hear us?" (p. 16). He expects a negative answer. From the characters' perspective, we are voyeurs, present for a play whose main set has cracks in its walls, along with electronic spying devices encouraging such voyeurism. But if we can identify with our onstage surrogates, then, like them, we are more properly "visitors." Irma herself underlines the importance of that word by breaking it into syllables: "And I demand respect for the visitors. Vi-si-tors!" (p.

29). The house "watched" (p. 43) or later "beseiged" (p. 8) by the rebels is the theater we ourselves have entered and now observe. George surely speaks as much for us as for himself when he defines his purpose in coming to Irma's "place": "It's to find satisfaction in your mirrors and their trickery" (p. 50). As the play progresses, its metadramatic awareness of us, the offstage audience, can apply without any loss of translation to those assembled onstage; what seems like threatening "roars" from the audience observing the royal procession turns out to be "cheering" or applause (p. 71). Roger's petulant "They give you the rush in this place!" (p. 93) will have a special meaning for the audience uninitiated in the tightly packed complexities of Genet's self-conscious theater. The Police Chief's "Think of me" (p. 94), like Hamlet's "You [that] are mutes or spectators to this act" (5.2.334–335), effortlessly includes those on- and offstage.

Yet *The Balcony*'s awareness of us is as much physical as verbal.[16] The play actually "waits" for us, or, rather, the brothel, its field of play, anticipates our presence in the "*unmade bed*" (p. 7) that is visible in the first three scenes through the onstage mirror's reflection. The stage direction notes that "*if the room were arranged logically,* [*the bed*] *would be in the first rows of the orchestra*" (p. 7). By scene 5 that reflected bed, earlier housing the audience only by a mirror's "implications," makes its way onstage, for we see that the bed and its surroundings are Irma's room, the "*same room that was reflected in the mirrors in the first three scenes*" (p. 28). In similar fashion, in scene 4 our presence, only implied during the first three scenes, is actualized or reenacted in the figure of the "*little old man.*" We enter this play at first indirectly and then directly; the cycle completes itself when Irma, in her epilogue, comments on our fate once we leave the theater. Even this exit has been anticipated in the Bishop's concern "about getting home" (p. 8).

The reaction of real-life audiences to *The Balcony* has ranged from unthinking ardor (the Emperor's-New-Clothes syndrome, in effect) to equally unthinking dismissal of Genet's work. Yet if we are seduced, as Roger will be, by its illusion, we are theatrical rivals become converts. Just before the first scene that introduces Roger and the revolutionaries (scene 6), we hear a "*window-pane*" and a "*mirror near the bed*" "*shivered*" by gunfire, and I would make a connection between this attempted destruction of Irma's theater (the window)—and its modus operandi (the mirror)—and Murray Krieger's definition of art as being at once a *window* through which we look back out into reality and a *mirror,* or self-contained world operating by its own autonomous aesthetic principles.[17] As it assaults our social or aesthetic bias, we, outside the play like that unwilling guest unable to escape before being seen by the host, are recognized and invited inside.

With open minds, eager to experience Genet's elimination of the boundaries between life and art, between off- and onstage, we can respond "No, not at all" to the Envoy's question, "Would it perturb you to see things as they are. To gaze at the world tranquilly and accept responsibility for your gaze, whatever it might see?" (p. 64). At the very least we can "eavesdrop" (p. 11), becoming voyeurs on the stage of our own wish-fulfillment.[18] At best we are willing participants in a radical theater that, in forcing us to challenge the standard definitions of reality and illusion, forces us to "doubt" ourselves (p. 85).[19] Anticipating his "apotheosis" (p. 84), George speaks of his future self, and, by implication, the present theater when he defines his image as "a pool in which they behold themselves" (p. 86). Thus stimulated, the "eyes" of this audience can develop "astounding qualities" (p. 89). In seeing our surrogates onstage, we can cultivate what one observer calls "consciousness," and another, "self-recognition."[20] In this sense, we are not only the ultimate audience, but also the ultimate actor; the play's final concern is our own identity.[21]

Of course, we never physically make it to the stage, except indirectly by that reflection of an unmade bed. However, two graphic statements of our presence are to be found in scene 8 and in the closing moments of the final scene. In the former, the stage becomes the balcony itself; as the shutters facing the audience are opened, the characters step to the edge of the balcony, which the stage direction locates as "*at the very edge of the footlights*" (p. 70). That sometimes hackneyed blocking of the modern theater, where the character standing on the periphery of the stage speaks his lines to some imaginary member of the audience, is here restored, *enhanced* by Genet's more pervasive concern for the "real" audience. Appropriately, the only dialogue in this otherwise silent tableau is that of our audience surrogate, the Beggar: "Long live the Queen!" His clichéd welcome contains Genet's symbolic theater: the mortal Queen dies even as the essence of her role, although not her inner self, is ratified by the stage enactment. The intrusion of that nonessential reality existing outside the house of illusions underscores the point: a shot is heard, Chantal falls, and the General and the Queen carry her away "*dead.*"

Yet, the most significant challenge for us to be more than eavesdroppers can only occur once the play has enacted itself, once it has had, to rework Virginia Woolf's eloquent phrase, its own vision.[22] Like Pirandello's Henry IV, as he gathers his actor-courtiers about him to fend off the real but inconsistent offstage world, Irma's final speech defines both the accomplishment and the failure of her illusory world in terms of the greater cost to her clients once they leave the brothel. Clearly, she addressed us no less than the onstage characters. Like a director, she will now be occupied in closing up the theater for the night, covering the stage set ("put the furniture-covers on"), and preparing for the next production when once again the lights must be turned up, costumes and disguises resumed, the set ("studio") readied, and roles distributed. She knows that her function, its "truth," lies both in its consistency and in her awareness of her role. But we "must now go home, where everything—you can be quite sure—will be falser than here" (p. 96). As actors in life's seemingly greater but potentially more fraudulent stage, our roles are now beginning, once we have observed its simulacrum on the theater's more circumscribed stage. Irma's instructions verge on the practical as well: "Leave by the right, through the alley." Then, just when we think we have been delivered back into reality, the theater, the illusion, reasserts itself. The sounds that literally end the play, the machine-gun fire, are of course not real, but only an illusion created by the sound crew. Irma's reference to morning—"It's morning already"—is, like the theater itself, a lie: if the production began at eight in the evening, then, even given its long running time, it is still dark outside.

We exit Genet's theater only to enter the real world's more public stage. Still, if we fellow clients carry within us our own "secret theater" (p. 35), even as in entering Irma's brothel "each individual [has brought] his own scenario, perfectly thought out" (p. 36), then our human task, our burden, will be to compare these inner and public theaters. Once we have done that, we can bring into enactment for our own audience, both as constituted by our sole self and by those others who interact with that self, what would otherwise die with the individual. If Irma's closing reference to "morning" is a tribute to the theater's spell, its figurative implications are anticipated when she speaks of her clients' pain in leaving a theater that starts only to finish as an "awakening [that] must be brutal" (p. 35). The reverse works as well: our entry into Genet's theater is also an awakening, a moment to see ourselves as another, the other, sees us. Irma tells us she can detect the clarity of the minds thus awakened through the eyes: "Suddenly they understand mathematics. They love their children and their country. Like you" (p. 35). That "you" seems at once singular and plural, simple and complex.[23]

5

This movement from the onstage to the offstage audience mandates a return to life itself. There, *The Balcony* implies, the concepts of theater and audience bifurcate to the extremes of shallow commercialism and, conversely, to a mysterious level beyond the comprehension of Genet's own complex theater.

When that shallow commercialism takes the form of the three photographers searching for the "definitive image" (p. 73), what is seen through the camera's lens has little to do with the truth, platonic or theatrical, but rather with what will sell in the tabloids. From the photographers' perspective, the outside world wants "to be bombarded with the picture of a pious man," and hence the end justifies the means: the General's monacle serves as the communion wafer, a rolled-up sheet of paper doubles as a marshal's baton. Such art is indeed *fraudulent,* yet not productive in the sense that the word otherwise has in Genet. In this reductive definition, their art presents "a true image, born of a false spectacle" (p. 75). Society's insistence on order, a rationale at variance with the playful, more relative mode of our modern theater that Genet epitomizes, is also at fault here. Carmen anticipates such commercial art through her pun: when she views that outside where "men show their naked selves" unrelieved by artifice and hence embodying no meaning beyond that of physical existence, then "it has all the unreality of a film" (p. 42). A Sartrean upside down saint achieving salvation through damnation, Genet equates the film's unreality with that of a picture showing "the birth of Christ in the manger." Loren Kruger speaks of *The Blacks* in terms that apply, I think, to the present situation: their beliefs assaulted by Genet's radical portrait of life as both shallowly and as deeply perceived, the "audience is not allowed simply to consume the myth in the manner of the photograph."[24] In *The Balcony* Chantal, who existed meaningfully when she worked in Irma's studio, is also reduced by the revolutionaries to something akin to a photographer's false symbol.[25] Again, the incompatibility between life uninformed by serious theater and theater as informed by Irma or Genet is underscored when Chantal is slain by the revolutionaries' own bullets.

However, when understood in a more relative context, life seems as mysterious to us as it had been reductive to the photographers. The Judge, who has now experienced both the theater's and life's realities, observes that "what you call outside is as mysterious to us as we are to it" (p. 85). The alternatives, therefore, are to acknowledge the world outside the theater as so relative or mysterious that it is beyond the reach of any clarifying metaphor, or to hammer it into the photographers' predictable and therefore false images. One can also explain it by the self-defeating allegory of the pious: the Bishop's affirmation of his authority "before "God Who sees me" (p. 11) reduces the concept of audience so far defined, and the Judge's equation of himself with the Devil, with the "King of Hell [who] weigh[s] those who are dead" (p. 17), is undercut by the Thief's sarcastic "You frighten me, sir," and further undercut by Genet's stage direction that the Judge speak "*very bombastically.*" Reality as generally understood, although indispensable to the theater's illusion—the "authentic detail" (p. 35) required at every performance—is also an irritant, hostile to the circumscribed actor-audience circuit of the stage.

Still, in Genet's symbolic, nonnaturalistic theater,[26] the parameters of actor and audience themselves constitute a significant presence. Through the metaphor of multiple audiences, the Judge and George define the arena of the play: above her attendants is the Queen, about the Queen herself is the image of the kingdom, above that image is God, above God are his subjects ("without whom God would be nothing"), above the people are the photographers, who are "on their knees before the people who are on their knees before God," and so on (pp. 82–83). For Genet, therefore, the Renaissance metaphor of the stage as a little world would deny the theater's literal presence.[27]

Because for Genet this stage usurps reality, it is in flux, a world of revolution, or what the Envoy calls a palace or theater of "continuous explosion" (p. 65). The principles of the theater, its "Comedy and Appearance," remain "pure," its "revels intact" (p. 36), but the mirror, *The Balcony*'s central image as well as the avenue of perception for the audience, is a "reality" without fixity (p. 41). Carmen's earlier criticism that Irma is too given to her "sober ceremonies" and lacks a sense of "irony" (p. 30) is well taken, for Irma will forsake her "destiny" (p. 67) as the director and indifferent observer to her clients' spectacles to become a real-life queen, temporarily abandoning illusion for the "useful" (p. 80). As the bishop recognizes, at any moment the stage's "ornamental purity, [its] luxurious and barren—and sublime—appearance" can be "eaten away" (p. 80).

When this destructive thrust toward the world outside the brothel meets the intrusion of reality, comically in the form of the three photographers, less so in the revolution outside the brothel, the collision admits multiple interpretations. Roger's castration is one such instance; is it his self-punishment for seeking power,[28] or a capitulation to the principle of illusion,[29] or his victory over the Chief in driving him into the aesthetic fixity of the tomb?[30] As it mediates what passes as reality outside, Genet's theater is too fluid to admit a single reading. Even that supreme moment for the onstage audience, when the little man sees himself and, with three actors impersonating his reflection, is in turn seen in three mirrors, must coexist with life as it is absurdly represented by the "*three almost simultaneous flashes*" of the photographers' cameras (p. 94).

Like a molecule, this theater has the physical stage at its core, around which revolve actor and audience. Furthermore, it is vulnerable, existing only to deconstruct: the telemachine that works so well earlier later breaks down. If tragedy requires implacable values,[31] *The Balcony* can offer none, but only what one critic calls a "becoming," and another calls a "process" in which its metaphor of the mirror continually mediates, but does not resolve, the conflict between art and reality.[32] We can identify the audience with life and the actor with the theater, yet what are we to do when the roles are reversed? Carmen longs to see her daughter alive in a real garden, preferring this anticipated role as audience to that of actor playing the martyred Saint Theresa. Yet once Irma reminds Carmen that her daughter is dead, the mother becomes both audience and actor, playing the saint in "flaming robe," under which is her heart, in which is an artificial garden where she can view her child's grave (p. 40). If appearance or illusion seem preferable to function or reality, the former are dependent on the latter, and even if they are capable of "consol[ing]" (p. 47) us as dreamers (p. 95), that consolation is itself an illusion. Irma's own pleasure in becoming the Queen who literally "acts" in the real world is undercut by her realization that she impersonates only herself: "In the center of the Palace is a woman like me." The Envoy, "*imperturbably*," reduces the picture further: that same woman is "standing on one foot in the middle of an empty room" (p. 63).

If Roger's castration or his impersonation of the Chief admits a number of conflicting yet equally valid interpretations,[33] then the relation between illusion and reality in Genet does no less: the two are in suspension,[34] or reality estranges an audience given to illusion,[35] or both reality and illusion are denied,[36] or both coexist as part of our larger existence.[37]

6

The relativity of this theater, its continuous implosion, its "life," in turn admits or, more properly, leads to, its opposite—death or fixity. In the Chief's tomb, as the Envoy reminds us, there are mirrors that "will reflect to infinity . . . the image of a dead man" (p. 69). Our own audience's eye itself a mirror, our living retina is imprinted with the stage's own image of death. The Bishop's line, "Here I stand, face to face with my death," is thus no less relevant to the offstage audience (p. 13). The most radical tenet of Genet's theater is not that it effaces life. Rather, Genet posits a third phase to theatrical presence and the metaphor of life as a stage—a pure stage at once avoided and sought by us, one of fixity or death, or what the playwright calls the "hieratic" dedicated to our "quest of immobility" (p. 61), or our "final immobility" (p. 13). Codependent, reality and illusion are therein perfectly balanced. Even when the theater's integrity is temporarily assured, such as by covering the windows with padded curtains (p. 8), its inhabitants still seek the nonintegral life offstage. As one of the characters exclaims, "You think we're going to be satisfied with make-believe to the end of our days" (p. 77). The liberation from such flux or relativity must be found in stasis, immobility, of which death itself is its most perfect expression.

Still, the conflict of opposites, although halted by immobility, is reactivated. As George goes to his death, in a theater of fixity beyond any stage representation, in a tomb made of a plasticized penis mocking the real-life agent of regeneration, the static darkness itself is opposed by the very onstage audience witnessing his immolation. The Bishop, Judge, and General, the first visitors to the brothel, yearn for the daylight world, one of action and "visibility" (p. 79). No longer dreamers but real men with political power, "dragged [from] . . . a happy state" of illusion, they will now "continue the quest of an absolute dignity" (pp. 79–80). Soon they will emulate the Police Chief who, when like them, emulated the pure image that they now both willingly and unwillingly fulfill as their function (pp. 79–80).

If Irma represents the principle of the Imagination,[38] she is also the audience that, even while accepting the stage's two hours' traffic as a patent falsity questioning any fixity we claim offstage, takes up the theater's challenge to "play" with life, to refashion it, to be what life denies us or, as in Genet's case, to usurp as our own an image that life has thrust upon us. We may enter Genet's theater curious and open-minded about what passes as reality, yet as the stage's seductive illusion verges on the real, it also becomes binding, lifelike, while life, in contrast, now seems new, fresh, an awakening from the confines of the stage. The theater's momentary therapy becomes a burden. One critic astutely observes that whereas in *The Tempest* Prospero with his epilogue frees us from Shakespeare's theater, Irma in her final lines only delivers us to our chains, to another theater,[39] to our illusion-bound world.[40] If it is always the next illusion we want,[41] then life in turn becomes a stimulant, part of the process. Jonas Barish eloquently captures this sense of equipoise between the modern audience and its theater that Genet in turn enacts in *The Balcony:*

> If the day ever dawned when men became truly able to "live in themselves," like Rousseau's imagined savages, if the dangers of theatricality ever ceased to threaten us in our daily lives, then perhaps our special need for the theater as an art form might also vanish: it would no longer

confront us with an account of our own truth struggling against our own falsity.[42]

7

As the third of Genet's five plays, *The Balcony* seems central not only chronologically but also philosophically to the issues I have raised. In *Deathwatch* the onstage audiences are comparatively static, ranging from the three inmates "circling around" (p. 121) each other to our most graphic surrogate, the Guard who more than any other character is "in the know" (p. 140). Even when Lefranc's "inauthentic" crime in killing Maurice isolates him from such concentric audiences, the principle of the onstage audience remains inviolate. As Lefranc utters his "I really am all alone!" Genet's stage direction instructs the Guard to appear "*smiling*" as he "leers" at Green Eyes, the "object" for whom Lefranc has unwittingly sacrificed himself.[43]

Seen in this light, *The Maids* is a more sophisticated play, for the sisters carry to the extreme, to death itself, the dualities of audience and actor. Finding their selves each in the other, as well as their combined idealized self in their mistress, they finally purify their inner theater by murdering the world, one embodied in the melodramatic story of the mistress and her lover. Playing her sister, Solange observes Claire playing both Madame taking the poison and, by extension, the despised counterimage of themselves.

In *The Blacks,* that despised "other" is "represented" upstage by blacks dressed as white colonials who serve as judges of the play performed by blacks playing blacks centerstage. Ultimately not a chauvinistic piece celebrating blacks, let alone whites, the play is so pervaded by the notion that we act the role given us by our audience, or by the audience socially dominant at the time, that here, where the audience-judges are also the judge, every metadramatic reference works equally well for the action offstage as well as on. Village can thus address both his fellow actors and us by switching a single pronoun: "Are they following me? . . . Are you following me?" (p. 74). Indeed, by this point those two pronouns seem interchangeable.[44] The final long scene of *The Screens* multiplies such onstage audiences to a factor of nine, with the transitions among them represented literally and figuratively by the porous screens themselves.

The character's complementarity as self-audience has an equally wide range. In *Deathwatch* the inmates are primarily aware of their physical selves; after some hesitation, perhaps even embarrassment, Green Eyes confesses that he likes "to cuddle up in [his own] arms" (p.

137). Because the lesbian twinship of the maids makes them a single, composite character, the focus of that play is essentially psychological. Claire's wish for Solange, "If only you could see ourself" (p. 54), becomes redundant when the servants' coequal self-love and self-hatred is also simultaneously played and observed by the sisters. Conversely, the blacks, although also servants, cannot initiate the self but can only imitate and thereby parody a self assigned by their white audience.[45] In *The Screens* the oppressed (the Algerians) also must assume a role established by their oppressors (the French Colonials), and it is only through the egalitarian nature of death that the stultifying, formative "look" of others can be mollified. Here, though, even Said's denial of the self, his attempted indifference to all those who perceive him, fails to free him when the Algerians threaten to convert him to a symbol of nationalism. In doing so, however, they become, as the blacks threaten to become, indistinguishable from the French audience who had earlier judged and thereby formed them.

Those larger implied offstage audiences in *The Balcony* parallel the historical audience that Green Eyes describes, the "terrific crowd of people in the streets" waiting like a theatrical audience for him "to show [himself] at the window" after the girl's murder (p. 135). In *The Blacks* it is this offstage audience who witness the black traitor's trial, for which the onstage play has been a diversion.

As the "real" offstage audience in *The Maids,* our role changes from that of dupes—until the alarm rings signaling the end of the sisters' dress rehearsal, we have assumed that we are observing Madame and a single servant—to coparticipants, as we form the crowd assembled, by implication, for Claire's funeral and Solange's imprisonment.[46] This elevation in our own role is underscored by Genet's curious stage directions that Claire, as she listens to Solange "*speak*" to an imaginary Madame, be "*visible*" only to us (p. 94), or at the end when, playing both herself and her sister, Solange faces "*the audience,* [*and*] *delivers the end of her speech*" (p. 99).

If we are collaborators in *The Maids,* we are, if whites, the opponents of the onstage actors in *The Blacks.* Not so much a diatribe against whites, I think, as against the more general notion of the domineering audience, *The Blacks* tries to "increase the distance that separates" actor from audience (p. 12). When we are asked to participate directly, the request is for the most trivial of actions; looking at the audience, Village asks if anyone would like to come onstage to hold Diof's (the Mask's) knitting (p. 69). Here we are denied seeing not only the real play, the execution and trial of the black traitor, but also a play in which blacks can be blacks since, still dependent on the discredited vocabulary of whites, Village and Virtue are at present deprived of a stage suitable for enacting their love.[47] If deprived of a meaningful role in *The Blacks,* we are, conversely, omniscient in *The Screens,* for the "spectacle's worth a look," as Said's Mother informs us (p. 161).

Opposed to the world of "solid accomplishment," as that phrase would be defined by those in power, by those for whom the theater is often a mere plaything, the theater for Genet, then, becomes the "home" of the powerless others, whether they take the form of socially insignificant clients, inmates, servants, oppressed minorities, or, as in the case of *The Screens,* an oppressed majority. Yet as this arena of play becomes serious business for those others, its actors lose their craft and venture into life itself, which in turn, generates a need for the theater.

8

There is a wonderful, childish innocence in Archibald's lines in *The Blacks:* "They tell us that we're grown-up children. In that case, what's left for us? The theater! We'll play at being reflected in it, and we'll see ourselves—big black narcissists—slowly disappearing into its water" (pp. 38–39). Locked in her self-chosen house of illusion, after a disastrous flirtation with being a real Queen, Irma also gleefully consigns her audience of adults to their own world. This same mood is echoed by Solange as she plays the Presenter in her closing lines: "We are beautiful, joyous, drunk and free!" (p. 100). The playwright himself is not regressive; rather he underscores the basic impossibility of remaining *homo ludens* even as he exposes the basic falsity of *homo sapiens.* That outside audience, as in *The Screens,* would "bottle" or confine Said (p. 138) just as it would the theater in making it the servant, the "reflection" (in the most pejorative sense of that word) of what passes as reality. Ommu realizes this: "To be their reflection is already to be one of them" (p. 135). Yet this child's existence is only defined by the presence of that same adult audience and its world.

There is a telling moment in *The Blacks* when the seeming opposites, black Virtue and the white Queen, or the worlds of play and of the playless reality of the powerful, realize their kinship as they recite in unison lines normally assigned to the dominant audience: "I am white, it's milk that denotes me, it's the lily, the dove, quicklime, and the clear conscience. . . . It's innocence and morning" (p. 45). For a moment, opposites—life and death (milk and lily), childhood and adulthood (innocence and morning)—are combined. Still, this is at best an interlude, and it is the tension between these two irreconcilable worlds, brought into the momentary and harmless confrontation onstage, that generates the dramatic energy in Genet. Similarly, the confrontation among real persons is displaced, mitigated, when some agree to be actors and others the audience to those actors, or when on our own inner stage we experience that moment of liberation as we play audience to our own actor.

Genet's theater is thus an attack on a self-assurance of which we would be unaware had we not entered his theater. Awareness, I think, and not change, is his object, despite the tantalizing political or social commentary that *seems* to inform his final two plays.[48] Art and life indeed may be irreconcilable or—conversely—may be interchangeable.[49] Yet theater is made possible by a stage where persons of flesh and blood become symbols, and where the audience, those clients entering this house of illusions, see patent imitations of themselves as meaningful precisely because they are imitations.

4

Brecht, *Galileo:* "And Yet It Moves!"

I will ask the reader's indulgence if, abandoning the *security* of the third person, I become shamelessly personal in this present chapter, perhaps even anecdotal at times. This is not the chapter I first intended to write.

I had acted in several of Brecht's plays, even impersonating the playwright himself in the role of the narrator for a production of *Mother Courage*. Yet, his dominant presence in twentieth-century theater notwithstanding, he was not among my favorites. For me, Brecht never penetrated our inner lives the way Beckett always does; even in the best of translations his dialogue paled beside the verbal wit of Stoppard. In him was none of that delicious hot-house imagery of a Genet; alongside the coy Pinter he seemed obvious, even didactic.

But one can't very well write a book on the function of the audience in the modern theater without discussing Brecht, with all his chest-thumping against what he saw as the passive role of the audience in the illusionist theater. Brecht's theory of estrangement, of course, denied the audience a comforting "fix" on the characters, and he insisted that the actor, like a spectator to his own performance, see himself as representing a social type, rather than becoming absorbed in a character.

Therefore, I dutifully—and a bit maliciously—decided to pick the one play that gave Brecht the most trouble, his only work based in detail on actual historical events. For despite Brecht's revising *Galileo* after the dropping of the atom bomb, thereby converting the romantic scientific hero of the pre-war version to a vastly contradictory character in the post-war revision, audiences for almost forty years now have usually felt an emotional identification with the character of Galileo.[1] Even when performed before people sympathetic to Brecht's avowed politics, the play seems to contradict the doctrine of its playwright. Ronald Speirs observes, for instance, that *Galileo* has never been especially popular in the German Democratic Republic, and speculates that this has "something to do with the demands that it makes on the intellect and the patience of the audience."[2] Indeed, Brecht's own championing of the spectator's equality with the actor might actually reveal a distrust of the audience, an autocratic teacher's inability to leave them to their own resources. Hence, he argues that the audience be fully lit rather than obscured by a darkened house, or that the performance itself continually call attention to its own artifice.

Several months after the present book had been accepted by the press, I received a call from my colleague Hernan Vera of the university's Sociology Department. The context for that phone call itself offers a striking parallel to the situation in *Galileo*. A year before, a controversy had erupted between the local university faculty union—the United Faculty of Florida, of which Vera is chapter president—and the administration of my university. It was alleged that the university's president, in sympathy with the then president of our chamber of commerce, had agreed to send out as speakers into the community faculty who would argue for (mostly) unrestricted economic growth for Gainesville—our town of some one hundred thousand people. These "growthers," as they were dubbed, would thereby counteract a rash of "non-growthers," faculty who, speaking as private citizens, were pressing for more restrictions on commercial development. After admitting that he had "embellished" the remarks of the university's president, the president of the chamber of commerce then resigned his position. However, unsatisfied, Vera and the union sent a long letter to the administration, asking to be reassured that academic freedom would not be violated. Essentially, the union argued that it was unethical for the administration to think of itself as a "person" with a distinct view that could be arrayed against those of the "non-growth" faculty.

When the university president replied in what the union saw as a short, almost generic letter saying, in effect, that there was no real issue involved, that the administration had always supported academic freedom, Vera, in an attempt to diffuse and then make productive his initial anger, appealed to the National Education Association, the parent of the local union, for funds to hold a three-day "Conference on Academic Freedom" on campus. Two months before the conference, I received that phone call. Vera's simple request was this: "Could you do something dramatic for the second night of the conference?" Something dramatic?—*Galileo*, despite my personal feelings, was the obvious choice. What was originally planned as a concert reading of the play, since Vera had asked for a single performance in a banquet room, quickly became a full-scale production when the board of directors of the Acrosstown Repertory Theater, our experimental theater in Gainesville, asked me if I would stage *Galileo* for what turned out to be an extended five-week run. Once I had to think of the work from a director's perspective, taking it through the early stage when I hammered out what we call the "director's concept," and taking it in turn through rehearsals to opening night, I discovered that I *adored* Brecht, that this play was one of the most challenging I had ever encountered.

1

To test Brecht's notion about the relationship between actor and audience, I decided to play *Galileo* on three circular stages (ten feet in diameter, and raised nine inches from the floor), located in the upper-right, upper-left, and down-side center of the large, rectangular room of the Acrosstown Repertory Theater. With these three stages resembling islands, the audience would surround them on all sides like an ocean. Crosswalks painted on the floor connected the three stages; an added crosswalk extending from the down-stage to the double doors on the theater's east side led to the lobby. If an actor moved from stage 1 (upper-right) onto the crosswalk to stage 2 (down-side), he would thereby pass through spectators seated on either side. Conversely, the spectators would have to adjust their posture as the action moved from one stage to another, although no audience member would have to turn more than ninety degrees. In effect, this arrangement was much more complex than the conventional proscenium stage, even as it incorporated but still went beyond both theater-in-the-round and an alley staging (the audience seated on either side of a central stage). If it made blocking more complex, these "islands" and their "ocean" also brought the actor into very intimate contact with the audience. The bulk of our lights were focused on the three stages, with auxiliary lighting on the crosswalks. During rehearsals, we learned to make those crosswalks playing areas in their own right. The large double doors to the theater themselves were used for significant entrances—for example, in scene 6 when Cardinals Bellarmin and Barberini enter, or in scene 11 when Galileo emerges to give his recantation speech. As a result, additional lighting was put on this area. On the question raised by Brecht of lighting the audience, I decided to meet the playwright halfway. Since a good deal of light spilled over from the stages to the surrounding chairs, the audience sat in something resembling the light of a not-too-dark cocktail lounge. Besides seeing the actors onstage, everyone could see fellow spectators in fairly sharp outline.

The three blue stages rested on a floor painted dark black, thereby establishing a fairly neutral playing area. On the theater's four walls—three were twelve feet high, with the upstage wall extending some thirty feet to a high-beamed ceiling—was painted a mural of the

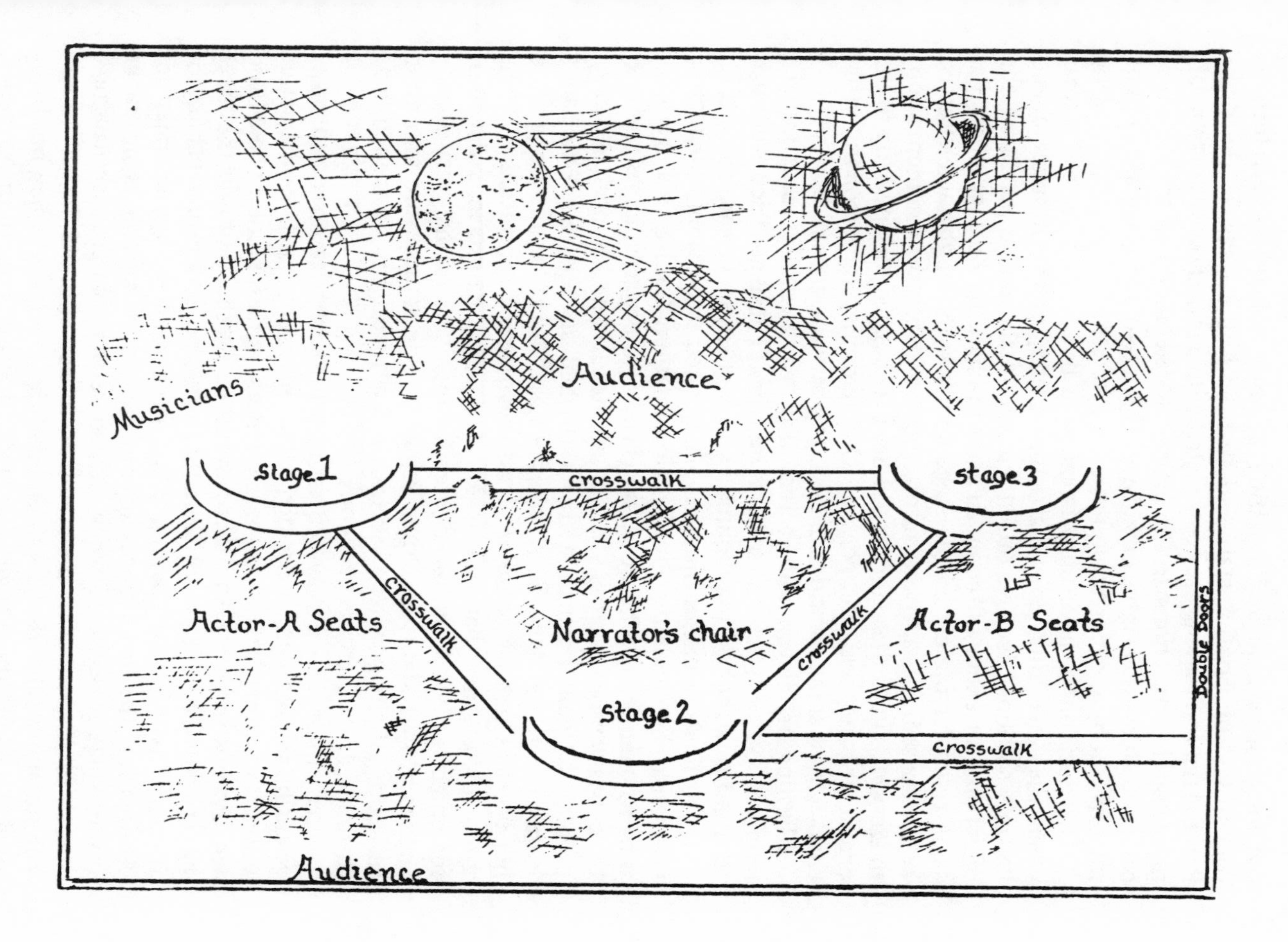
Musicians
Audience
Stage 1
crosswalk
stage 3
crosswalk
Actor-A Seats
Narrator's chair
crosswalk
Actor-B Seats
Double Doors
Stage 2
crosswalk
Audience

cosmos, nonrealistic and boasting brightly colored planets over a background of shooting stars and assorted Milky Ways. In this fashion, the neutral playing area contrasted with a mural that was, to recall my general instructions to the artist, "a celebration of the heavens, colorful, glorious, bright, expansive, joyous—outer space as it might exist free of human corruption or even cynicism."

The decision to have no offstage area but instead to seat actors, when they had finished a particular scene, in the nearest of two "actor's sections" located on either side of the house produced the effect on a spectator of seeing an actor in-character onstage, then that same actor, having exited the stage and now out-of-character, seated beside oneself. If that spectator discreetly whispered a comment about the production to the actor, would he, I speculated, be speaking to the character, the real-life person who had just impersonated that character, or some hybrid soul hovering between art and life?

Clothing my eleven adult actors in brown monklike robes put the emphasis on each actor's face and delivery. These generic, even proletariat brown robes, highlighted by a single piece of jewlery or cloth (our Cardinal Inquisitor hit upon a bright red sash), would identify or symbolize the character. Until his recantation, Galileo, for example, wore a golden pendant shaped like the sun; afterwards, it was replaced by a heavy brown cross. Mr. Matti had about his neck a heavy, pretentious golden chain with intertwined strands, Sagredo had a jaunty beret, and Mrs. Sarti, a set of heavy brass keys hanging from her waist. These *personalized* accessories thereby contrasted with the uniform costumes that said, in effect, "We exist ultimately not in or for ourselves but as public figures, as members of that very society Galileo at first shuns and then rejoins." The actors wore minimum makeup, a light powder base with a few highlights, just enough to distinguish actor from spectator.

Furthermore, in a play requiring a host of telescopes and other scientific instruments, I decided to use no props but have the actors mime everything instead, including letters, purses, money, books, and writing instruments. And there would be no sets—simply the three bare stages. The one exception to this would be an occasional chair, for instance, two in the opening scene when Galileo demonstrates for Andrea that the earth moves around the sun, or a single chair on the center stage in scene 13 when Galileo delivers his great confessional speech to Andrea, who sits attentive, indeed stunned, like a student behind an invisible desk. I should add, however, that when not being used in a scene, these chairs were located just offstage in the audience, facing backward (to prevent unwary spectators from occupying them).

To make music a coequal in the production, I commissioned a

colleague in our music department to write a score for *Galileo* for bassoon and flute. That score would be played live between scenes as a nonverbal, indeed, emotional, *commentary* either on the prior scene or on what was to come. At certain significant moments in the dialogue this music also accompanied Brecht's text—during the opening lines of scene 3, for example, as Sagredo looks through his colleague's telescope and, with Galileo, sees what no man has seen before, or during Galileo's confessional speech in the penultimate scene. For the between-scene music, my initial "instructions" to my composer friend consisted of a paragraph or so of prose describing what I thought had happened or would happen in a particular scene. For example, scene 3 moves from tension, as Galileo tries to seduce Sagredo with his new theory of the universe, to the comic entrance of the Curator, who is angry that he has been publicly embarrassed by this scientist passing off another man's invention as his own; it moves further to Galileo's romantic union with Sagredo as both realize "there is no support in the heavens" (p. 62), and even further to Sagredo's reassessment of what they have seen and his prophetic warning that Galileo not go to Florence, with a brief motif for Virginia who comes upon the two scientists and is shunted aside by her father in patriarchal fashion. The bassoon, low in the register and dark in tone, would represent the Ptolemaic order, and the flute, high and light in tone, the Copernican order. What my colleague gave me, after hibernating with his assignment for two months, went beyond and was far more complex than my expectations. His final score would have a profound effect on the audience's reception of the play, and of Brecht's text in particular.

An acting style that called attention to itself, to the fact that the momentary artifice of the stage world is being sustained by audience as much as by actor, seemed proper for Brecht. At the same time, I wanted all the characters to be three-dimensional, psychological beings, and not just social types. I was, in a sense, trying on one hand to be faithful to Brecht and his notion of character as social type, and yet also responsive to the needs of modern actors who prefer impersonating characters who remind them of themselves or of people they know. (Just try to get an actor these days to portray a character as a symbol or as an allegorical figure!) Therefore, the acting style would fluctuate between realistic and "artificial,"—that is, the actors' being aware of the audience, at times playing to them, including the spectators in the play by directing a line or even a phrase at them.

I also love doubling, even tripling parts. Hence, a single actor would play the First Senator, the Philosopher, Barberini (who later becomes the Pope), and the Customs Official in the final scene. In part, this multiple playing would be dictated by the particular skills of the actor, as well as by the obvious limitation of being able to double only those characters who never appear together in a single scene. But this concept also embodied psychological, even symbolic considerations. Might there not be a telling irony, for example, in having the Customs Official who allows Andrea to cross the border with the *Discoursi* earlier play the Pope who attempts to suppress Galileo? The actor who played the Curator in the first three scenes later became the Cardinal Inquisitor, and hence the audience was able to see one actor—we did not try to deceive the audience as to the single source of the two roles—change from the comic, practical, businesslike Pruili (the Curator) to the rather sinister, single-minded, evangelistic Inquisitor.

For the crowd in the Carnival scene (scene 9), I used seven young children, including two of my own, and they reappeared as the children taunting Old Marina, the supposed witch, in the final scene. These children were not only the barometer for the conflicts between the adults when they leapt passionately but unthinkingly, childishly, at Galileo's theories, but also the promise, for good or for evil, of the future. In that final scene I placed the Boy, who realizes he has come to the wrong conclusions about the old woman, between his playmates, who are clinging to their fear that the Old Marina is a witch, and Andrea, who begs them, indeed, begs the entire audience, to look carefully with their eyes, to "think it over" (p. 128). Because the children are the future, an extension beyond the immediate play, I had them wear ordinary school clothes, not robes, to remind the audience that ultimately *Galileo* is set not in the 1630s, or even the 1930s of Nazi Germany, or the postwar 1950s, but today, *now*, even as our Gainesville audience, aware of that growth/non-growth conflict that had been the stimulus for the production, would translate Brecht's pseudo-history into *their* present.

All this, then, albeit described here in the most general fashion, constituted my director's concept. That concept would be affirmed, challenged, enhanced, and at times discarded during that exciting period between the first rehearsal—actually, even during the read-through preceding the first rehearsal—and opening night.

2

Initially, I wanted to distribute among the cast Brecht's narrations fronting each scene, with an actor doing a given narration—usually the last actor to speak in the preceding scene—stepping out of character. Since we had no sets, I also added to Brecht's little poems or suggestive prose passages the descriptions of the set itself. Thus, the narration for the second scene consisted of the four-line poem ("No one's virtue is complete . . . The truth about his telescope") and also the passage extending from ". . . the Great Arsenal of Venice overlooking the harbor . . ." to ". . . and his friend Sagredo, on the other side" (p. 55). But during the first read-through I realized that Mrs. Sarti's part was small—in the Laughton version she only appears in scenes 1 and 8—and since I had a very fine actress cast in that role, I decided, instead, to transfer all fourteen narrations to her. The question was soon raised: should she deliver the narrations as Mrs. Sarti? as a neutral observer (rather difficult, since some of the narrations are ironic, or take positions)? as a representative member of the audience (if this were possible)? Or should we take some other option? After testing out all of the above during rehearsals, my actress and I concluded that she should deliver the narrations as her real-life person, not as a representative member of the audience but rather as a single, *normal* spectator responding to what had just happened or, as is often the case with the narrations, knowing what is about to happen and offering something of a prejudgment on the forthcoming scene against which each spectator might weigh his or her own response.

There were also some obvious places in the text where the actors might address the audience directly, such as Sagredo's "Can you see the Pope scribbling a note in his diary: 'Tenth of January, 1610, Heaven abolished'?" (p. 65). I had blocked this passage with Galileo standing on stage 1, having just told Virginia to "run along to mass"(p. 64), while Sagredo from stage 3 delivered his warning about the power of the monks in Florence. The line in question would be spoken as he moved on the crosswalk toward Galileo, a crosswalk cutting through the audience sitting on the up-side of the center stage.

I told the actors to find other places in the test where such direct addresses to the spectators might be appropriate, and, predictably, on those rehearsal nights when some of the technical crew or theater staff took time off to watch us, that is, on those occasions when we had a "real" audience, no matter how small, such places or opportunities did indeed emerge. During the actual run, with the house full, the frequency of such direct addresses took a quantum leap. Given the intimate relation between actor and audience and the nonrealistic bareness or—shades of Grotowski—"poverty" of our stages, having the actor alternately play to the world onstage and then to the encompassing audience seemed no great disjuncture. Sometimes such direct addresses would be made in a general manner, with the actor focusing on a particular section of seats or, just as often, involving the entire audience by turning in a circle onstage during the delivery of a line. At other times, a single audience member might be addressed: in scene 8, for example, when Andrea begged Galileo to "listen to this dedication" (p. 88) in a new book by Fabricius, only to be rebuffed by his teacher, he turned in desperation to someone sitting on the up-side of the central stage, thrusting an imaginary book before the spectator. But here I anticipated the next section since most of this interchange with the audience could be tried only in performance; the rehearsal audience, no matter how involved or friendly, was never, *is* never quite the same as the real thing.

At other times, accidents during rehearsal led to our rethinking this relation between actor and audience. As mentioned above, my original idea was to have the actor step out of character when he or she exited the stage to sit in one of the two actors' sections in the house. I even flirted with the idea of having no designated section for actors but asking, instead, that the actor take any available seat. But given our full houses, and the need to have the actors sit toward the center to facilitate their taking the stage for the next scene, this idea was quickly abandoned. One night, however, I noticed that when our Andrea took his seat in the actor-A section, after saying a tearful farewell to the teacher whom he had first greeted coldly, he was still too *high* from the emotion of the scene, was still in character. On the spot, I asked my Galileo to deliver his lines—"I gave him his first lesson; when he held out his hand, I had to remind myself that he is teaching now" (p. 125)—not to Virginia, as the script indicates, but to the *former* Andrea now seated with the audience. The effect was *electric,* for in a production designed to bring actor and audience closer, whatever barrier remained was now even more blurred. When Galileo returned to the world onstage with his question to Virginia—"How is the sky tonight?"—that world was reasserted yet also qualified since our Andrea, in the audience, now looked with his fellow spectators as Virginia mimed opening the shutters. When she replied, simply, "Bright," Andrea showed his pleasure as a spectator. His subtext would go something like: "The night is indeed bright since my teacher has taught me, by his failure, by his savage self-assessment, the most important of all lessons." His response would itself be reflected by that of the real-life audience surrounding him. We even learned how to intensify this effect by having one of the actors seated nearby push Andrea's chair a little forward as he exited the stage, so that everyone in the audience could have a clear view of this man both in and out of character. And while our lighting was otherwise *neutral*—no gels, no colors, with the lighting limited to following the action as it moved from one stage through a crosswalk to another stage—I made a rare exception for this one moment. As Virginia pronounced "Bright," we raised the stage illumination about 20 percent.

This *discovery* that the actor, while seated with the audience, could also continue in character led to numerous other erasures of the distinction between the stage and the house. At the end of scene 10, for example, once Galileo and Virginia heard the stern words of the Lord Chamberlain "that the Florentine court [was] no longer in a position to oppose the request of the Holy Inquisition to interrogate [Galileo] in Rome" (p. 107), Galileo slumped to a seat just off the stage in the actor-B section, head in hands, a beaten, humiliated old man, comforted by Virginia who, sitting next to her father, clung to him, cradling him like a mother. The two actors held this position throughout scene 11, leaving their seats only at the end so that our Galileo could exit out the double doors in order to come back through them when he gave his recantation in scene 12. Or, at the end of scene 13, after Virginia's "Bright," our Galileo, like a stage hand, removed his chair from the stage, placing it in a space between the chairs of two spectators sitting on the up-side of stage 1, and there, still in character, watched with them the final scene where Andrea smuggled the *Discoursi* over the border.

Until the final week of rehearsals, I did not insist that the actors, after finishing a particular scene, confine themselves to the two actors' sections. Until then, they were free to wander about the theater, to take a breather, as long as they were ready onstage for their next scene. Insisting that we now rehearse under performance conditions had wonderful benefits. For in good Brechtian fashion, as audience to their fellows onstage, seeing the play not just from the limited perspective of their own scenes, nor from the remove of backstage, the actors became like fellow directors. Actors, of course, often suggest bits of stage business to the director, mostly involving their own roles. Or, if they are critical of another performer, they might, subtly, suggest that the director do something about so-and-so since so-and-so is holding down a particular scene. To be sure, I got my normal share of such *contributions*. Still, with all the actors now being alternately character and audience, I found them offering a scholarlike *reading* of the larger play that went far beyond anything I had ever experienced in the theater.

In scene 2, for instance, six of the actors in the actor-B section formed the audience for the public ceremony onstage, presided over by the Curator and involving Virginia (holding the telescope), Galileo (the guest of honor), and his assistant, Sagredo. I had decided that when Virginia came downstage to present her father's "optical tube" to the members of the senate (p. 56), she would simply hand it to the actor playing the First Senator and, at his invitation, take an empty seat to his right. But the actors had noticed that in the Laughton version there is no time given to showing the courtship between Virginia and Ludovico. They meet at the end of the scene and then by scene 6 are going together to the ball. Indeed, the actors had charged that Brecht, at least in the Laughton version, drew the two women characters, Virginia and Mrs. Sarti, too quickly; one actor even suggested the playwright was a male chauvinist, limiting Virginia to the role of a "bimbo," and Mrs. Sarti to that of the practical, unintentionally comic housefrau.

During one rehearsal, after the First Senator had properly offered her that seat to his right, Virginia by mistake took instead an empty seat to his left, right beside Ludovico. Later in the rehearsal, Ludovico came to me and proposed the following bit of stage (or, more properly, *offstage*) business: the Senator offers the seat to his right; Virginia, however, sees the handsome Ludovico two seats to his left and boldly asks the Senator if she might instead sit near the young man, so that the Senator, an old married man not realizing her motive, inadvertently brings the young couple together. This seemingly small piece of business had larger ramifications. As Galileo talked to Mr. Matti about his iron factories, Virginia and her new-found companion engaged in some flirtatious conversation, thereby establishing a courtship, however hurried or accidental. Yet, torn between Ludovico and her father—something of a platonic lover, and, later, Virginia's "husband" after Ludovico abandons her—she impulsively tried to unite them with her line, "Here's Ludovico to congratulate you father" (p. 58). This division between father and lover was then reexpressed at Cardinal Bellarmin's house when, as they prepared to go into the ballroom, she again broke from Ludovico to return to her father with the news that the hairdresser kept four women waiting and took her first because of Galileo's reputation.

As a result, our Virginia, far from being mere window-dressing, became more a tragic figure, neglected and yet also controlled by her father, wanting to enter the larger world *circling* his own and yet, at the end, opting to remain with him. By scene 13, she had changed into something of a sterile "old wife" to Galileo, bickering with him, irritated by and in turn irritating him, yet not wanting to leave. They were a couple who had, in a way, grown to resemble each other, to sound, even to move, like each other. All this, in effect, came from my actor's observing, interpreting, and then, like a director, reblocking Virginia's exit to the audience in the play's second scene.

One night when I had to miss a rehearsal of scene 8 because of a prior engagement, I gave the directorial authority to my assistant director. My general concept for that scene had been that it would move from the lethargic mood of Galileo's two assistants forced to redo

Aristotle's experiment with floating bodies, to Andrea's abortive attempt to change the experiment to one on sun spots when the messenger brings a copy of Fabricius's latest book on the subject, to the diversion caused by Ludovico's return after eight years, and, at length, to Galileo's resolve, on hearing that the Pope is on his deathbed, to resume the forbidden research, without thought of Virginia's marriage or any personal consequences. The next day, however, the cast met me with "We have some changes we'd like to make in scene 8"—and what changes! Now, when Galileo ordered Andrea to "clear that stuff away, ice, bowl, and needle" (p. 92), Andrea and the Monk suddenly bolted from their chairs and began dashing madly from stage to stage, throwing away old equipment, pulling out new materials, in the process pushing about a startled and then contemptuous Ludovico and thoroughly confusing Mrs. Sarti. Contrasting with the sense of boredom, even an irritated complacency in the scene's first half, this new mood of excitement, this sudden physical energy erupting from Galileo's exhilarating yet potentially fatal change of mind, was now expressed not just by Brecht's dialogue, which I had thought would be sufficient, but by this frantic stage movement, an exaggerated, even comic, nonverbal complement to the text. When I asked who was responsible for this splendid change, my assistant director said, quite rightly, "The cast." My scholar's mind silently amended the reply with "the actor as audience."

This incident brought to mind an actor friend, also a teacher and scholar, who has observed that there is very little relation between his work onstage and in the study.[3] As a scholar, he plays an ideal, platonic audience to the entire play about which he is writing, but as a character, by definition, he sees the world of the play only from the limited perspective of his character. Confined as an actor to thinking like a totally self-absorbed "person," his view of the play is as small as the view of the scholar or teacher is large. Indeed, my friend argues that as an actor-character competing with the equally limited views of other actor-characters, he tries to *win* every scene in which he plays. Yet, given this additional role of playing audience to their fellows, my actor-characters in *Galileo* began to develop that larger view.

Someone suggested, for instance, that in scene 13 Andrea might wear the sunlike pendant that Galileo had worn until his recantation: in effect, the symbol of scientific inquiry would pass on from the teacher to this former student now turned fellow teacher. Galileo does in fact observe at the end of scene 13 that it is Andrea who "is teaching now" (p. 125). Likewise, another actor suggested that the set of keys that the actress doubling as Mrs. Sarti and the Narrator had tied about her waist—"a set, but only one of the possible sets of keys to the play's meaning," as another actor observed—be transferred to Virginia when she crosses with Galileo to the upper-right stage as he delivers his recantation. The actor's reading here was that now, with no prospect of marriage or of leaving her father, Virginia has become his "house-keeper"—and she should, therefore, *take over* the keys.

We gave Galileo a cane in scene 13 to stress his blindness and general physical impairment, but the actor playing the senile Old Cardinal in scene 5 asked if he might first use that cane. His reasoning was that this absurd old man, believing he is "at the center of the earth" (p. 73), would by contrast prefigure Galileo near the end of the play. The Cardinal is really spiritually blind, whereas Galileo, able to see himself as he confesses his personal failures to Andrea in scene 13, is only physically blind. "Like Shakespeare's Gloucester," the actor playing the Pope observed, "he can now 'see it feelingly.'" A single cane, in essence, now embodied alternative symbols.

Furthermore, seeing fellow actors from the audience's vantage point made us all in turn very conscious of those moments onstage when one actor plays audience to another. In this light, the opening scene was typical. Andrea watched Galileo sarcastically describe the "map of the sky according to the wise men of ancient Greece" (p. 47), and then imitated his teacher's disdain for such a cosmos with the line "locked up inside . . . It's like a cage" (p. 48). At this point it seemed *right* to have Galileo, as he made his prediction about the coming "millenium of doubt" (p. 49), leave Andrea on stage 1 and cross to stage 2, as if he were trying to lure his young student further into the new Copernican cosmos. At first, our Andrea clung to stage 1—"You're off again, Mr. Galilei"—watching his teacher, both fearing and desiring to join him. When he did cross to Galileo on the center stage, the light on stage 1 went off, only to go on again when Mrs. Sarti stood in Andrea's former place, like an audience watching Galileo demonstrate the new cosmos as he converted the chair on which her son sat to "the earth." In turn, the would-be student, Ludovico, entering stage 1, looked first at the ancient map and then for a few seconds at Galileo and Andrea, before coughing politely to catch Galileo's attention. Crossing to stage 2, Galileo, again like an audience, observed Ludovico while reading the aristocrat's letter of introduction. At the same time Andrea watched Ludovico with disdain and watched Galileo with some anxiety, fearing that this new "sun"—for Galileo liked to have adopted sons (pun intended) revolve around him—might displace him in the scientist's affections. Again, we raised the lights on stage 1 when Mrs. Sarti, a second time, watched Galileo treat this new student a bit too casually: "Why do you bother your head with science? Why don't you just breed horses?" (p. 52). A third time, the Curator, also from stage 1, saw Galileo, to whom he had just given a scudo, rush back to stage 2 to toss the measurements for an optical tube to Andrea, who from near the double doors had in turn watched Galileo greet this second unexpected visitor. The scene ended with Galileo, then Andrea, and then Galileo again looking through the lenses that Andrea had just brought onstage. This time, both teacher and student faced the upstage audience, with Andrea spotting the "washerwomen by the river" (p. 54) somewhere in that audience, and with Galileo first looking in the same direction and then tilting the two lenses upward to see the mural of the cosmos painted on the high wall behind the top row of seats.

In scene 6 Virginia and the Inquisitor, on stage 3, watched an embarrassed, angry Galileo trudge behind the two Cardinals as they crossed to the actor-A seats. They then mounted the stage for that chilling moment when the Cardinal, at once superfically charming and somewhat sexually provocative ("Your youth and warmth will keep him down to earth" [p. 81]), tries to determine just how much the daughter knows of her father's scientific experiments. As they crossed to stage 1, the Inquisitor's character changed to that of an evangelist bent on driving this too-obedient daughter from her godless father. His final line was split between a seemingly gallant "Go to your dancing" and a sinister "and remember me to Father Christopherus" (p. 81). Since I wanted the Inquisitor to exit to the other side of the house—-that is, not to follow Virginia to the actor-A seats—I asked my composer to write some seven seconds or so of music to accompany that cross. Instead, I got fourteen seconds that sounded like a grotesque parody of a medieval chant. My Cardinal Inquisitor used this additional time to great advantage—first watching from stage 1 as Virginia took her seat, then slowly crossing between the rows of spectators, occasionally looking back at Virginia, sometimes looking at the audience with a face conveying his own newly hatched campaign against her father, and then, with four seconds of music remaining, slowly taking his seat among his fellow actors in the actor-B section, as if he were a spectator deliberating on what he had just seen. At length he slowly, gracefully felt his way into the waiting chair.

In its overall structure, *Galileo* itself is something of an *audience* continually watching and reflecting upon itself. If I had thought a modern audience could sit through the fourteen scenes without a break—with the various cuts I made in each of the scenes, the playing time was roughly two hours—I would have preferred having no intermission. Clearly, *Galileo* establishes a tension between a scene's opening and its ending that parallels the ongoing dramatic tension between scenes, a tension growing, without interruption, from the play's beginning to its ending. Still, I broke for intermission at the end of the

Carnival scene, for that scene, with a new set of characters and only indirectly related to the plot of the first eight scenes, serves as an audiencelike response to the potential, for good and for bad, of Galileo's decision to continue his experiments. I underscored scene 9's special position by using the children as the crowd, even as I doubled the actors who had played Cardinals Barberini and Bellarmin with the two ballad singers. I further separated this scene from its eight predecessors by a blackout at the end of scene 8. As Galileo thundered out, "Take the cloth off the telescope and turn it on the sun" (p. 97), Virginia came running back on stage—she had exited to get the bridal gown to show Ludovico. Like an audience realizing what has happened and why Ludovico has exited, she cried out "Father! Oh, Father!" (a personal addition to the text, I must shamelessly confess!). That three-second blackout followed immediately. After this, the lights came back up full force on all three stages to signal the Carnival scene.

In similar and much more obvious fashion, the final scene resembles a Greeklike chorus to the four scenes of the "second act" as I had fashioned it. Scene 13, of course, ends with Virginia's "Bright." Galileo's ultimate discovery is not the new cosmos but himself, his human status, his limitations, even weaknesses. However, this optimistic, nevertheless penultimate, scene is not the final word. On the surface the final scene appears almost "light." First there is the comic interchange between Andrea and the Customs Official where, because of the latter's bureaucratic mentality, Andrea is successful in hiding the *Discoursi*. As the Customs Official exits to prepare the papers, Andrea himself plays teacher to the Boy, who wants to "bash" old Marina because he is convinced by the most flimsy evidence that she is a witch. Still, the scene ends ambiguously, its tone at once optimistic and pessimistic. In our production, on stage 3 Andrea implored the Boy and his youthful companions to "think it over" (p. 128), while on stage 1 the children clung to their decidedly unscientific handling of the evidence: "Old Marina is a witch. / At night on her broomstick she sits / And on the church steeple she spits" (129). I stationed the Boy on stage 2, midway between Andrea and the children, between, if you will, fact and superstition. In good Brechitian fashion, the play ended only with the promise, the hope but not the certainty, that things will be better in the "new age." During the short blackout, while the actors assembled on the center stage for curtain calls, our Customs Official broke into a hearty laugh, poised somewhere between pleasure and cynicism. I like to imagine that Andrea's line, capped by that laugh, was directed as much to the real-life audience as it was to the onstage audience of seven children: "You saw it with your own eyes: think it over!"

3

Our ultimate collaborator, indeed, a collaborator whose responses and even, at time, lack of response shaped the production from the moment rehearsals ended until the final day of the run, was the *real* audience. To be sure, their vital role had been anticipated, and to a large extent set up. Two audiences to the same production, of course, are never the same; the mood of a matinee crowd is not that of the audience for a weekend evening performance. There were also some atypical audiences: a presold house of scholars whom we found fairly staid or, to be charitable, reacting more internally; and a high-school matinee audience who, as one of my actors observed, seemed more attuned to videos than to live theater. Still, the audiences' reactions fell within clear limits. And if their responses became more intense, even more favorable, during the five-week run, the change itself was orderly, consistent, an indicator, I would hope, that the production itself got steadily *tighter*, and more assured. My practice as a director is to sit with the audience on opening night but, after that, to watch performances from the booth. There I make notes for the actors and technical crew—critiques, suggestions, pat-on-the-backs—that are religiously posted the next day on the dressing-room mirror. Since this particular production was to be the source of a revitalized chapter (I trust) on *Galileo*, I also made notes on the audience's reaction and on its role, at time imposed, at other times chosen.

Although possibly realized in other productions, Brecht's fear that the audience would sympathize too much with his major character was not realized in our *Galileo*. To be sure, the audience was very much on his side in the opening scene when Andrea, boasting that a "coachman brought it" and that the box was inscribed " 'From the Court of Naples' " (p. 47), confidently presented the "astronomical instrument" to his teacher. Galileo easily, even comically, dismised this straw man, and although our audiences in this college town paid slight attention to his lust for making money, they relished, even if the insult was self-reflexive, his scheme to "sell it to the university" since "they still teach it there" (p. 47). Nor, until the parallel "seduction" scenes—scene 3 between Galileo and Sargredo, and scene 7 between Galileo and the Monk—did Galileo's present seduction of Andrea, despite his mother's legitimate protests, seem ominous.

Galileo's character darkened quickly in the following scene, however, when his curiosity about the instrument Ludovico described led to his passing off the telescope as the "fruit of seventeen years patient research" (p. 56). Nevertheless, even these qualifications appeared to be swept away at the end of scene 5 when Clavius—played by our Andrea—announced that Galileo is "right" and that it is now the theologians' turn "to set the heavens right again" (p. 74). Here the audience seemed more impressed with the fact that Galileo's findings had been upheld than concerned with the earnestness, albeit expressed with some mild sarcasm, in Clavius's challenge to his fellow churchmen. Later in the play our Andrea was even able to restore some of that romantic, unqualified image of Galileo when, after neurotically pacing the stage as he recited the core of Galileo's findings—"The moon is an earth because the light of the moon is not her own"—he challenged the audience with a statement delivered to two or three spectators in the first row: "You can't make a man unsee what he has seen" (p. 112). But as our Andrea himself observed, this line is mostly bravado, only partly conscious. Like our audience, those twentieth-century beneficiaries of Galileo's scientific experiments, Andrea clings to an idealized picture of his teacher. By the end of Galileo's confessional speech in scene 13, Andrea's pleasure in the bold researcher of scene 1, indeed of the first three scenes, would metamorphose to a more profound pleasure, one tinged with sadness, at this man who now knows of himself as well as the heavens.

Yet, if not consciously acknowledged by the audience, the qualifications to Galileo's character came early. His celebration of the "millenium of doubt" (p. 45) always seemed to puzzle them, and we emphasized the radical implication of this line by having Galileo abandon his student on stage 1 and deliver the line, indeed most of the entire speech, on the crosswalk leading to stage 2. This physical distance between them seemed to dispel the very comradeship conveyed by Galileo moments early when he had stood next to Andrea, the two men, as one, holding the same discredited astronomical instrument. Furthermore, audiences generally gave a nervous laugh when Galileo called Andrea "stupid" (p. 49) for saying the sun moves: the rightness of the scientific point was at variance here with the teacher's crude, almost violent manner as he grabbed his student by the scruff of the neck and with his other hand dragged the chair noisily to the other side of the stage. Mrs. Sarti's "Well, I hope we can pay the milkman in this new era" (p. 50) seemed, in contrast, as practical and disinterested as Galileo's demonstration (albeit practical) appeared self-centered: to Galileo's mind Andrea's (understandable) ignorance reflected poorly on his teacher. Galileo's psychological "appetite," his devouring young men for his own psychic need, was especially obvious when, despite his scorn for the aristocrat, he feigned friendship as he plied Ludovico for more information about the "tube affair" (p. 51) he had seen in Holland. If the audience had by now moved from an initial identification with Galileo to a fuller, more critical response, they were clearly unsettled when, at the scene's end, Galileo crudely told Andrea to "get out of the way" and, snatching the two lenses from him and pointing them toward the roof of the theater (our "sky"), burst out with a loud "Ah." This cry of immense, almost animallike satisfaction was accompanied by the bassoon playing the Galileo theme, but now sounding ironic rather than expansive.

By the next scene, Galileo's patent lie that the optical tube was the result of "seventeen years patient research" (p. 56) was not lost on the audience, and if Ludovico had seemed something of a sap in that opening scene, his sarcastic response to the scientist's hurried self-defense ("I improved it") always brought a cynical laugh from them: "Yes, sir. I am beginning to understand science" (p. 58). Exposed by this young man whose mother had sent him for lessons since "science is necessary nowadays for conversation" (p. 52), Galileo exited slowly, even thoughtfully, to his chair in the actor-A section. Virginia's question to her escort, "Isn't father a great man?" (p. 58), could now only appear pathetically hopeful. When Galileo in scene 3 repeated the lie to the third young man, Sagredo, by admiting only that he "had heard about" the telescope, our Sagredo looked nervously, almost apologetically, at the audience nearby. Once again, as Galileo tried to justify his theft—the instrument he made was "twice as good as any Dutchman's," he needed the money, he likes to buy books (p. 61)—he left Sagredo on stage 1 and, alone, crossed to the center stage. We reestablished this sense of isolation near the end of the scene when, after convincing Sagredo that scientific proof would be sufficient to convince any skeptics, Galileo left him on stage 3 to cross to Virginia on stage 1, there asking her to read an overly flattering letter to Cosimo De'Medici. Distanced from his colleague, Sagredo stared helplessly, even forlornly, at the audience as he observed that the Prince is a mere boy of "twelve" (Brecht made him nine, but our Prince looked older). Galileo's "The only way a man like me can land a good job is by crawling on his stomach" (p. 64) was delivered to the audience as if he were purposely ignoring a dubious fellow scientist. He then scolds, bluntly, "I have no patience, Sagredo, with a man who doesn't use his brains to fill his belly," a line that always struck me as a more desperate variation on those excuses for his avarice given earlier in the scene. Galileo's final dismissal of Sagredo's warning, "I am going to Florence (p. 65), sounded almost petulant, and, once it was delivered, Sagredo shrugged his shoulders in frustration, seeking out someone in the audience who would take more seriously his sonlike warning to this difficult father figure.

Cardinal Barberini's entrance in scene 6 dealt the final blow to any facile acceptance of Galileo. A sophisticated, humane man, in contrast to the more bearish Cardinal Bellarmin, Barberini is as much scientist as theologian. He modestly admits to having "read a few papers on astronomy," and his realistic "It is harder to get rid of than the itch" (p. 77), directed to the audience, always produced a sympathetic laugh, even as it challenged Galileo's obsessions with both science and the self. Then, too, Barberini appears at least Galileo's equal as they battle each other by quoting scriptures that support their opposed positions regarding the establishment and the individual. Barberini's line—"Your findings have been ratified by the Papal Observatory, Galileo. That should be most flattering to you" (p.79)—was split at the first period between a stern tone and one more sympathetic. At once churchman and scientist, this more complex character came across at least as likeable and certainly more politic than Galileo. When the Cardinals left the stage to take the crosswalk to stage 1, Galileo followed behind, head bowed, a figure at once cruelly discredited and yet also a little foolish. My Galileo observed that this scene seemed to destroy the scientist's unwarranted optimism, to take some of the Renaissance exuberance out of the portrait, and that from this moment on in the play he could no longer fully be his own charming, arrogant, carefree self.

The following scene (7) invariably left our audience divided in their response to Galileo. Not a political cleric, and not part of the high Vatican establishment, the Monk embodied the virtues of country life, of simplicity, and of a concern for the community, even as his delight in physics, he found, was incompatible with his empathy for his parents and the peasant class they represented. Here was a scene Galileo at once *won* and *lost,* for his successful strategy to return the Monk to the fold of science (to whet his student's diminshed appetite, Galileo hurled a manuscript on ocean currents onto the floor) seemed born at least as much from the need for self-vindication (given the treatment he had received from the Cardinals in the previous scene) as any concern for the intellectual welfare of this third disciple. As the Monk hunched over the manuscript, the "apple from the tree of knowledge" (p. 85), Galileo directed his description of this churchman-reconverted-to-scientist to our Narrator, seated on the up-side of the center stage. Yet her face, clearly showing a mixed pleasure, almost an anguish, at what he had just done, qualified Galileo's joy and thereby partly unsettled him. Much lower on the social scale than

Barberini, the Monk is, paradoxically, an even more potent opponent to Galileo; he seeks no political gain but, like the true shepherd of the flock, is concerned only with "the inward peace of less fortunate souls" (p. 84).

The "typical" audience reaction I have been describing so far came from what was already there in Brecht's text, as informed by our production, with most of that *informing* having been established during the rehearsal period. Perhaps a more profound but no less intentional way of collaborating with the audience was our treatment of the characters as they appeared over the full course of the play. Virginia is a case in point. As my actors quickly noted, at first glance she appears merely a submissive child adrift in a patriarchal world where Galileo's real desire is for sons— Andrea, Sagredo, and the Monk—rather than daughters. In fact, Virginia has only one small scene, or rather part of a scene, without her father—that conversation with the Cardinal Inquisitor closing scene 6. But from the start we resisted the temptation to make her a minor, *auxiliary* figure. Instead, from her very first appearance she was played as an intelligent woman, suppressed in the males-only world of her home and of a commercial society. In the second scene Galileo limited her to holding the telescope, like some magician's assistant; yet when he sat down to talk with Matti, the iron founder, our Virginia, as I observed, experienced a conflict between her growing interest in Ludovico and a father who, the ceremony over, unceremoniously abandoned her. Her line to Ludovico, "Did I do it nicely?" (p. 58), was therefore something of a *female* ruse to flatter a man who might take her from home, *springing* her from her father. Still, to her own mind Ludovico was hardly ideal; his "I thought so" was delivered with that sense of male superiority she had already experienced too often.

After the intermission, indeed, almost as if the character had been changing again between acts, Virginia seemed to become even more assertive. Her "What's in your book? Will they say it's heretical" at the start of scene 10 (p. 104) was startling, its tone a mixture of concern and (almost) scolding. Our Virginia even asked if she might put in this same question a touch of contempt, even if it be unintentional. Without fail, Galileo's chauvinistic dismissal of her question, "You hang around church too much" (p. 105), led to a nervous, seemingly reluctant laugh from the audience. It was as if Virginia's strength, emerging from her decision to forget marriage, grew in direct proportion to Galileo's weakness, his lack of confidence born of both political pressure and inward doubts. By scene 13, Virginia and Galileo had become that old married couple, fending off the world, irritated, for instance, by the knock on the door when the messenger arrived with a goose. If anything, Galileo seemed henpecked when Virginia chided him for not being able to identify the goose at first. When Andrea arrived, he was clearly a rival for Galileo's affections.

In rehearsals Virginia, indeed all the characters, seemed to *leap* from one stage of their development to another, without that smoother, more logical psychological progression that characterizes conventional drama. Confirmed by the audience's reaction during performance, this was to be expected in the fashioner of an epic theater, a playwright who saw character as suddenly affected, even radically changed, by society and its politics, by external pressures rather than by exclusively inner or psychological drives.

At one with these leaps in personality was the fact that some characters appeared erratically over the fourteen scenes. Andrea, for example, was introduced in the opening scene, then not again until scene 8, and, after that, only much later in the final three scenes of our act 2. Conversely, other characters were used up quickly in successive scenes, never to appear again: the Curator, for example, was a dominant presence in the first three scenes, and then vanished from the play. In this case, we were able to establish the character in an orderly, conventional manner, and, the actor's part completed, to bring him back later in an entirely new role as the Inquisitor. Nor did we do much to disguise the actor's second role: the single red sash for the Inquisitor replaced the pendant jewel that had marked the Curator.

For such reasons, an additional imaginative burden was placed on an audience forced at times to comprehend a character within the miniplay of his few but sequential appearances, and asked at other times to retain over several scenes an image of the actor's last appearance, which would then be qualified, even transmuted, by an appearance much later in the action. In fact, several audience members remarked to me that the characters seemed to "float" through the scenes with the irrationality of a dream. Others observed that, like planets rotating around the centrally placed Galileo, the rest of the cast appeared to be extensions of or—conversely—antitheses to his given personality at the time. The audience, in effect, was asked in ways unthinkable in the "well-made play" to add each new piece to a larger, constantly evolving pattern of *Galileo,* one that would be completed only when, in scene 13, the central character came to terms with himself. Indeed, the subtitle for this chapter echoes Brecht's original title for *Galileo:* "And Yet It Moves!"

This special, indeed vital, role of the audience led to some experiments half-way during the run itself. Since Ludovico doesn't appear in the second act—he walks out of his engagement to Virginia in scene 8—I used our Ludovico as the Lord Chamberlain in scene 10. There, in a single and very brief stage appearance he informs Galileo that the Prince has no time to see him, let alone accept his book, and, after some leading questions about the scientist's eyesight, he informs him that the Florentine court will no longer oppose the Holy Inquisition's request to interrogate Galileo (pp. 106–07). For the first two weeks of the run we played the Chamberlain as a cold bureaucrat; but once I realized how engaged our audience was in collaborating with us in fleshing out, or rather patching together, the characters, I asked my Lord Chamberlain to try, within the space of just a few lines, to divide the character into three moods. Initially he would appear hesitant to confront the old man with the bad news, indeed, so hesitant that he would deliver the excuse about the Prince's having to judge a parade at the Riding Academy without facing Galileo. Then, when he did face him and realize that the scientist was no longer the imposing figure he once was, the Lord Chamberlain would gather courage, speaking more bluntly, almost gleefully. Finally, after crossing to stage 1 as Galileo and Virginia try to escape, the Lord Chamberlain would stop them, this time speaking in that cold, bureaucratic tone, almost like an automaton. Our audiences, not to mention the actor charged with such quick shifts in character, seemed to have no trouble adjusting.

Perhaps one doesn't usually think of Brecht as a comic dramatist, but it was the audience response to the play's humor as much as this issue of character change that fashioned the complex tone of our production. Whatever growing qualifications there were to Galileo's character in the first three scenes, the humor, almost without exception, emerged from him. For instance, as the Curator entered in the first scene (he came with the bad news of the honorarium's being turned down), Galileo rushed up to him. Believing that the scientist was eager to see him, the Curator held out his hand, only to be confronted suddenly with Galileo's hand palm-up as he begged, indeed *demanded,* a scudo from Priuli. Scudo in hand, Galileo then rushed from the startled Curator to toss the coin to Andrea, who was waiting outside the window, instructing him to "run to the spectacle-maker" (p. 52).

By scene 4, this humor, *with* rather than *at* Galileo, was so pervasive that we played the scene in almost slapstick fashion. Hearing the Chaperon (who replaced the "Elderly Lady" in the text, and was played, I should add, by none other than Virginia) "oh" and "ah" over his oration on the heavenly spheres, the Philosopher left the stage and, as he spoke of the celestial harmony, grossly flirted with his new-found admirer. Indeed, his "architecture of the celestial globes" (p. 67) was delivered, double entendre and all, to her bosom and met with her suggestive "What diction!" Having come into the theater expecting a *serious* Brechtian inquiry on the issue of free speech, the audience must have thought by the end of the scene that they had stumbled instead into some Broadway comedy. Galileo himself joined in this comedy, adding a leering "And everything on Taurus the Bull" in his reply to the Chaperon's nonsensical question, "Can one see the claws on the Great Bear?" (p. 68). When the Philosopher and Mathematician refused to look through the telescope, even this rejection of Galileo was displaced by the comedy. Moreover, after a concerned Mrs. Sarti rose from her *Narrator's chair* (located in the center of the spectators on the up-side of stage 2) and offered the Prince "a piece of homemade candy" in a last-minute attempt to give Galileo more time to make his case, the audience without fail laughed not at her domestic strategy but at the Mathematicians's line (assigned in the Brecht/Laughton text to the Elderly Lady): "Not now. Thank you. It is too soon before His Highness' supper." Taking the candy from Mrs. Sarti and eating it himself, the Mathematician led a frustrated prince to the actor-A seats.

However, after the following scene (scene 5), where Clavius upheld Galileo, the humor was never as carefree, even if earlier it had been only superficially so. From my vantage point in the booth, I could see the audience change in mood, the laughter at Galileo's line, "Thou shalt not read" (p. 85), said to the Monk as he clutched the manuscript, being more studied than before. Even the defiance of Ludovico and the decision to turn the telescope on the sun brought that same divided, introspective response.

The final scene of our first act, the Carnival scene on April Fools' Day, had its own dialectic. The sudden presence of the children—they would rush on stage, half of them supporting Galileo, the other half opposing him—seemed to reverse the play's increasingly solemn mood, even to the degree that the two adult ballad singers were not taken seriously in their warnings: "Good people, what will come to pass," etc. (p. 99). The audience would also break into laughter when the "Newsboy" (assigned to the actor playing the Inquisitor, his lines in the text those of the Ballad Singer) appeared at the double doors wearing a comical, obviously modern cap and hawking his pamphlets "fully illustrated with pictures of the planets, including Venus" (p. 102). Yet the otherwise *cute* kids soon turned ugly as, blocked for a time by the two ballad singers, they scrambled to get to the Newsboy, turning over chairs, and occasionally stepping on the foot of a spectator as they charged in pursuit out the door. Our former Virginia, now the "Loud Voice," then delivered her "Galileo, the Bible-killer" in an abrasive tone. When my stage manager announced after the blackout a fifteen-minute intermission, the audience, confused (estranged? distanced? still pondering the ambiguous second half to this first act?), would slowly, in staggered groups, leave their seats.

The humor in the much shorter second act was even darker, whether it was the Inquisitor's response to the Pope's decision to "show" Galileo the torture instruments—"That will be adequate, Your Holiness. Mr. Galilei understands machinery" (p. 110)—or Andrea's barb to the Monk (assigned in the text to the Monk), "Oh ye of little faith" (p. 113), when seconds before the bell sounded Galileo's two assistants mistakenly believed he had not recanted. Indeed, only after Galileo's confessional speech to Andrea would the audience once more appear relaxed in its laughter.

The issue itself of who sent the goose always led to discreet whisperings among the spectators, as if they were participating in a guessing game. In rehearsals my actors, who all became *Galileo* scholars during the run, would debate the source: was it Andrea (my own candidate)? someone forever anonymous? Or, as one of my actors argued after reading everything he could get his hands on about Galileo, the young John Milton? This relaxed state, among both audience and actors, spread to the final scene, where Andrea gave the Boy a Galileolike lesson, reminiscent of the one given him in the first scene, on using one's eyes to determine the facts. Both Andrea and the Boy played that scene in a patently natural style, almost as if they were not *acting* at all.

Our audience was also involved by the staging itself, by the fact that we could make them adjust their position by moving the action from one "island" to another. In scene 8, for example, the conversation between Mrs. Sarti and Virginia, as they sewed the trousseau, took place on stage 1, while on stage 2 Galileo and his two assistants mimed working in the laboratory. But the knock on the door from the messenger bringing a book from Fabricius ended that stage-1 conversation, and the audience was now obliged to turn to stage 2 as Galileo, much to his assistants' displeasure, insisted that they "stick to fiddling about with blocks of ice in water" (p. 89). Ludovico's entrance and his brief lover's conversation at the door with Virginia turned all eyes back to stage 1, until, after Virginia's exit, he himself crossed somewhat reluctantly to stage 2, there to embark on the soon-to-be disastrous conversation with his potential father-in-law. Once Galileo decided to "clear this stuff away" (p. 92), we threw lights on all three stages as the assistants rushed madly about, taking from imaginary shelves (equally) imaginary materials for the new experiment, at times even leaning into the audience to fetch a piece of equipment. As they raced from stage to stage, with Galileo and Ludovico all the time standing still on stage 2 conducting their testy conversation, the audience resembled spectators at a tennis match, their heads moving in unison from side to side.

In scene 11, we put the Pope on a balcony to the left of the light booth, with the Inquisitor standing alone on stage 2, looking upward along with the audience. As the Pope spoke, the audience at times strained to see him—since their vision was partly blocked by the trusses and beams in the ceiling—while at other times they focused on the Inquisitor, who was visually, although not verbally, responding to the Pope's indecision as to what should be done with "this bad man" (p. 109).

In the recantation scene (scene 12) Galileo entered by the double doors, made his way through the audience, crossed to stage 2 where Virginia took the keys from Mrs. Sarti, and then, still delivering his recantation, crossed to stage 1. All this while the audience, from the various possible vantage points in the seats surrounding all three stages, followed him intently. Suddenly bolting from the center stage to stage 3, opposite stage 1, Andrea delivered his "Unhappy is the land that breeds no hero" (p. 115) as all eyes, *abandoning* Galileo, turned to that corner of the room, only to return just as quickly to Galileo with his rejoinder, "Unhappy is the land that needs a hero."

This visual and no less physical participation of the audience made them a very clear presence in the play, for, not *allowed* to sit quietly and stare straight ahead as they would in a proscenium theater, they and their heads constantly moved about, like currents of an ocean surrounding the three stages, constantly changing direction. Thereby aware of their audience, of its physical presence, at a level beyond their usual experience in more conventional stagings and—surely—with more conventional plays, the actors found moments, beyond those we had anticipated in rehearsal, to play to—and play *with*—that audience. In scene 6, for example, the Inquisitor, suspecting that Virginia had been covering for her father when she told him that Galileo "doesn't talk to [her] about the stars" (p. 81), would abruptly leave her, cross to the far down corner of the stage, and smugly but with growing irritation deliver to the audience the aphorism "They don't eat fish in the fisherman's house," a line not heard by Virginia yet conveying to the audience what the Inquisitor saw as a daughter's unnatural desire to protect her father. Then, leaving his *confidants* in the house, suppressing his anger, and putting back on an affable face, he would cross back to Virginia, who could now only wonder why he would so suddenly yet briefly break from what seemed to be a cordial conversation.

At times, a line was split between an actor in the audience and the larger *real* audience. Galileo, for example, directed "The first sight of the book!" to the Narrator, and then, refocusing his gaze to include three rows of spectators seated behind her, offered the audience the remaining "His mouth watered and his scoldings were drowned" (p. 123). Such sharings with the audience were magnified in Galileo's confessional speech, as he directed some specific passages to individual audience members and others to the house, sometimes speaking as if he were passing the dialogue through the back of the spectator's head and into his or her conscience.

No less significant was the audience's response to the music. In the first act, there was always music when the Narrator spoke. After the overture to the second act, however, there was no musical accompaniment to the Narrator's line preceding scene 10. Instead, she intoned in silence, "The depths are hot, the heights are chill, / The streets are loud, the court is still" (p. 10). Inevitably, the audience at first looked surprised, almost as if they felt *cheated* that the pattern had been broken. Then, as the Narrator got to the phrase "the courts are still," they realized, with some satisfaction, that the accompanying silence had been dictated by the text itself.

As someone whose scholarship is a blend of metadramatic and performance criticism, I was also very interested in any theatrical allusion in Brecht's text—and, no less, in how it would be received by an audience made very conscious of their role in the performance. The frequency of such references in Brecht, of course, pales beside those in Genet or Stoppard. Still, there are some. Andrea's "Exit Ludovico" (p. 96) always brought a *knowing* laughter from the house, as if we all were sharing a metacritical in-joke. And in scene 13, when Andrea recreated an imagined scene in which his supporters, joined by the crowds in the streets, engage Galileo in a debate—"We said: 'He will die . . .' You came back: 'I surrender but I am alive'" (p. 121)—this miniature play-within-a-play was enacted before the real audience as well as before Galileo, an audience of one onstage.

In trying to move away from the illusionist theater so as to make his own stage more *real* or epic, Brecht constantly calls attention to the artifice of the stage and, hence, only underscores the play's metadramatic dimension. In asking the audience to imagine props mimed by the actors, in doing without sets, in breaking the barrier between on- and offstage by direct addresses, I believe we and our audience-as-character were being faithful to his principles. My most flagrant act of infidelity, a metacritical one at that, was to add to Galileo's cynical assessment of Andrea's mini-play, "It makes a picture" (p. 122), a complementary line from my own feeble brain: "It would make a good play." In defense, I should point out that this *interpolation* always brought a big, reassuring response from those offstage.

Despite such growing intimacy with the audience, whether planned in rehearsal or suggested during performance by the audience itself, a play remains an obvious play, artifice that is, paradoxically, lifelike or at least relevant to the real world offstage. With our audience, for *our Galileo,* the issue was one of degree, rather than the antithesis suggested by *life* and *art* or *offstage* and *onstage.* As the major thematic concern moved from scientific to self-discovery, as the play itself turned from history or the public world to Galileo's inner world, the *characters* onstage and offstage seemed to grow closer to each other. The artifice of the theater gave way to the reality of the situation, that theatrical "presence" where, for a specific period of time, two groups come together: *actors,* in their real-life bodies, drawing on their real-life experiences, moving in space and time before an equally alive *audience,* present and ratifying with their eyes and ears what would otherwise be merely "literary." This dissolution of the otherwise antithetical terms *actor* and *audience* encouraged me to borrow a custom I had observed in the Chinese theater when I taught and directed plays in that country two summers ago. As the lights came on for the curtain calls, actors applauded the audience even as the audience applauded actors, each group thanking the other, in effect, for a mutual effort.

4

In my original and now rejected version of this chapter I had been particularly concerned with the degree to which Brecht's theories about the audience held up during an actual performance. Did or could the audience really *work*—intellectually, as coequals with the actors—in the way he envisioned their role? There I straddled the issue, concluding that the personal predicament of the hero does move the audience, does make them identify with him, but that this fact did not deter from Brecht's presentation of a "social problem."[4] Given his notions of estrangement, Brecht's audience *is* asked to work harder, to weigh issues against a constantly shifting dialectical presentation. Still, their role is not that radically different from what it would be during the performance of a work by any gifted playwright. I found myself at length agreeing with critics like David Grossvogel, who speaks of the theater as having "an anthropomorphic quality that defies rational efforts [such as Brecht's] to alter it,"[5] or with Heinz Politzer's contention that "in time" such epic theater "grows into theater, great theater pure and simple."[6] From this perspective, I found a bit grating one critic's dismissal of *Galileo* as a "fortunate misfortune."[7]

Now, having staged the play, having watched that audience with the bifocal vision of director and scholar, I think that Brecht *does* demand of anyone staging his work that they offer the audience a collaborative role more graphic, more self-conscious, and at times perhaps even more threatening or challenging than do the playwrights of his despised illusionist theater. However, Brecht has no monopoly on involving the audience, and I hope that the discussion of three playwrights so far—with three to come—will sustain this point.

For me, though, Brecht's most graphic difference from other playwrights is evident during rehearsals. At most impressed by, and at very least unable to avoid the strategy I had envisioned of having our audience surround those three islandlike stages, my actors were encouraged during that period of experiment to work with me in playing to a (then) theoretical audience that would be, we imagined, intimate with those onstage, sharing the same room, seeing the actors, and, when the actors took seats in the house, seen by them. These speculations influenced everything from blocking to delivery.

When that real audience materialized, their presence constituted, in essence, a second round of *rehearsals*. From boredom to sighs of pleasure to laughter to that tennislike situation where their attention was continually bounced from one stage to another, the spectators' every reaction became a potent force. We found that successive nights, if they did not present totally new situations, offered options nevertheless—to try something different, to refine an experiment initiated the night before, to reject this, to consider that, even to reconsider the other. For me, the deepest level of the audience's involvement was theatrical rather than political or intellectual. And I say this even in light of the political situation, that growth/non-growth controversy, that had been the stimulus for staging *Galileo*.

I can now take, with more confidence, two sentences from my otherwise abandoned first draft:

> By stressing the interaction between actor and audience, Brecht links his theater with society: both are public domains. And so when a Marxist critic finds in *Galileo* a call for a "social transformation . . . which will allow the productive energy of the individual to benefit both himself and the rest of society,"[8] this political aim appears inseparable from the principles of the theater, whether it be Brecht's or that of Shakespeare's age.

My experience with *Galileo* has shown me that the above is, although certainly not absolutely true, at least plausible—perhaps.

5

Stoppard, *Rosencrantz and Guildenstern Are Dead:* "Incidents! All We Get Is Incidents!"

For Brecht the ultimate audience is outside the theater, in the political world, in that society who inherited the dilemma created by the Vatican in the Renaissance or by the officials of Los Alamos. For Stoppard the concern for the audience seems confined to the immediate dramatic experience. In fact, here is a playwright so aware of his audience that, for some observers, his seeming violation of the stage's fourth wall amounts to a limitation: Stoppard is too playful, and too self-conscious of that playfulness, we are told, and as a consequence is not sufficiently concerned with the integrity, nor with the originality of his onstage world.[1]

Clearly, the audience—for better or worse—assumes the role of character in Stoppard's plays. The most graphic example is, perhaps, *The Real Inspector Hound,* where an audience of two affected drama critics go onstage and become embroiled with the inner-play's farcical plot.[2] *The Gamblers* presents an equally intrusive onstage audience who complicate the plot by confusing the jailer with his prisoner. In turn, characters misread audiences in Stoppard: in *The Engagement,* Mr. Cartwright, observing a crowd just offstage, concludes wrongly that they are observing him. Such acute recognition of the audience might suggest what Stoppard's own Guildenstern would call some "un-, sub- or supernatural" force observing a human world populated by stage characters whose "fault" is their assumption that they are real and are, moreover, the ultimate observers.[3] Ruth, in *Night and Day,* is given an interior monologue, denied to all other characters, so that she can comment directly to us about the play's absurdly competitive male world. With his companion Fraser, Albert finds the world just "tenable" when viewed from the height of his bridge. Does Stoppard's observer, then, see the attending playworld as nothing beyond an object for inspection? Has he taken the Sartrean *look* to its inevitable and absurd extreme? If the object is insignificant, is the role of the audience, on- and offstage, itself reduced? When old Carr, in *Travesties,* serves as audience to his own past, we see him as quite the opposite of an omniscient and therefore trustworthy audience, for Carr bungles the narration, leaving us to sift coherence and meaning from his disjointed story.

Often we must supplement the suspect or biased or even shallow readings of the story offered by these onstage counterparts. We are as involved as the characters themselves in penetrating the mystery in *Artist Descending a Staircase,* where vestigial remarks on tape provide our first clue to the death. Thereafter, the radio play's chronological regression to the initial encounter between the artist and Sophie, followed by a return to the material presented in that opening scene, invokes our mutual participation in what might be described as something of a cosmic detective story. *After Magritte,* as Ronald Hayman observes, offers us a "visual riddle" with the rising of the curtain, yet whatever assumptions we bring to that riddle are in the course of the play comically overturned.[4] In *Jumpers* that opening tableau is not only a riddle but a peculiarly obscure one: our sight of Dorothy Moore on her swing is partially blocked, and the audience-critics who were our untrustworthy guides, perhaps even parodies of ourselves in *Inspector Hound* here materialize as the equally untrustworthy Inspector Bones.

In Genet the conflation of man as actor and audience requires our theatrical redefinition of what formerly passed for reality, and thereby obligates us to be shapers of an illusory world whose artistry is at once original and fraudulent. Genet's pessimism is thus far removed from Brecht's optimism. In *Galileo* the actor's own audiencelike consciousness of his role allows him to overlay the character's *psychology* with a sense of its being re-presentation, and parallels the intellectual consciousness of the offstage audience, *cool* in the midst of performance and, as a result, able to assess the action both within the confines of the play and in the encompassing world of social forces reflected in its onstage mirror.[5]

Especially in *Rosencrantz and Guildenstern Are Dead,* however, Stoppard's characters seem torn between the roles of actor and audience, one role enlarging and yet also vitiating the other, even as attempts to separate them prove impossible. Yet in slowly grasping, in reading correctly—if only dimly so—a "play" in which they had assumed they were at worst functionaries, at best indifferent and hence unaffected observers, Stoppard's pair, I believe, evolve into the play's chief actors and therefore into significant beings. They are the real issue rather than mere messengers delivering Hamlet's end in the form of a letter.

In act 3 these indifferent spectators-turned-unwilling-actors advance to the position of incipient playwrights. Thus, in *Rosencrantz and Guildenstern Are Dead* it is this trinity of audience, actor, and playwright that constitutes the *end* the play. The playwright's consciousness of the offstage audience, perhaps dismissed too easily as a sign that he is merely playful, is inseparable from the more profound, although no less darkly comic, view of man. In Stoppard this generic man flounders, has occasional flashes of success, but at length observes himself acting in a playworld with a predestined script that, although in small part, he will in turn fashion.

1

If we know Shakespeare's *Hamlet*, it would apparently follow that in such a "pre-critical state"[6] there will be no surprise for us in Stoppard's "adaptation." His title deliberately reminds us of the fate of Shakespeare's two time-servers. If we could approach Stoppard's play in this way, then at best it complements, fleshes out, *Hamlet*'s somewhat hurried portrait of two minor characters. As a "parasite"[7] to Shakespeare's tragedy, then, Stoppard's can boast only the marginal originality of a parody. The fact is, however, that the opening action of *Rosencrantz and Guildenstern Are Dead*, while acknowledging its debt to Shakespeare's portrait, is purely Stoppard's. Nor is it the sole example of an addition on his part that has no precedent, or at best is only implied, in Shakespeare. In effect, we are given no warming-up period anticipating the modern playwright's subsequent departure from his source.

Although the play's title leads us to assume that the characters we see in the opening tableau are reworkings of Shakespeare, Stoppard's own stage direction immediately blurs their identity. They have, we are told, no *"visible character"* (p.11); nor will their names, let alone their geographical location, be announced until the play is well underway. Our upturned expectations—*are* they Rosencrantz and Guildenstern?—mirror their own divided state. They know why they are here—they have been "sent for," to use their recurrent phrase—but that small knowledge is itself surrounded by a tantalizing uncertainty as to the purpose. The coin toss embodies this copresence of certainty and uncertainty: the probability that tails will turn up equally as often as heads is contradicted by a mysterious run of heads that apparently has begun before we ourselves encounter the characters and now continues in our presence.[8] Seemingly superior to Rosencrantz and Guildenstern because we know the plot, because, playbills in hand, we assume to know their story, we are also *like* them, waiting for the play proper to begin, for, surely, two onstage characters monotonously tossing and retrieving coins cannot pass as serious dramatic action. Surely, to be "sent for" cannot be the end but only the means to some as yet undisclosed end. Confined to our seats, we examine the stage set; they do likewise. Along with his philosophical anxiety over a seeming defiance of probability, Guildenstern still has time to check out *"the confines of the stage"* (SD, p. 12), and as he *"goes to look onstage"* with his back to us, by definition he duplicates our position in the house.

When he isn't examining the stage, Guildenstern sits, both audiencelike and criticlike, while Rosencrantz, the actor retrieving coins and announcing "heads," stands. When Rosencrantz turns shallow critic with his nondiagnosis of the coin toss, Guildenstern, who had been standing, now *"sits despondently"* (SD, p. 15). When this audiencelike Guildenstern turns actor by coyly raising his foot as the Player makes his prediction of "Well . . . heads," the Tragedians, normally actors, themselves turn audience as they "crowd round" the tableau and, like spectators, offer signs and sounds connoting *"relief and congratulations"* (p. 29).[9] Once Hamlet enters, such onstage audiences become more frequent, indeed, become more involved with the set, for Hamlet's entrance with Ophelia coincides with a *"lighting change sufficient to alter the exterior mood into the interior"* (SD, p. 34). Parodying the attentive audience, the attendant lords are *"frozen"* in position (SD, p. 35) during the first of the play's three dumb shows.

With the entrance of Claudius and Gertrude, and the subsequent explanation as to why they have been sent for, this frozen audience *"unfreezes"* (SD, p. 35), as the former spectators become unwilling actors, participants in Hamlet's story. Now they desperately cling to that privileged position of spectator—or try to combine both roles; instead of seeking out Hamlet, that is, instead of *acting* on Claudius's command, they purport to wait like an audience for "somebody interesting [to] come on" (p. 41). Even this hybrid role is dismissed as "an appalling business" when they find themselves "intrigued without ever quite being enlightened" (p. 41). Guildenstern invokes a particularly suggestive metaphor for this state in which one is quasi-spectator and quasi-actor: they are "like two blind men looting a bazaar for their own portraits" (p. 39). Thinking that their task is to "glean" what afflicts Hamlet, their real task will be to see enacted by the Tragedians, by Hamlet, and by themselves in act 3 their own condition or end, one only implied in Shakespeare through Hamlet's letter to Horatio. The object of both their speculation and search will be not Hamlet but themselves, that very "portrait" of men searching for an image or identity. The more Rosencrantz and Guildenstern try to retreat to the old role of cynical observer, the more they are drawn into the action of the play.

This paradoxical relation betwen audience and actor, character and audience, is subsumed in the Player's extended discussion of the obligations of his audience. In fact, the Player's first words as he spots Rosencrantz and Guildenstern are "an audience!" said *"Joyously"* (p. 21).[10] Yet the Player's own definition of an audience has been prefigured in Guildenstern's tale of the unicorn. As that account progresses from the initial "mystical encounter" with the fabulous beast to a "common experience" once the unicorn is witnessed by others, the play offers the first sustained statement on the power of the audience, or of the observer's eye. Multiple spectators reduce the same phenomenon to a shared or "common" experience. Yet if this diminishes the wonder of the beast existing in the solitary imagination, this sharing balances such loss with a communal vision closer to that reality that is "common" or applicable to us all. This shared theatrical experience, where the playwright offers an audience what, unshared, would otherwise be merely idiosyncratic, makes the movement from the unicorn to the "horse with an arrow in its forehead" to an ordinary deer a proper one.

But does an audience of more than one reduce the wondrous to the mundane? The Player still asserts the principle behind a productive collaboration between actor and audience. Without an audience for some time now, the troupe is "rusty," and while they would have preferred a larger crowd—as an audience Rosencrantz and Guildenstern are "disappointing," although "about average for voyeurs"—the diplomatic Player assures them that quality is more important than quantity (p. 24). More relevant to the present issue is the Player's notion that actor and audience, or "performance" and "patronage," are "the two sides of the same coin." If his metaphor alludes to the play's opening action, it both distinguishes and unites actor and audience. Assuming, as they do, that they are real and that the Tragedians are "unreal" players, not people, Rosencrantz and Guildenstern cannot imagine that such binaries have any application to their situation. Nor do they pick up on the hint when the Player links the fate of the Tragedians with that of their spectators: "It [your fate or ours] could hardly be one without the other" (p. 25). At present, the two can only accept advice that, they assume, defines and thereby limits the audience's role in the production: "Keep an eye open, an ear cocked" (pp. 39–40). Buoyed up by the "fact" that they are now doubly privileged spectators, observing the Tragedians' play as well Claudius's plot for Hamlet, Guildenstern likens their status to being given "an extra slice of childhood when you least expect it" (p. 40). Still, here he forgets that the essence of the child is to ratify the play of others by entering into the communal pretend world of children.[11]

The rigid separation between actor and audience cannot hold: to observe is to participate, a paradox brought home to us because our suspension of belief has been a factor since the opening line. The actor playing Guildenstern announces each coin toss as heads; in actuality the coin will turn up heads roughly half the time. Our own playing along with the game, allowing onstage what we know to be an impossibility offstage, thus sustains the illusion as we silently collaborate with the two actors assigned the lead.

We participate in the "building up of suspense" (p. 12).[12] Of the four possibilities Guildenstern raises to explain the overwhelming presence of heads, three are linked to determinism, with only one allowing for the force of human will: "I'm willing it. Inside where nothing shows, I am the essence of a man spinning double-headed coins" (p. 16). This final *minority* opinion actually constitutes the actor's *truth* in performance. No less than the playwright or the two actors, we are the "un-, sub- or supernatural" force allowing for the improbable to occur, to *seem* real. In this way, the play as an inevitable bonding of actor and audience is predetermined.[13]

Still, *play* itself, that ability to interpret and thereby refashion otherwise immutable facts, cannot be so predetermined. Even as the actors need our collaboration, our participation, the Tragedians need more than mere witnesses from the characters Rosencrantz and Guildenstern.[14] The Player ominously informs his would-be audience that while "it costs little to watch" their performance, it costs only a "little more if you happen to get caught up in the action" (p. 23). Even more ominous is his line, "We're inclusively players, sir" (p. 27), because his audience mistakenly assumes it does not apply to themselves. Less threatening is his clichéd observation that the actors do onstage "the things that are supposed to happen off" (p. 28), for this allows Rosencrantz and Guildenstern to distinguish between their roles as *actors* in real life and as spectators to a present reality that they assume is ultimately beyond their concern, let alone their influence. Yet the Player's witty "every exit being an entrance somewhere else" reveals that theater and reality are merely reverse images of each other, a level of relativity originally denied by the conscious, absolutist mentality of the play's two central figures.[15]

Initially, Rosencrantz and Guildenstern are unwilling, parodic actors, taking bows before, rather than after, their final performance onstage—and absurd bows at that. Then, like an actor playing to the

Tragedians' audience, Guildenstern initiates a segment of action by challenging the Player to bet him that the year of one's birth doubled is an odd number (pp. 30–31). Guildenstern suddenly confesses to feeling a bit "on"—that is, functioning as an actor—although he does not recall the Player's earlier account of his profession as being so "on" (p. 34) that he cannot exit from the stage to real life. Predictably, this primitive attempt at acting proves disturbing. Guildenstern realizes that, his wishes to the contrary, they have somehow "been caught up" (p. 39), while Rosencrantz now finds himself "out of [his] step here" and over his "*depth*" (p. 38). They plaintively want to return "home" (p. 380) to that immune—if it could ever remain so—position of observer. Since we know nothing of that place, unless it be Shakespeare's tragedy, their real home, as Robert Wilcher observes, must be the present play.[16]

Their home is, in fact, not a matter of geography but of language, this play *of* and *on* words. When Rosencrantz asks his partner, "What are you playing at?," Guildenstern replies, "Words, words. They're all we have to go on" (p. 41). Hamlet's own "Words, words, words," his cynical answer to Polonius's intrusive question, "What do you read, my lord?" (2.2.191–192), likewise champions the notion that the *play* of language is a counterforce to playless facts. Fearing that they are indeed being drawn into a play, his voice like that of one crying "*in the wilderness*," Rosencrantz demands, "What's the game?" Guildenstern echoes, "What are the rules?" To this chorus Hamlet enters, significantly "*reading a book*" (p. 44). They now act, *play*, at first engaging in a verbal sparring whose metaphor is sports, in particular, tennis. In Stoppard's suggested blocking, they figuratively hurl words back and forth like tennis balls. Such linguistic play admits a larger play, the "hypothesis" (p. 47) in which Guildenstern impersonates Hamlet while Rosencrantz is given the option of playing himself or his partner. Again, they find this movement from seemingly secure observers to participants alarming—"What in God's name is going on?" (p. 42), and "WHO DO YOU THINK YOU ARE?" (p. 44). As their reality, here defined as that past when "people knew who I was" (p. 38), is displaced by the theatrical presence shared with us, we ourselves are drawn in as collaborators. The issue now is not what was, but has become "our situation" (p. 48).

The supposedly predetermined play, already brought into question by the ambiguous opening, now becomes increasingly open-ended. We have, accordingly, moved from the coin toss (a "bit of a bore" [p. 13]), to gymnastics (the "tumble" first proposed by the Player), to "gory romances" (p. 22) such as *The Rape of the Sabine Women,* to these early examples of acting or playing on the part of Rosencrantz and Guildenstern, to the now more frequent entrances of Hamlet and Shakespeare's characters—to what? The random coin toss, where the participant could rightly feel "abandoned" (p. 20) or insignificant, now leads into a more creative field of play that, no less, demands "some direction" (p. 20). When the Player removes his foot from the final coin tossed onstage, Rosencrantz discovers "it was tails" (p. 34); all philosophizing about the improbable coin toss is erased. Thus, we move into Stoppard's yellow zone, a "mystical experience" but, appropriately, one "shared by everybody" (p. 20).[17] We are being knocked out, as Helene Keyssar-Franke phrases it, of the familiar and, I would add, seemingly real world.[18] James Calderwood has suggested in his book *To Be and Not To Be: Negation and Metadrama in "Hamlet"* that at the heart of the theatrical experience is what he calls *theatricide*. Once given to the stage's illusion, we participate in a killing-off of reality as narrowly or rigidly understood, even as we enter a fraudulent world that, on its own completion, with the delivery of its final lines, will self-destruct, thereby allowing us to move back into life.[19]

Before the play "a coin showed heads about as often as it showed tails," and "then a messenger arrived" (p. 18); the implication is that with that arrival, with the play's becoming its own messenger, the improbable now becomes possible. In Rosencrantz's words, formerly "we were sent for" and now "we're here" (p. 19). Pragmatism is displaced by the imagination, by that creative effort among playwright, actor, and audience, or by what the Player calls "trust" (p. 30). In short, we move from facts to language. Alfred is the joyous player of this alternative world. Losing" often," now he has nothing to lose. A creature purely of play, denied even a single gender, accomplishing nothing but an impersonation, he is at first carefully inspected by Guildenstern and then asked, "Do you like being . . . an actor?"(p. 32). Tragedians, Rosencrantz and Guildenstern, and the offstage audience are now all "on" (p. 34), about to "entertain the offered fallacy," as Shakespeare's Antipholus of Syracuse says.[20] "Which way did we come in?," Guildenstern cries, as act 1 closes with Hamlet's first dialogue with the pair. As Rosencrantz and Guildenstern step into this new fluid world of the theater, Hamlet—the ultimate role for any actor—greets them with "Good lads, how do you both?"

2

With act 2 *we*—actors, characters-turned-actors, and audience on- and offstage—plunge fully into the Tragedians' heightened theatrical world, surrounded as it is by Stoppard's own theatrical world. No longer merely voyeuristic, the spectators' vital role is signaled by the Player's dismay over Rosencrantz's and Guildenstern's having abandoned their promised performance in the preceding act: "You left us," he says *"Bitterly";* that "somebody is *watching*" is "the single assumption which makes [their] existence viable" (p. 63). In a profession based on illusion, on the insubstantial, to have spoken even that fraudulent language and made the gestures of the actor's craft in "the thin unpopulated air" is, for the Player, a fate worse than death. To deny one's role as spectator is to limit one's role as a meaningful actor.[21] The court performance that the two offer as an apology for their earlier vanishing act allows the actors a second chance, or a second "slice of childhood," a fresh audience, Rosencrantz assures the company, who know nothing of the Tragedians' usual "perverted desires," while the actors "know nothing of them, to your mutual survival" (p. 65).[22]

That absent audience only implied in the Player's complaint now generates its opposite, the veritable plethora of onstage audiences, in this second act. It is no less a person than Hamlet, the very object of the twins' observation, who initiates the process when he calls upon them to "mark" Polonius as he enters, "that great baby you see there . . . not yet out of his swaddling clouts" (p. 55). Even Guildenstern plays the audience to the Player's speech about the missing audience as he *"claps solo with slow measured irony"* (SD, p. 64). Like Moon in *The Real Inspector Hound,* he is even something of a resident critic—"Brilliantly re-created. . . . Rather strong on metaphor, mind you. No criticism—only a matter of taste." Such onstage audiences are all audiences to each other, and hence "all fellows."[23] As they analyze Hamlet's reference to "hawk" and "handsaw," Rosencrantz and Guildenstern *"stare at [the] audience"* (SD, p. 58) located "southerly" from where they stand, a direction echoed in Hamlet's "When the wind is southerly I know a hawk from a handsaw" (p. 55). Rosencrantz shouts out "Fire" to prove that "it [free speech, but perhaps the audience as well] exists" (p. 60); we will recall Oliver Wendell Holmes's argument against shouting out "Fire" in a crowded theater. As he delivers the test word, Rosencrantz *"regards the audience, that is the direction [southerly], with contempt"* (p. 60). Does he envy what he thinks is our own less involved status? As Claudius takes Rosencrantz upstage, Guildenstern turns to face us (p. 72). Stoppard's blocking here thus serves as an emblem of the division between political and theatrical commitments. As Rosencrantz *"looks out over the audience,"* Guildenstern surely refers to us as well as the characters from Shakespeare's play in saying, "They're waiting to see what we're going to do" (p. 85).[24]

The pair's dialogue with Hamlet becomes their major concern as they proceed to offer a rather pessimistic diagnosis of that first two-line interchange with the Prince: "He was scoring us all down the line" and "He murdered us" (p. 56). Because they fear being "out of [their] depth here" (p. 68), they try to regress by asserting past roles as spectators—"Keep back—we're spectators" (p. 79)—but the fact remains that Rosencrantz and Guildenstern are now caught in the play. They can even anticipate their own final action, or disappearance, in act 3 when, struck by Polonius's death, Guildenstern can only wish that "more tears" will be shed for them when they die (p. 86). "And why us? Anybody would have done" (p. 92). Perhaps the lines apply to us as well.

If Rosencrantz and Guildenstern must be actors as well as spectators, the issue is, in whose play? Claudius offers them the minimal role of messengers to bear unknowingly Hamlet's death warrant, a role that for them is self-effacing, not to mention self-destructive, once the mission is completed. In Shakespeare's play they are fully cognizant of Claudius's seedy politics, but since they cannot know the full ramifications of his designs against Hamlet, their sin remains one of omission, if not commission. Stoppard, it should be noted, chooses not to stress the amorality of these former undergraduate friends turned political hatchet men, and thus, alongside the ironic destruction of Claudius's messengers of death, he casts the pair in a new role that really comments on the nature of the theater itself.[25] A live medium of presence sustained by the imaginative effort of actor and audience, Stoppard's theater now contemplates its darker side, one of absence and death, a dimension concomitant with its own reliance on illusion, on metaphor, on all "that which is not" as a means of mirroring "that which is." "To be" is here inseparable from "not to be," but this second, integral half of the equation is figured not in Hamlet, but in these undergraduate parodies. Concerned with their skins, attempting to limit their lives to the spectator's role, begrudgingly stepping into what they still hope is a minimal level of acting, the two thereby only sustain the play's own rush toward nonexistence.

The signs to this dark side, or role, come early, as when the *"two cloaked Tragedians,"* anticipating the Rosencrantz and Guildenstern of act 3, *"sway gently in unison,"* as if imitating the motion of the boat bound for England; or as when the two discover the spies dressed like themselves, as Rosencrantz barges into the rehearsal asking pathetically and hopefully, "I don't know you, do I?" (p. 82). Significantly, such clues to their ultimate role come from the rehearsal, or a play-within-the-play. When the two try to reclaim the roles of observers, as Hamlet lugs Polonius's body offstage, we know, from Shakespeare's text as well as from Stoppard's air-tight link between actor and audience, that what they observe, the disposal of a dead body, is their own fate. Even Hamlet's mistaken murder of Polonius will be reversed when he consciously substitutes their names for his own. Like Polonius, who also felt secure as an audience behind the arras, they will be thrust, literally and figuratively, into the action.[26]

Now the rehearsal usurps the stage, expanded into scenes either only implied or nonexistent in Shakespeare; the theater here thus feeds off itself, devouring its own Ur-text. We move from the quasi-real mood of act 1, that Greeklike chorus of two spectators greeting us in the opening tableau, to purely fictive characters, to players—*actors* or, using the Player's definition, "the opposite of people" (p. 63).[27] Now everything is defined in terms of the theater, even the most private of emotions. When the Player asks Rosencrantz to "think, in your head, *now,* think of the most . . . *private* . . . *secret* . . . *intimate* thing you have ever done secure in the knowledge of its privacy," Rosencrantz's "*shifty look*" becomes an actor's gesture, a bringing to the surface of something that, outside the theater, would have remained interior. Once started, this process cannot be revoked. Rosencrantz's "*dissembling madly*" cannot in any way obscure the fact that the Player—and the offstage audience, who have already been addressed by the Player *("He gives them—and the audience—a good pause")*—has seen him "do it" (p. 64).

As this self-conscious, seemingly exclusive theater[28] asserts itself, the coffin, the box with the lid on it, becomes the metaphor for the very act of illusion. For a time the theatrical world excludes offstage reality, yet Stoppard's medium, built on illusion, also effects its own destruction. We might characterize this theatrical world as one of essence, *dead* in that it has been extracted from existence; people and spectators exist, actors and characters do not, and yet, as we have seen, the division between the two is at best moot. The *life* of the stage world, ironically, is here the enactment of two characters moving towards death, nonexistence, their dismissal from the stage, through a play whose metaphor is the confined boat, the closed box of the theater, and a verbal trick where two names are substituted for one. This paradoxical relation between reality and illusion, life and death, existence and essence, random life offstage and controlled but fraudulent *life* onstage, is caught in Rosencrantz's own contradictory cries: "I'm going" (p. 73) and "Nobody leaves this room!" (p. 69). (Stoppard, we may recall, defines the immediate purpose of his plays as that of entertaining a room full of people.[29]) Here language is both essence—the verbalized significance of an object—and death. "It is *written*," pronounces the Player like some theatrical god (p. 80).

At present, illusion is all-encompassing. Trying to break out of the play, refusing to "stand for it" any longer, Rosencrantz sneaks up behind a female figure, ostensibly the Queen, and with "*desperate frivolity*" exclaims, "Guess who?!"—a line doubly ironic since Rosencrantz has already questioned his own identity. Then this encounter with the *real* Queen turns to mockery as he spins round the figure only to discover he has been holding the transvestite Alfred. If this displacement of an assumed reality by illusion shocks Rosencrantz, for the Tragedians it is nothing more than the opening of the dress rehearsal in which Alfred will play not Gertrude, the seemingly real, flesh-and-blood individual, Claudius's wife, but a Player Queen, the *essence* of the Queen or of *a* queen, and therefore a role not demanding physical verification, let alone verisimilitude. A mirror for reality, to the degree that, as Norman Berlin argues, we can see life clearly only in its mirror, the present stage world threatens to become exclusive, making us all so "inclusively Players" that, by definition, life is excluded, or at very least diminished.[30]

Yet in a strange reversal, the theater employs its illusory, nonexistent nature, its *death,* to affirm life, as it makes a countermovement back to reality, to the world offstage. Little wonder that the discussion of death is "held over" from the previous act: "Whatever became of the moment when one first knew about death?" (p. 71). We are now presented with that moment reborn onstage. The Player well knows that a performance arrives "at the point when everyone who is marked for death dies" (p. 79) and that this moment and its "conclusion" are issues of aesthetics, no less than of morality and logic (p. 79). The question now becomes: can the theater justify itself by enacting and thereby giving present meaning to this final act, the same self-cancelling act that is the topic of Shakespeare's own gravediggers at the start of *Hamlet*'s act 5?[31]

Still thinking that life is meaningful without the theater, Guildenstern answers "no"—there can be no theatrical approximation for death; but the Player is just as emphatic with his "yes."[32] If the theater cannot define life by enacting death convincingly, then we are presented with a mere spectacle; yet if the seemingly impossible can happen, if we are allowed to draw a significance from our own actions, and from our own ultimate nonaction, then the medium is justified.[33] The messengers speak to these issues. "Life in a box is better than no life at all" (p. 71), although the assertion would be meaningless if we were dead, or at very last unconscious of being in the box. Negativity itself is relative here: is one's situation hopeless if he or she does not know it is hopeless? Does being a conscious spectator to one's own actions provide sufficient incentive for an existence where it is all *"written,"* predetermined, fraudulent in the sense of being inauthentic, and doubly illusory in being an artifice already spun from the mind of a playwright, be he Shakespeare, Claudius, Hamlet, or Stoppard?

By definition, this enactment of death, at the heart of a medium existing only to yield to life, cannot come until the end. In a sense, Guildenstern is right: the enactment of death "isn't death." Still, the Player is no less right: in a larger sense death is what we think it to be and what we are willing to accept. His anecdote is revealing: when he once tried for a realistic onstage death by hiring an actor already condemned to die for sheep stealing, the audience found the intrusion of reality a *"disaster"* (p. 84). "Audiences know what to expect, and that is all that they are prepared to believe in" (p. 84). Stoppard's next stage direction is timely: *"The SPIES die at some length, rather well,"* although as yet Rosencrantz and Guildenstern cannot see this theatrically convincing action as a portent of their own destiny in act 3. Ironically, Guildenstern's attempt to redefine death as simply "failing to reappear . . . now you see him, now you don't" will later be enacted. On one subject both Guildenstern and the Player agree, on a line taken from *Hamlet:* the function of the theater is "to mirror life" (p. 81).

With its multiple deaths, its omnipresent theatricality, and its originality in showing action only suggested by Shakespeare, act 3 promises to be a triumph of illusion that in turn most mirrors life.[34] Our presence will be critical; by our suspension of belief we allow these onstage shamans to enact our own end. In its boat, in its box, within the confines of the stage, Stoppard's theater can invest existence with that which is not—no mean task in a medium that owes its own *life* to that which is not.[35]

3

The final act pushes Rosencrantz and Guildenstern from concerned spectators and hesitant actors into the role of incipient playwrights, even as the ship's set greeting us in act 3, by delivering the twins to a theatrical place only reported in *Hamlet,* also delivers Stoppard's play to the offstage audience and to that real world encompassing the stage. We are all in one boat, sailing to destinies respective to our positions in the play.[36] The question opening the blackened stage of this final act, "Are you there?" (p. 97), may include us as well. Our own witness to the production and our superior position to characters who, since act 1, have tried but failed to remain with us as fellow spectators, are signaled by this consciousness of the play's offstage audience hastening the dissolution of the imaginary barrier once separating on- from off-stage. As this final, most original of acts itself transcends Shakespeare's text, we, having little pretext to anticipate its incidents, become mutual passengers with these Everymen. Hamlet can now be pushed upstage, hidden under an umbrella, while our fellows stand downstage staring out at us. If we occupy the position of the offstage ocean, then our witness is in part responsible for the direction of Stoppard's theatrical *narrenschiff.* For the first time Hamlet himself acknowledges and then is rudely acknowledged by us: he comes downstage, "*regards the audience,*" and when he "*spits into the audience,* that spit is returned as he "*clasps his hand to his eye and wipes himself*" (p. 116). Our presence is also announced in more subtle ways: we are, properly, the "larger" movement in which the smaller movement of the play is "contained" (p. 122). With the pronoun "you" at last having its more catholic application, a line like "You are Rosencrantz and Guildenstern. That's enough" (p. 122) surely embraces us as well.[37]

Now Rosencrantz and Guildenstern, at once thematically *tragic* and theatrically *comic,* become the dominant actors—and spectators—in the ultimate action of their own death, the perfect action, as Shakespeare's clowns well know, in that it is complete, subject to no further ramifications. As Guildenstern impersonates the English King while Rosencrantz, typically, is given the option of playing himself or his partner, they act out, in anticipation, that final event, even as they carry with them the "prop" that can only lead to their deaths. For the first time they define themselves as actors who "perform" (p. 108). And they perform now in a world given to the word. Death itself takes the form of a letter. This ultimate action, the one closing off the possibility of any further action, has been announced from the start, they realize, in the "message" delivered by that man appearing outside their window, and announced for us in the play's own title greeting us on the playbill.[38]

The lighting change in act 1, we will recall, announced Rosencrantz's and Guildenstern's involvement as actors in Claudius's scenario, as well as their loss of the privileged position of spectators. Here in the final act, with the raising of the stage lights, the coming of dawn, the two are revealed in their final posture, that of futile playwrights trying by some authorial fiat to adjust their destiny. When Guildenstern stabs the Player, it is an *original* action, one willed by a character who had earlier taken pleasure in his lack of will power and hence lack of responsibility for his condition. Appropriately, his action is comically anticipated in a stage direction: his partner "*makes a stab at an exit*" and then "*changes direction*" (p. 113). With escape blocked, the only alternative now seems to be to seize control of the script. But such control is futile in two senses: the Player stabbed by Guildenstern only feigns death and, what is more, actually proves his point that the illusion of death, although not the actual event, is within the range of theatrical enactment and, as a consequence, alone has meaning for an audience.

In addition, Guildenstern now sees his own fate even more graphically than he could during the rehearsals of *The Murder of Gonzago*, where he failed, or purposely failed, to recognize himself in the two spies. Once dubious not only about the theater's ability to enact that event but also about dying himself, he is now guardedly optimistic: "Well, we'll know better next time" (p. 126). His own death, or, more properly, disappearance, from the stage will have the surface comedy of a vaudevillian's act: "Now you see me, now you—*(and disappears)*" (p. 126). Concerned earlier about payment for their services, jealous that a partner may have received more, they are now beyond material desires, as fully fictive as was Alfred, who in receiving nothing expected nothing. They now have a purpose, even if the full meaning of that phrase "We're delivering Hamlet" is beyond their present comprehension. Hamlet, character *and* play, disappears through one of the barrels, as Stoppard's own Tragedians and these newly invested courtiers, also freed from Shakespeare's text, emerge from those same barrels, from a theatricallike womb that itself seems to reverse the ashbins borrowed from Beckett, who served as master to this former apprentice-playwright. For Shakespeare's act 5 we now get Stoppard's own act; or as Guildenstern says, perhaps also making oblique reference to the gravediggers' scene, "I knew it wasn't the end" (p. 115). Only at the moment death is closest can Guildenstern, the more intellectual of the two, be comically philosophical about the subject: "what is so terrible about death?" (p. 110); and, "As Socrates so philosophically put it, since we don't know what death is, it is illogical to fear it" (p. 110).

This newfound serenity about death is inseparable from the celebration of the theater itself. Although he dismisses it as "merely competent" (p. 123), the Player's convincing imitation of death seems real, *The Real Thing*. Invariably, no less than Rosencrantz and Guildenstern, the audience, if only for a second, swallows the effective illusion.[39] Surely, this faked death proves disconcerting to audiences both on- and off-stage. We had not imagined that Guildenstern would be capable of adjusting his own script, nor are we prepared for the seeming irony when the Player, who had dismissed real death as less meaningful to an audience than its simulation, actually *dies*. Thus, the

Player's *rebirth* only celebrates the powers of illusion, not death. No less than Shakespeare's *Hamlet,* Stoppard's play champions the power of the theater. By enactment onstage we diffuse the one event otherwise most terrifying to us. The theater becomes a hymn to life, and the artist, as Yeats well knew, is always gay, despite the apparent tragedies of existence.

Perhaps from linking the play with the so-called theater of the absurd or from stressing its bleak image of mankind, some of the critics of *Rosencrantz and Guildenstern Are Dead* respond as if it were a novel. There is, surely, a world of difference both aesthetically and philosophically between the two media.[40] Our collaboration as playwright, actor, and audience—with those roles now interchangeable—is, Thomas Whitaker argues, a meaningful and an optimistic one.[41] The process of enactment—or, as Guildenstern says, "Well, we'll know better next time"—outweighs its end, whether that end be defined as mortal or theatrical. To be more literal about it, the boat never reaches England, and so during the performance that we witness its destination is quite rightly dismissed as nothing but a "conspiracy of cartographers" (p. 107). Conversely, the present imitation, whether in the form of a map or a play, is the real thing and something we *can* believe in.

One perceptive critic announces that the play "worked" for her;[42] this judgment, a theatrical one, is echoed in Rosencrantz's line, "We've arrived" (p. 121). Again, the play's movement toward its final enactment is now of less consequence than the issues it raises along that way. Significantly, the final variation of the persistent refrain "Give us this day our . . ." is "Give us this day our daily cue" (p. 102).

Rosencrantz and Guildenstern themselves end differently from what we see at the start. If their profoundly (for them) theatrical growth seems small to us, it is growth nevertheless, like the barren tree in *Waiting for Godot* that by the start of the second act has sprouted a few wretched leaves.[43] They discover the ultimate script, however late, when they find in place of Hamlet's their own names on the letter. Even if the "circumstances [were] ever so slightly beyond [their] control," it "was quite a good play nevertheless" (p. 115), and this collage unites the lines of the Player and Rosencrantz, respectively. When they see Hamlet's name on that letter, they decide not to alter Claudius's script (and by implication Shakespeare's) by informing the Prince of the facts. And when Hamlet himself turns playwright, substituting their names for his own, they are given a second chance to make a change. What they had feared, moving from spectator to actor-participant, let alone to apprentice playwright, turns out to be comic and peculiarly satisfying. Although Rosencrantz considers jumping over the side of the boat, he thinks better (p. 108) and instead finds its planking "nice" (p. 100). Guildenstern also confesses to being "very fond of boats," even liking the "way they're—contained" (p. 100). Hamlet, the character and the play they had feared, is now reduced to a lantern's light shining through fabric at the top of the stage.

So delivered, the play stresses the copresence and the interdependence of actor and audience.[44] Rosencrantz now sees their destiny, unalterable as it may be, as "a play" and themselves as being "on top of it now" (p. 111). At its end *Rosencrantz and Guildenstern Are Dead* brings before us all those responsible for the illusion. The pair disappears, to try "better" tomorrow, and then as *"the whole stage is lit up"* (SD, p. 126), the tableau offers the King, the Queen, Laertes, and Hamlet *"all dead."* The onstage audience—Horatio, Fortinbras, and "two Ambassadors from England" (the countermessengers for Rosencrantz and Guildenstern)—witnessing this "dismal" sight is promised by the playwrightlike Horatio, in lines taken directly from *Hamlet,* that he will serve as Presenter for the next performance. His words are Shakespeare's, of course, but they now perfectly duplicate what Stoppard has achieved.[45] For the final emphasis is on theatrical enactment; Hamlet's body will be placed "high on a stage" to be viewed, and the actor playing Horatio, confronted with one audience—us—about to depart, promises to retell the story to Fortinbras and those two ambassadors, the new or next-day's audience. What he offers in the way of a preview is something of a plot outline: "of carnal, bloody, and unnatural acts, / of accidental judgments" and so on. His last words, and Shakespeare's and Stoppard's as well, themselves stress the delivery of the play to a waiting audience, in turn stressing that audience's reception and therefore ratification of the dramatic message, "all this can I / Truly deliver" (p. 126).

If we, the ultimate audience, have experienced, along with our surrogate audience and fellow actors, the essence of the thing, the theater's enactment of the universal nonevent that, no less than birth itself, demarks the limits of our earthly existence, then it is no less true that in the play's delivery of life we have also been participants. Against an otherwise gloomy philosophy of nonexistence, this is indeed the "miracle of the playwright's collaborative art."[46]

6

Williams, *A Streetcar Named Desire*: "Whoever You Are—I Have Always Depended on the Kindness of Strangers"

Williams's epigram for *Streetcar,* the lines from Hart Crane's "The Broken Tower," suggests that the audience is the primary, or at very least the initial, *character* in the play: "And so it was that I entered the broken world / To trace the visionary company of love."[1] Like Blanche, perhaps even like her playwright, if we see Williams's own complex life and personality divided between his two protagonists, we voyage into this world, the single stage set before us. Before a word of human dialogue, the set itself speaks to us. Its atmosphere of *"decay"* is attenuated by a *"kind of lyricism,"* and if the neighborhood is *"poor,"* like other run-down sections of inner cities, it also has a *"raffish charm"* (p. 3). On the steps of the building we see two women, one white, the other black, an image of America's melting pot, an extension of ourselves. Eunice and her neighbor testify to the fact that New Orleans, as it exists before Blanche's own audiencelike entrance, is a *"cosmopolitan city where there is a relatively warm and easy intermingling of races"* (p. 3). Then two men, Stanley and Mitch, enter a set that as yet is still an exterior one, with its interior revealed only slightly when Stella comes out on the first-floor landing. The mood at present is familiar, familial, reassuring, even comic, as Stanley tosses a package of meat to his wife, his gesture at once literal and symbolic. Crying out in protest but laughing *"breathlessly"* (p. 4), Stella catches this gross extension of Stanley's own self, to the accompaniment of laughter from that racially mixed onstage audience of two. Unless they have read Crane's epigram printed on the playbill, the audience might anticipate a domestic comedy, a southern Maggie and Jiggs. Although his dialogue is minimal, Stanley still eloquently addresses us, *plays* for our approval in a stage world that, like him, is physical, direct, literal, unpoetic, or, if poetic, then unintentionally so.

Similarly, Blanche speaks to us before her first line. Solid and literal as it may appear, *Streetcar*'s single set is suddenly *broken* when, with a lighting change, the exterior walls of the Kowalski apartment dissolve to reveal the interior. Thus, the theater's own technical "magic" coincides here with the entrance of Blanche, who will later confess that she prefers such "magic" to "realism." And at the end she can be removed from the set only by a patently theatrical trick: the doctor must conceal his true self, that efficient and emotionless professional who has come to take her to the asylum, and assume the role of her Rosenkavalier. Blanche is, in Williams's stage direction, *"incongruous to this setting"* (p. 5). In contrast to the raffish charm, the comic mixture of crude yet wholesome sexuality of the attendant characters, she has an *"uncertain manner,"* an *"expression . . . of shocked disbelief"* (p. 5). Her entrance, to invoke the passage from Crane, "breaks" what had seemed a monolithic comic world. Blanche's own status is ambivalent: the white dress and that uncertain manner suggest that she is a *"moth,"* drawn to this stage, desiring it even as she becomes its victim.[2] If the entry of Stanley and Mitch has been easy and natural, Blanche's is arduous. With *"faintly hysterical humor,"* she recites a depressing litany of travelling from one streetcar to another before getting off at what, for her, is the ironically named Elysian Fields (p. 6).[3] Eunice, in contrast, fits in happily with this same world, the stage set that alternately seduces and rebuffs the intruder, for if the visitor is anxious, Eunice is assured and practical: "Well, why don't you just go in" (p. 7). When Blanche expresses reservations about entering an apartment whose owners are absent, Eunice again assures her, "We own this place so I can let you in" (p. 8). I note that the printed text devotes almost six pages to this movement into the set, the mutual act of the audience, the characters at home onstage, and the visitor from Laurel.

In Ionesco the audience plays an imaginative collaborator with the old couple. In Pinter we are investigators, like Goldberg and McCann, sifting through what meager facts the playwright or his Stanley offers us. Genet enacts our own irrepressible desire, indeed our need to be the "other," and to validate our own fraudulent reality by the theater's mirror image, paradoxically true because of its artifice. For Brecht, of course, the audience is the literal recipient, the goal of the play's artfully suspended dialectics. Stoppard's Rosencrantz and Guildenstern come from us, would prefer to remain uninvolved spectators like the audience surrounding them, yet when the messengers discover not once but twice the contents of the letter they bear to England, they will assume our burden of knowing the plot. In this context, I think the audience in *Streetcar* is asked to assess but, ironically, refrain from judgment, while Stanley and Blanche compete for our attention, offering us antithetical perspectives on the play's otherwise single world.

I recall my actor friend, mentioned in the chapter on *Galileo,* who tries to *win* every moment he is onstage, as if he were in competition with his fellow actors for the audience's favor. At the same time, he divests himself of his real-life personality for a fiction and, one step further, gives up his autonomy to be a member of the company, a good ensemble player. I see Stanley and Blanche, both the characters themselves and the actors assigned these two roles, in this fashion. Together, they constitute the play, define its boundaries—in a sense, *need* each other. Representing two different concepts of theater, two different scenarios for *Streetcar,* and the two genders, these two rival actors cannot share the same billing. Embodying the divided nature of our own being, the very division of our brain into the rational and the imaginative, or of our otherwise single self into a public and a private being, they play to the audience, to us, so that we become the arbiter, seated offstage, to be sure, yet housed within the same theater.

Stanley *wins* in the sense that, with Stella's concurrence, he dismisses Blanche from the set. Still, Blanche's line—the subtitle of this chapter—"Whoever you are—I have always depended on the kindness of strangers," appeals to the audience, and is significant for our experience with the play, however deluded Blanche is as she mistakes the doctor for a gentleman caller. She implores the audience, those strangers in the darkened house, to be *kind* to her, to "entertain" what she represents, that alternative world she has attempted unsuccessfully to impose on Stanley's New Orleans. When the play concludes and the two lead actors appear for bows, this same line can as easily be Stanley's as they hold hands; the fictive antagonism between the two actors dissolves. But during the play itself we can do what Blanche and Stanley cannot do for each other—"tolerate both," as Stella says (p. 74), admit both into the fuller interpretive spectrum of a play whose ambivalence or lack of resolution has been at once praised and condemned.[4]

1

The world entered and then witnessed by the audience, the *real* or tangible world of *Streetcar,* is Stanley's. This is the undeniable, the egocentric, *fact* of the play,[5] and the set itself, along with the implied geography just offstage, reflects his character: provincial, controlled, exclusive, decidedly physical, and able to transform, by persuasion or by violence if necessary, anything coming into its orbit.[6] If Marlon

Brando has been faulted for taking over the play, at least in its first half, for suppressing the ugly elements in Stanley while stressing the appealing crude charm of this ugly American, the fact is that his character, as drawn by the playwright, seduces us no less.[7]

Her illness notwithstanding, Blanche may be a titantic figure, allegorical, a signifier for a tradition whose depth far surpasses anything that Stanley can or could offer. Still, Blanche is literary, in a curious fashion *a*theatrical, clearly not public in the way that the medium of the theater demands, and hence she is at variance with that single set. Stanley may also be a Brechtian type, perhaps no less allegorical than his adversary, and surely there is a psychological substructure, an actor's subtext, to his character. Yet his real force in the play, I think, is physical, immediate, and, again, at one with what we can *observe* in *Streetcar* without qualification, without being figurative. In this sense, Stanley's is the play's real *geography,* both spatial and psychological. His theater is the *realistic* one that we *see,* as distinguished from Blanche's inner, imaginative stage, which we only hear of or see imperfectly, and only symbolically, in its exhausted representative. Stanley is therefore both microcosm and macrocosm, and Williams's first extended description of him sustains this balance: *"Branching out from this complete and satisfying center are all the auxiliary channels of his life, such as his heartiness with men, his appreciation of rough humor, his love of good drink and food and games, his car, his radio, everything that is his, that bears his emblem of the gaudy seed-bearer"* (p. 25).

When Stanley's set is concentrated, as in the poker game where four men huddle around the table, then Mitch, an even more divided character, with his membership in the New Orleans Athletic Club and his obligation to his mother, observes that "poker shouldn't be played in a house with women" (p. 63). When Mitch leaves that table and, outside the bathroom, engages Blanche in conversation, Stanley repeatedly and derisively calls for him to return to the game. Stanley pervades the set. Even as the transparent walls allow us, the offstage audience, to move easily from the exterior street to the interior apartment, so there is "no door," as Blanche herself observes, between the two rooms of the Kowalski apartment (p. 16). The bowling alley, or the garage, or the Four Deuces are just immediately offstage, within the confines of a neighborhood that Stella defines as a "mixed lot" (p. 17). Yet these implied extensions of the set are contained in Stanley himself, sometimes literally, as when he comes onstage in his flashy bowling jacket, and sometimes symbolically, as on the morning after he and Stella have made love when he goes "to get the car greased" (p. 71).

New Orleans itself becomes his domain, for Stella's retort to

Blanche's dismay over living "in these conditions" is that New Orleans, the extension of their neighborhood, which is in turn an extension of the apartment, "isn't like other cities" (p. 12). She assures her sister that, like Stanley, the city is "not that bad at all." The state itself, Louisiana, reflects the set, since for Stanley it is the Louisiana of Huey Long, whose political motto becomes his own: "'Every Man is a King!' And I am the king around here" (p. 131). Even when Stanley travels, the time he spends away from home so intensifies the need for his physical presence that Stella "can hardly stand it," "nearly go[es] wild." Blanche's sarcastic "I guess that is what is meant by being in love" is met only with a *"radiant smile"* (p. 19). Even Stanley's reference to nineteenth-century France, when he speaks of the Napoleonic Code, is at once egocentric and provincial since he invokes the legal doctrine to secure his share of his wife's estate. And although he is of Polish ancestry, Stanley insists on defining himself as "one hundred percent American" (p. 134). For him, China is deflated to the "Chinaman's" where the poker players go for take-out food, and when Pablo curses his host's luck, in his native Spanish, Stanley bursts out, "Put it in English, greaseball" (p. 163). Even Blanche, in the midst of her luxuriant, maddened vision of dying at sea, indirectly acknowledges that New Orleans, Stanley's domain, the presence of the play, will be the site of her death. For that fatal unwashed grape comes from the French Market, and is physically present in the bunch of grapes that Eunice herself has bought for Blanche as something of a going-away present.

Stanley's exclusive, almost claustrophobic, reductive world *is* the reality of *Streetcar,* the only physical reality enacted in the play and the main component of Williams's theater of presence. It is "where you are now," as Eunice tells Blanche, and since this is obvious, "You don't have to look no further" (p. 6). Nor can Stanley budge from this reality, this presence; in his words, "You're damn tootin' I'm going to stay here" (p. 36). In this sense, Mitch's compassionate promise to Blanche not to "step out of bounds" (p. 108) has a geographical or theatrical, along with an ethical, implication.

Still, Blanche must challenge this world. Incapable of accepting what is literally before her eyes, of what has no profound implication beyond its own presence, she demands that Stella "explain this place" to her (p. 12).

Looking *"apprehensively toward the front door"* (p. 23), she fears this theatrical presence, this pressure; when Stanley enters the apartment for the first time, she *"hides behind the screen"* (p. 23). Opposed to the communal, public nature of the apartment complex, not to mention a public medium such as the theater, she complains that there is "no privacy here" (p. 111). And alluding to her own sexual and alcoholic addictions, she still finds her sister's "fix" worse than her own (p. 73).

Blanche's own world, her internal "set," is essentially unseen, beyond enactment, an imaginative, expansive one created by language rather than by physical presence—the verbal half, in effect, to the visual half of the theater embodied in Stanley.[8] Nor does the bathroom, Blanche's temporary refuge just off the Kowalski's bedroom, yet remaining unseen by us, prove an adequate alternative; Stanley's increasing outbursts at her for monopolizing that room are simultaneously comic and sinister. Despite half-hearted attempts such as re-covering the bedroom chair, she cannot alter the given set. In scene 6 there is even a touching but aborted play-within-a-play when Blanche and Mitch come back after their first date to discover that the "lord and lady of the house"—in her sarcastic yet also romantic rewriting of their characters—are absent. By a sort of verbal fiat she tries to transform the set as she stands on the doorstep, calling first upon the Pleiades, the Seven Sisters, indeed, invoking them the way a poet would her muse. Significantly, they "are not out tonight." Once in the apartment, Blanche somewhat lugubriously tries to convert the Kowalskis' home to the Left Bank of Paris by playing with Mitch at being Bohemians (p. 103). Yet Mitch doesn't understand a word of French, and Blanche's difficulty in finding the key prefigures her failure to rearrange the play's physical presence (p. 101).

Her world thus hovers on the periphery of the set confronting the audience, indeed, stretches cosmically beyond it. Still, that world cannot be staged. Blanche's spiritual home is Belle Reve, her paradise lost, but the geography of the surrounding town of Laurel, albeit specific, remains unseen: a school, whose principal is appropriately named Graves; two hotels, the Flamingo and the Tarantula Arms; an accounting firm, Ambler and Ambler; and on the outskirts of Laurel, the Moon Lake Casino and the nearby army base for whose recruits Blanche's home is " 'Out-of-Bounds' " (p. 121)—we will recall Mitch's use of that term.

Yet against the reductive geography of Stanley's Louisiana, Blanche, as Roger Asselineau phrases it, "again and again opens up vistas . . . far beyond the narrow limits of the claustrophobic apartment to which she is physically confined."[9] However, fraudulent, however fictive the romantic world she tries to "create" (p. 104), her United States includes Miami, Dallas, Texas, and the potential reaches of Western Union, while her references to the world outside this country embrace Poland, France, Germany, Russia, England, the Caribbean, and China (although the Chinese lantern itself has been purchased on Bourbon Street). Her references through fiction and music have both historical and spatial dimensions—the "land of the sky blue water" to which they "brought a captive maid" (p. 30), nights in Arabia, and Poe's ghoul-haunted "woodlands of Weir" (p. 12). As she translates and interprets them, her first and last names call up the white woods of romances (p. 59). At length, the geography of this unrealized but cosmic set extends into space and eternity: Blanche is interested in astrology; she sings about the "paper moon, sailing over a cardboard sea" that exists only through an imaginative effort she equates with love (p. 120); and at length she invokes heaven itself to which that "unwashed grape" from the French Market will have "transported her" (p. 170).[10]

But again, this internal, imaginative set is not, *cannot* be, enacted, and is thus an irritant to the play's theatrical presence. From Stanley's perspective, Blanche—her set—must first be attacked, as in the rape scene, and then dismantled, either through a one-way ticket back to Laurel or a one-way journey to the asylum. Her imaginative effort is both an achievement and a burden, inseparable from her neurosis. She is a lonely individual who cannot find a haven of love or a haven *in* the present theater. Blanche's "traveling wears [her] out" (p. 27), and her understandable but ironic wish is "to *rest*"(p. 95). In Stella's view she was always "flighty" (p. 124).[11]

The offstage audience alone shares this unenacted vision. Coming from a world larger than the stage, our mind's eye provides an actual locale that is correlative to Blanche's otherwise verbal, imaginative, or literary geography. The onstage audience itself can only parody, even if unintentionally, her unenacted world. For Stanley, Belle Reve is simply a "place in the country" (p. 30), and its occupant, a criminal who has "raided some stylish shop in Paris" (p. 37), a creature of mere "Hollywood glamor" (p. 39). Blanche translates her sister's first name as "star" (p. 10), but such extraterrestrial origins have in Stella's case clearly been sacrificed to her husband's more mundane, albeit vital, physicality.

2

Blanche is thus the literary artist adrift in a highly theatrical, sensuous theater, while Stanley embodies what is immediate, here and now, tangible. As a literary artist, Blanche professes a vision that is correspondingly private and in a sense hostile to such a realistic medium as the stage.[12] She wants—to cite again her well-known line—"magic," not "realism" (p. 145). If there is a theater for her, it is inner, verbal, and escapist.[13] Her theater is characterized by what

Ruby Cohn has called the role-playing of its sole actor,[14] but it lacks the prerequisite plot capable of bringing such role-playing to a comic conclusion, to a resolution within the control of its chief actor. Stanley opens her wardrobe trunk, the symbol of her art and artifice, and pulls out a handful of dresses. Yet that same trunk also contains the papers charting the decline and subsequent death of Belle Reve, that unseen stage on which Blanche has first been a Southern belle—waited on by servants as well as by her sister—and then an abandoned woman who takes family and servants to their graves (p. 33). Buoyed up by drinking in scene 10, she drags that trunk to the center of the stage; yet the scene she enacts, just before Stanley's own drunken entrance, takes place on a night when she goes with admirers for a moonlight swim at the rock quarry and where her last line is the grimly ironic "be careful to dive where the deep pool is—if you hit a rock you don't come up till tomorrow" (p. 151).

As the feminine principle of art, the woman whose charm "is fifty per cent illusion" (p. 41), Blanche thus assaults the reductive masculine realism of Stanley's stage, which coexists with her for a time but is incapable of union except through its sterile, cruel parody in rape. A rival visionary, curiously like an Iago challenging the world of domestic, if noisy, marital bliss, hammering out her vision by language rather than by physical force, she is a would-be creator whose work is aborted. Her sexuality is thereby the avenue to its opposite, death. Appropriately, the line from Elizabeth Barrett Browning that Blanche reads on Mitch's lighter is "'I shall but love thee better after death!'" (p. 57). And the American authors she tried to teach her drug-store Romeos in Laurel are all dead ones: Hawthorne, Whitman, and Poe. That death waiting on the other side of her sexuality is made manifest when the Mexican woman comes onstage selling "Flores para los muertos" (p. 148), in the same scene in which Mitch, earlier the God who "sometimes" comes "quickly" (p. 116),[15] has abandoned her. Blanche's imagination is dead because it cannot find a home onstage. She coexists with the stage's physical half but is also incapable of uniting with it to establish the balance of the verbal and the visual elements that characterize live theater. Blanche is the Grim Reaper (p. 22), at once a creation of a cruel, patriarchal world and, to an equal degree, its self-induced victim, simultaneously its scapegoat and sacrificial figure.

In the midst of Williams's own high art, she represents a fraudulent art—or an unrealized artist, to be more charitable and also more accurate. Blanche defines this art, unintentionally, as that of a Barnum and Bailey world, "just as phony as it can be." Still, hers is also an art calling out for ratification, for enactment: "But it wouldn't be make-believe / If you believed in me!" (p. 120). That cry falls on deaf ears onstage. However, that same "if" travels offstage to the more comprehending, sympathetic audience who, knowing the larger artifice of which she is a component, has no bias against her, who sees her as the necessary but as yet incomplete half of Williams's verbal-visual theater. To his own mind, Stanley is the entire world, but then he is a character in a play, engaged rather than detached, unlike the audience, who observes him and knows that he, too, is at best an artifice, a creation of the playwright.

3

We witness, in effect, three plays, one enacted, one implied, and Williams's larger play, *Streetcar,* containing them both. Stanley's authority is challenged and then brutally reasserted as the play itself gravitates from Blanche's *feminine* charm, which for a time almost usurps the stage, to Stanley's *masculine* force, which drives her from it. This deliberate division is the play's achievement, I think, rather than evidence of a split between Williams's moral and artistic sentiments, or between his ethical imperatives and his characters, who exist not in themselves as fully realized human prototypes but as examples of those sentiments;[16] nor is it a split between his use of the trappings of tragedy and his compromise in tracing only its aftereffects.[17] In a less judgmental sense, the split has been defined as one between the romantic and realistic temperaments, either of its chief characters or within the single mind of the playwright, or between the artistic and the practical,[18] or between Blanche's heightened consciousness and the luxuriant unconsciousness of Stanley.[19] *Streetcar* offers its divided halves not as ends in themselves, nor for the purpose of some resolution between them, but rather as a challenge to us. Confronted from the start by those lines from Hart Crane and confronted again by the seductive stage set ("*You can almost feel the warm breath of the brown river beyond the river warehouses with their faint redolence of bananas and coffee*" [p. 31]), we have been drawn into this divided play and then represented onstage by the surrogate audience figures framing the apartment house and, later, by characters making their entrance like us, albeit from backstage rather than the street outside the theater. Now, individually and collectively, we become the final arbiter of a work founded on such basic division, on the elemental conflict embodied in Stanley and Blanche.

In the final scene, we are enacted once more by the Doctor and Matron, the last characters to enter that set, during the penultimate moments of the performance. They come, of course, to remove Blanche; yet when the Doctor abandons his cold, professional manner and assumes the stance of a gentleman caller, he gives form, however temporarily or fraudulently, to her otherwise unrealized world. As I have suggested, Blanche can be removed from the stage only on her own terms, only when the actor impersonating the Doctor "plays" her "Rosenkavalier" (p. 99), the same role Mitch has forsaken. The Matron offers only force, a crude and self-incriminating power not unlike Stanley's. She is described as *"divested of all the softer properties of womankind"* (SD, p. 175). Williams comments on the doctor's change as *"he takes off his hat and now he becomes personalized. The unhuman quality goes. His voice is gentle and reassuring as he crosses to Blanche and crouches in front of her. As he speaks her name, her terror subsides a little"* (p. 177). Whatever the metadramatic overtones in this description, it is also, literally, a director's instructions for an actor asked to change character—and within seconds. If the onstage characters have summoned the late-arriving visitors, this *final* audience, if Stanley has driven Stella to the desperate action of removing the intruder, still the Doctor's sensitivity to Blanche, his recognition that she will exit the stage not by force but only through artifice, attests to Blanche's own power, to her imaginative inner world that, if it cannot find enactment on the present stage, anticipates a stage—the asylum—just in the wings.

From the perspective of the other onstage characters her line, "Whoever you are—I have always depended on the kindness of strangers" (p. 178),[20] is ghoulish, an absurdly pathetic vestige of the fraudulent world in which she has tried to live, and which she had tried to superimpose on Stanley. Still, for the actress speaking that line, and for the character she impersonates, it seems logical, wonderfully sane, and quite the proper social response for a Southern belle exiting the stage *"holding tightly to [the Doctor's] arm,"* the way a debutante might act when entering a ballroom. She gives herself to the Doctor, allowing him *"to lead her as if she were blind."* The play's two worlds, romantic and practical, artistic and realistic, verbal and visual, Blanche and Stanley, here coexist in a single line, but now without contention. She exits triumphantly, *grandly,* about to take that voyage—to the Caribbean perhaps—of which she has long dreamed.[21] She anticipates another play; her role is not yet exhausted.[22]

Thus it is the audience that frames the play; it is our insight, as one critic calls it, that is the final "good" or justification of *A Streetcar Named Desire*.[23] Blanche's imaginative reality is possible only through our witness.[24] The play's ambivalence, sexual or thematic or artistic,[25] is not, I believe, a sign of weakness. Far from distrusting his audience as Pinter appears to do,[26] Williams may actually entrust it with too much, asking, especially in this ending, that we sort out our own ambivalence or, perhaps, that we hold in suspension the play's contradictory claims on our sympathies. With the exception of Stella, the onstage characters themselves cannot, or will not, or do not entertain the conflicting worlds represented by the two central figures. Like an audience, the poker players rise as Blanche moves toward the door, but their expressions are those of indifference or incomprehension.

As Stanley kneels before Stella, searching for the opening of her blouse, he seeks her approval with his "Now, honey. Now, love. Now, now, love." Williams's stage direction for him is complex. If he speaks "*soothingly,*" as if trying to justify their decision to send Blanche away, Stanley also speaks "*voluptuously,*" as if asserting the priority of their physical marriage, which is assaulted, as he sees it, by the sister's presence. In fact, he first addresses Stella "*a bit uncertainly,*" before expressing confidence that his world is now restored with a second round of "Now, now, love. Now, love. . . ."

However, there is no clear sign that Stella has reconciled herself to the decision, or that she can now affirm Stanley's world in the same way she could before Blanche's visit. Stella's own earlier rhetorical question, "What have I done to my sister?" (p. 176), echoes in her silence during the play's closing moments, in her very position onstage, divided as she is between a husband present at her side and a sister who has just exited, madly and yet serenely. If anything, Stella's nonverbal sobbing—in effect, her final "line" in *Streetcar*—seems to convey relief that Blanche is gone yet profound sorrow at the fact, as if part of her were now missing: "*There is something luxurious in her complete surrender to crying now that her sister is gone.*" Bringing husband and wife together in a mutual embrace implies that in reconciling with her husband, Stella restores the world of *Streetcar* to that blue-collar marital comedy anticipated before Blanche's arrival. Thus, it perhaps reduces not only the play's open ending but, more important, the vital, difficult role that Williams has thrust upon the offstage audience. Neither for Blanche nor for us is the theater allowed to become an asylum[27] or escape—a world unto itself.

Like Blanche, we enter a "broken world" whose pieces are not so much joined as distinguished; like Blanche, we come "to trace the visionary company of love." The play's *voice,* like the theatrical experience itself, is an "instant in the wind," in Hart Crane's words, the mere two-hours' traffic of the stage. It is all artifice, phony, self-sacrificing to that life—reality—waiting beyond the confines of the theater. It is the audience offstage, engaged and yet also detached, who are asked at the end—as audiences always are—to make, from the playwright's enactment of a broken world, a whole.[28]

7

Beckett, *Nacht und Träume, Catastrophe, What Where*, and *Quad*: "Make Sense Who May"

If Beckett is not *the* twentieth-century playwright, surely the range of his experiments, his easy movement among the media of stage, radio, television, and the cinema, and, no less, the extraordinary achievement of plays like *Waiting for Godot* and *Endgame* establish his preeminence in the theater. In this chapter I consider four recent plays, two written for television. What *audience* means in Beckett includes and, in certain ways, goes beyond that term as applied to the six playwrights considered so far; a final chapter on Beckett, therefore, serves both as a summary and, perhaps more important, as an expansion of the issues raised in this study. After surveying what Beckett reveals about the role of the spectator offstage, the use of audiences onstage, and the more general concept of audience, I turn to his *Nacht und Träume, Catastrophe, What Where*, and *Quad*.

1

Audience surrogates abound in Beckett's plays.[1] In *Endgame* they are immobilized upstage in a way that makes the phrase "riveted to their seats" seem tame. From their ashcans, Nagg and Nell—Hamm's parents—observe and occasionally comment on their son. And when they cry out once too often for the physical necessities—a Sprat's Medium biscuit, among other delicacies—they are promptly silenced, indeed, rendered inoperative as an audience when Clov screws down the lids on their containers. Beckett's *Play* opens with its three characters, Man, Woman 1, and Woman 2, staring ahead at us, all talking at the same time and hence unintelligible to those offstage. Like a precurtain audience with its initial blur of conflicting conversations, they, too, will be quieted by the first intelligible onstage line as

Beckett's invisible curtain rises. In *Rockaby* we watch—and hear as well—the single visible character, W, play audience to V (or voice) offstage or, from her perspective, her own internal self. V tells of her mother sitting like an audience before an open window, desperately, futilely searching for someone to appear in a window across the street, wanting both to play the spectator and to be observed as an actor might be observed by an audience—in this case one that never materializes. In V's narration, this failure to be seen drove the mother mad. One day she left her station before the window and went into the basement, there to sit until she died, even as her daughter sits at present in that same rocking chair. I should add, though, that since she is seen by us, W succeeds where her mother failed.

During the television play *Eh Joe* we occupy the position of the woman just off-camera who addresses Joe. In staring at her, he also stares at us. As the camera moves in on Joe—Beckett specifies nine distinct movements—we likewise move in on Joe, or rather, by the technological trick of the medium, he moves closer to us. We must wonder, then, if Joe represents us, if there may be a pun in the title, "A Joe," signifying not the "other" but an Everyman, our self projected on the screen. In her final speech, the woman pronounces only the words italicized in the text; that is, most of the dialogue as printed never makes its way into actual production. Do we not therefore fill in these Derridian "white spaces" with our own silent dialogue as we identify with Joe? Or do we find ourselves split, like him, between the voiceless body seen on the screen and the inner voice (Joe's voice? our own?) coming from offscreen, from our direction? In the final close-up of Joe, when the camera is inches away from the face now occupying the entire screen, the medium of television itself becomes a mirror for the audience.

Represented onstage, commented on, drawn onto the stage by this collapsing of that imaginary fourth wall, the audience in Beckett is also a force inside his plays—and sometimes a powerful one. The single spotlight in *Play* is stationed at the rear of the theater, as if it came from the audience. Thus, when the characters forget their sordid love-triangle story and begin commenting on what to them must seem like a light used in some interrogation room, they speak directly to us. Indeed, only when the spot shines on the actor can she or he speak. In this way, our presence activates the play, as the characters' own focus changes from the past to the present in which they share the same space with the spectators. Furthermore, when *Play* repeats itself, our own role changes. Now hearing the story a second time, we can concentrate less on its details and more on the delivery of the actors, on the nuances in their narration, in essence, on the present collaboration between character and spectator. Since each of the three onstage characters is unaware of the others, in fact imagines he or she speaks only to us even although all three tell similar versions of the same sordid tale, we alone can make the connections between what to them are single, entirely personal, even interior monologues.

At one with this emphasis is the open-ended nature of Beckett's plays, the way each demands that the audience complete what the playwright has only "started." No one speaks, nothing moves, in fact, there are no human presences in *Breath*, and thus, in-between the opening birth cry and the closing deathlike groan, the audience alone determines the meaning of the tableau before it—a horizontal line of trash, on which a light fades up and then fades out. In *Come and Go* a line is whispered by one of the two onstage characters to the other after the third has made a brief exit into the darkness surrounding the bench. The dramaticule's most significant line, it goes, in effect, unheard, a violation of stage convention that everything should be heard or, rather, overheard by the audience. As I have also discovered when performing this play before audiences ranging from school-children to psychiatrists to participants at a conference on modern drama, the audience, forced as a consequence to fill in the line, invariably supplies from its own experience a tragic happening for whatever the onstage informant hopes God has hidden from the pathetic victim just offstage.

2

The significance of the spectator is no less pervasive onstage. In *Footfalls* the relation of M and V, actor and audience, is a coequal and, indeed, mutually procreative one. The onstage M is essentially a physical creature, the offstage V, a cerebral, imaginative one. If V dominates the play's second section as she comments on her stage life, which consists of rigidly prescribed pacing before us, it is M in the play's third section who builds a story upon what she has heard V say, thereby advancing the play. By *Footfall*'s final section, M and V have drawn closer to each other, erasing the distinction between actor and audience to the degree that, together, they assume equally the other-wise antithetical roles of playwright and audience as they project themselves into characters, Amy and Mrs. Winter, in a play-within-the-play.

Just as frequently in Beckett, an onstage character plays audience to himself, or herself. In *Embers* Henry can at length figuratively see himself, that man divided between his own passion to retreat into himself and the demands for a public life foisted on him by both his wife, Ada, and his father. After avoiding the creative act, he gains insight in the Bolton-Holloway story he manages to tell, for clearly Bolton and Holloway enact the divided nature of Henry's own earthly life. In *That Time* the single onstage character listens to voices A, B, C, reenactments of himself at different stages in his life. As the initially separate narratives begin to blend, as parallels and repetitions grow among the three stories and their otherwise distinct vocabularies, so the onstage character, hearing himself, draws his past, to which he has been audience, into his present witness. In *Film*, O's face, otherwise hidden from us by an oblique camera angle and by a hat, on top of a handkerchief, pulled low over his forehead, can be seen by us only when he dares to face E directly, the camera that, in the final frames of *Film*, metamorphoses into a mirror image of himself.

If the audience is represented onstage by surrogates, such as the Auditor in *Not I*, they are just as often acknowledged by the characters themselves, sometimes by implication, as when Pozzo in *Waiting for Godot* asks, "Is everybody looking at me?" Sometimes we are acknowledged more directly: Estragon "*halts, facing auditorium,*" when he describes the audience as "inspiring prospects." On several occasions, even props literally go into the audience: Hamm throws offstage the whistle that he has earlier used to summon Clov, and Krapp in frustration pushes a banana into the house.

This relation between onstage actors and offstage audience is inseparable in the instructions for blocking that Beckett gives directors. Winnie in *Happy Days*, the three characters in *Play*, and the three old women in *Come and Go* face the audience directly and in the first two plays the characters never move from that position. Except for those few moments when Clov wheels Hamm about the stage, the central character of *Endgame* is likewise positioned at centerstage, facing us. C, the subject of an examination by A and B in *Theater II*, looks upstage, his back to us, thereby duplicating our own position. By thus turning away from us, the faceless character violates the stage convention that dictates that blocking should allow for actors to face the audience in full- or half-profile, even if it means constantly moving them about in theater-in-the-round so that they can play equally to the sides of the house. Because C thereby resembles us, we may seem to be on trial through our onstage representative. A and B recount the episodes, some comic, most of them pathetic, of C's life, after which A moves upstage, stares in C's face after lighting a match, and then apparently wipes a tear from C's eye. Only if the stage and house were reversed, while the position of A and C remained unchanged, would we be in the conventional theater where the audience, distinct from the characters, watches them unwatched through the fourth wall.

Beckett's plays also acknowledge the spectator in metadramatic references in the texts themselves. Clov refers to "making an exit," Hamm, to a "soliloquy" and his fear of *Endgame*'s own "underplot," in which the small boy, sighted through the upstage window by Clov, threatens to intrude on and possibly destroy Hamm's insular onstage world. At such moments the characters' awareness of being in a play underscores our own present reality. In this light, Norman Holland has observed that one of the features of post-modern art is the artist's striving to establish a relation between the text and its audience; contemporary critics, including Holland himself with his reader-response theories, have made that relationship explicit.[2] Properly, the "creator" is not the artist alone, but the audience as well. Or, as Holland phrases it, we experience "systems thinking," where the components—artist, actor, and audience—are mutually and equally responsible for the creative act.

3

Given this relation between character and audience, expressed in the complementary movements from offstage to on and onstage to off, perhaps more than those of most twentieth-century playwrights, the text of a Beckett play is its *performance,* an intimate, temporary happening created by actor and spectator. What I have called "theater of presence,"[3] the actress Barbara Becket and the director Charles Lyons, in speaking of their experience staging Beckett's works, label as "present consciousness"—the requirement that the actor, in collaboration with the director, first "establish" but then "dissolve" the "character's consciousness of his or her history."[4] Stanislavski's principle that the actor recreate a past, a history for the character, can in Beckett exist only as a "preparatory technique." A history may launch an actor into the part, but at length must be discarded, like the first stage of a rocket, literally obliterated before the audience. This "concentration upon the immediate circumstances of the character" thereby becomes the joint responsibility of actor and audience. In this sense, Vladimir and Estragon do nothing more or nothing less than we would do if we, instead of they, were waiting, whether onstage or at a bus stop: we talk to pass the time. Our mutual process, not goal or closure (or finding Godot), then becomes the issue, the essence of the performance.[5]

The characters, indeed, have an almost pathological fear of being alone, of being unheard or unseen. In *All That Fall* Maddie pities the woman who sings "all alone in that ruinous old house," and later, when Tommy doesn't acknowledge her, she cries out sarcastically, "Don't mind me. Don't take any notice of me. I do not exist." After a life spent being abandoned by or rejecting women, ranging from his mother to a nurse pushing a carriage in the park, the sole character in *Krapp's Last Tape* searches frantically for the spot on the tape that records the one brief union he experienced with the woman in the punt. When he is offstage drinking in private, he is reduced to mere sounds—a bottle clinking on a glass, booze being poured—so that, painful as it is, he returns three times to the stage, to confront both himself on the tape recorder and, by extension, the audience.

In fact, Beckett's characters do everything they can to draw out the audience, to make it visible. Hidden for most of the play behind the mound, so that the audience sees only his raised hand holding a newspaper or his bowler hat, Willie, in *Happy Days*, at length emerges. Winnie is unsettled by his appearance—"Is it a kiss you're after, Willie . . . or is it something else?"—for since Willie is "*dressed to kill*," perhaps he appears only to silence his wife, to kill her. Still, she pronounces his appearance a "happy day," before bursting into a Franz Lehar song (ironic, given the occasion) from his operetta *The Merry Widow.*

However, this desire to be seen and heard generates in turn a fear of being exposed, either to others or to oneself. In *Film*, O tries to avoid E, or what Beckett calls the "angle of perceivedness." The woman in *Not I* tries, as the title suggests, to deny her own story: she tells not of herself, not I, but of a fictitious character. But we (and she, at length) penetrate that defense. In *Cascando*, Opener tries unsuccessfully to deny that he has any relation to the character Woburn. Like Croak in *Words and Music*, he regressively assumes the stance of a technician, someone who merely opens and closes the story. By the end of the work the would-be narrator can no longer remain aloof; the story becomes his own.

Whatever the subject of Beckett's "story"—whether it be expressed in the theater, radio, television, or cinema—its enactment ultimately celebrates *theater* itself, that performance sustained by the mutual presences of actor and audience. The Listener's face in the closing moments of *That Time* breaks into a "*smile,* [*albeit*] *toothless for preference.*" In both *Embers* and *Footfalls* the sad facts of a real life, existing outside the play and for which the performance serves as a flashback, are replaced by a fiction, sad yet, by its very artificiality, not as threatening as existence itself. In *A Piece of Monologue* the Speaker's growing consciousness of his role as narrator, as opposed to his being the subject of his own tragic story, allows him to draw closer to our reality, our presence at his performance; for his final lines are, in effect, technical instructions to the play's lighting operator: "Unutterably faint. The globe alone. Alone gone."

The motto of *Film* applies to characters generally in Beckett, both onstage and off: "Esse est percipi." Beckett's most recent works, I believe, sustain and expand these dimensions of the audience I have traced so far.

4

In the familiar Beckett room—or womb, or tomb—of *Nacht und Träume,* the outside exists only in the form of "evening light" from a window upstage-right. If the dreamer A, stage-right, is lit from above as well, then this blend of artificial and (deceptively) natural light, moonlight, signals the transitional nature of the setting—it is not the unrelieved darkness outside Holloway's living room in *Embers*—as well as that of the ensuing play which moves between A and B, "his dreamt self." The symmetry, as far as it goes, is comforting: A, at a table on audience-left, his right profile showing; B, at an identical table on audience-right, his left profile showing; and a general movement from A to B and back to A. Our initial impression might be that A is both author of his dreamt self and, when B appears, audience to his own enactment. Like *Play, Nacht und Träume* repeats itself, and like *Ghost Trio* repeats, to some degree, camera angles already established.

But this apparent symmetry is itself balanced by asymmetry. Most obvious, A is essentially passive: he is first seen sitting at the table, hands resting on it, his head bowed; then as he dreams he rests his head in his hands. In contrast, B is more active and is also acted upon: a hand, L, appears; B looks up at its invisible face (invisible to us no less than to him); then after L has withdrawn, a right hand, R, appears, and in the fashion of the offstage presence in *Act Without Words I* first offers B water and then wipes his brow. B next interacts with R in a complex joining of hands, and, when he lowers his head as A did on the desk, L reappears and rests on B's head. In addition, A and B do not occupy parallel positions on their single stage. B is on an "invisible podium about 4 feet above floor level." While we cannot see the floor on which A's table rests, if we properly assume that the bottom of his table is at floor level, then B's raised table, the support for which is also invisible, must appear to drift above the floor, in space or perhaps establishing a second, higher floor.

Only when we survey the seven-part structure of *Nacht und Träume,* however, does this curious combination of symmetry and asymmetry take on a larger significance:

1. A appears, with Schubert's song *Nacht und Träume* first hummed and then its last three bars sung
2. As A fades to a "minimal" light, B appears, lit by a "kinder" light
3. B, with A still visible, goes through the various interactions with L and R
4. As B fades out, A fades up on audience-left
5. When B reappears, to repeat the interactions with L and R, although—significantly—at a "slower motion," A disappears from the screen as the camera "moves in slowly to a close-up" of B
6. A is then "recover[ed]"
7. B fades out, and then A does

If the dreamer is *real,* is the human stimulus for the dream, then section 5, as I have described it, denies the copresence of A and B since the close-up removes A from the screen. Otherwise, A is always present, even if lit by "minimal light" and even when B is not present. Or, through reverse mirror, section 5 duplicates section 1—when only A was present—although this time with the movements of B, L, and R slowed down. Then, too, in section 5 the camera moves for the first time. Except for a second move when it recovers A (Beckett's step 28), it is otherwise stationary, including B only when the light fades up on him. That light—to repeat—is said to be "kinder" than the minimal light afforded A. If A is lit both by the evening light from the window and by stage lighting above, the source of B's light is off, or rather above, camera range.

It is this asymmetrical exception and the curious "favoring" of B through the kinder light, as well as by the atypical close-up, that encourages the audience to interpret a drama that is otherwise obvious, even comforting, in its symmetry. To adjust the line from the ending of *What Where,* the audience must "make sense . . . [if they] may."

Section 5 serves as an apex in the play's structure. By duplicating, although in reverse fashion, the opening section where A alone is seen, it reverses the direction of *Nacht und Träume:* A now seems the dreamt self, the projection of B, the dreamer. I am reminded here of the saying Stoppard cites in *Rosencrantz and Guildenstern Are Dead:* "A Chinaman of the 'Tang Dynasty—and, by which definition, a philosopher—dreamed he was a butterfly, and from that moment he was never quite sure that he was not a butterfly dreaming it was a Chinese philosopher" (p. 60). If B is the *play* imagined by A, who is stimulated by the Schubert even as B is stimulated by A, then in step 5 the fictive world—or Beckett's fiction within a fiction—challenges reality, at very least duplicating it, at most (or worst, depending on one's perspective) threatening to absorb it. But if A is relatively passive until he projects his dreamt self, it is no less true that B's dream is short-lived, offering us little more than—to use Beckett's revealing direction for the camera—a single segment "recovering" A before first B and then A disappear. The fictive nature of this dream, or theater, offers only an illustory, short-lived paradise—the "kinder light" and the solicitous actions of R, and then, as if he had thought better of B, the actions of L as he joins R in the tableau of united hands (like those in *Come and Go*) by gently touching B's head. Still, the theater, the dream, by itself cannot generate a play; if it transcends life, it still needs life as its base.

Only in performance, then, can A and B, audience and actor, possess a double authority. Only when those positions are momentarily reversed at the start of section 5 can art temporarily make a claim equal to reality, even although each is constituted by different elements. However unequal in life, all of us can boast an autonomous, powerful status in our dreams or in our moments of wish-fulfillment: the beggar's unconscious visions are no less unique, or satisfying, or glorious than the king's. Outside the dream (B) reality waits to dissolve that vision, even as the stage's illusory power, no matter how compelling to its audience, at length dissolves when we leave the theater. Enoch Brater observes that the play ends not with the fade-out of A (section 7) but with the audience. When both B and then A disappear from the screen, "suddenly we are all alone, facing neither dream or dreamer, only our own reality in the shape of an empty rectangle."[6]

5

Catastrophe shows us the theater from the dual perspective of the rehearsal (its setting) and a performance before an audience, since, in point of fact, it is a play about its own rehearsal. Its *stage* offers at once a literal stage—that portion, the "*plith*" (later named the "*pedestal*"), on which the protagonist (P) acts as if he were in rehearsal—and the illusion of the house. The Director (D) and his female Assistant (A) are located somewhere in the first few rows of seats, as they would normally be when a production moves from the rehearsal room to the main stage. Morever, lurking somewhere in the back of the house in the "*booth*" is the lighting operator, Luke (L). Any distinction, therefore, between performer and actor, or between people involved in theatrical production and their audience, is blurred since *Catastrophe* simultaneously shows us the stage and the house. D—and A, when she is allowed to make suggestions or when her opinion is solicited by D—at once directs P and, like an audience, observes him: "Like the look of him?," he says to A, or later, "Let's have a look." If the invisible Luke at the back of the house suggests our own offstage and, by theatrical convention, invisible presence, then D joins Luke and, by implication, the real audience when half-way through *Catastrophe* he announces he will "go and see how it looks from the house" and exits, "*not to appear again.*" Figuratively, and technically (if the real-life director in charge of *Catastrophe* chooses to place D at the back of the house), everything he says from that moment until the end of the play comes from the audience.

Metadramatically, then, *Catastrophe* is about as close to reality as a play, or a play about a rehearsal, can get without dissolving into one of those *happenings* that were popular in the American theater in the 1960s. I refer to experiments in which an audience, primed by the person minimally *directing* what would most likely happen, would be assembled, say, on a busy city street corner to wait until the first traffic accident, or quarrel, or even mugging occurred. The principle here was that the presence of a group designated as an audience would elevate such an accident, catastrophic or not for its unwary participants, to the level of theater, or a *happening*. This principle, in a sense, is reversed in Beckett's play. Our presence offstage, or beyond the illusory offstage of *Catastrophe,* is the point of direct reference during a performance that, of course, is not an accident but is carefully rehearsed. No less than the audience that D anticipates for his unnamed play, we are the people "in the stalls" who "see [P's] feet," the ones to whom D also refers when he cries, "let 'em have it." He arrogantly—and Beckett, ironically—even anticipates our reaction with "Terrific! He'll have them on their feet. I can hear it from here." As in Ionesco's *The Chairs,* there is a recorded "*distant storm of applause*" which, upon P's raising his head in seeming defiance of D, "*falters*" and "*dies.*" But the gap between the internal applause (that "*distant storm*") and that of the real-life audience will remind us, if we need reminding, that *Catastrophe,* however close to reality, is still of a different order.

Antonio Libera argues that D is here a tyrant attempting to manipulate audience response by the technological apparatus of the modern theater, and in the process deleting any verbal text.[7] D's creation, P, is paradoxical. Stripped of speech, even of his clothes, except his ashen "night attire," he seems nothing more than a puppet of the Director, bowing his head in submission to his secular creator. If P, arms folded across his breast, resembles the statue of a saint, the act is a parody, not a confirmation, of religion. Noting that Beckett dedicates the play to Vaclav Havel (the Czech dissident artist whom the playwright does not know personally), Libera links D's image of P with what he calls the godless, secular ethic of Communism. P's seeming defiance of D's command when the actor raises his head may be a hopeful sign, then, that man can resist his demonic creator. Or the act itself may be deceptive, D's illusion of freedom that, in reality, has been no less scripted than every other moment in the play.

For me, of more immediate concern is *Catastrophe*'s commentary on the negative, or noncollaborative, dimension of a play's relation to its audience. If the mutual accomplishment of actor and audience during performance is the temporary suspension of belief that allows for an illusion to become compelling and significant, here that collaboration is parodied in a theater that serves the ends of the state, or, as is too often the case in the commercial Broadway theater, is reduced to an "entertaining illusion."

A remains as the one visible audience member after D exits to the back of the house, and in my own metadramatic reading she, like the female assistant in *Radio II*, contrasts with D's tyrannical figure. If A tries to appease D, or takes his notion of control to the extreme by suggesting that they gag P, she is also concerned that P is "shivering," and in the second half of *Catastrophe* she becomes *"irritable"* at D's high-handed manner. It was A who first suggested that P raise his head; and if A, as in Libera's reading, is not just amoral Nature or a mere extension of D, then here she inspires P's final act of defiance, an act that silences the thunderous applause D hears, or imagines he will hear. Given the political overtones of Beckett's dedication of the play to Havel, the same act, itself in defiance of D's divine or demonic plan, would potentially bring applause from a real offstage audience. Significantly, after P raises his head, he looks directly at us, *"fixes the audience,"* as if asking us to respond, if we want or dare to respond, to an action that, however brief, asserts the right of the performer. This human action, the raising of a head, challenges the technical or physical theater—lighting, blocking, props, costumes—that so preoccupies D.

Increasingly occupied with directing his own plays, the playwright, through D, seems to parody himself, or to present an uncompromising reverse image. D's concept of theater is as closed and literal as Beckett's seems open and suggestive. If the ultimate significance of the audience in Beckett lies in the interpretive burden placed on them, then D would deny us that role just as he denies the actor's equality with the director, right up until the final seconds of *Catastrophe* when P, who is, of course, ultimately Beckett's and not D's creation, raises his head and *"fixes"* us.

6

The line that most directly confronts the audience of *What Where* is the play's penultimate line, V's "Make sense who may." As in *Catastrophe,* the stage here includes the audience; downstage-right of P, the performing area, is V, a much smaller area housing—probably on a table—a *"small megaphone at head level."* V, or voice, is at once a director giving the cues (in the form of stern commands) for entrances and exits, the disembodied voice of the actor named Bam, and an observer of the stage action.

In one way, Bem, Bim, and Bom appear to be characters independent of the onstage Bam, even as V is identified as the voice of Bam only in the dramatis personae. That is, from the perspective of an audience not having the printed text in hand, there are five characters—in his first line V refers to "the last five"—four of them onstage, and one represented by a voice issuing through the megaphone to the side and separated from the larger stage (P) by darkness. The four actors on P perform for V, trying and yet failing to produce some sort of statement, the "it" in "say it" that would inform V of "what" has happened and "where." The visual pattern here duplicates that employed when the characters are given dialogue. This repetition is echoed in the second half when each of the four characters plays both the person sent to elicit the *What Where* from the unnamed "he" and, failing to do so, the prisoner led offstage by one of the other characters. Offstage, as we learn, each of the four, like "he," is given the "works," yet despite the weeping, screaming, and begging for mercy, each remains silent or is unable to produce the information that V seeks. V, then, is a director and an observer who finds his actors unable either to say "it" or to force someone else to say "it." In *Footfalls* both V and Mrs. Winter are similarly frustrated by the fact that Amy (in the inner story) constantly revolves something, "it," in her mind. That play ends with M asking, "Will you never have done . . . revolving it all? *(Pause.)* It? *(Pause.)* It all? *(Pause.)* In your poor mind." In *Catastrophe* V pointedly asks the two onstage actors to repeat their dialogue, and the second time, "anything" changes to that more generic "it." In fact, *What Where* might be a one-character play, a monologue, where V, the single character, bifurcates himself or herself into four onstage surrogates who, four times, try to produce for their creator some sort of truth about life. Thus, the play becomes something of a psycho-drama, in which V plays audience to himself, represented by Bam, Bem, Bim, and Bom trying to find life's meaning. I note that the "We" of the first line becomes "I" in V's final speech when he is alone on his smaller stage; likewise, the earlier line "In the present as were we still" is replaced with "In the present as were I still."

Within the play, V (Bam) may enact his own failure to uncover any meaning in life beyond the physical fact that time passes. *What Where* starts in the spring and progresses through summer and autumn, so that in the end the isolated V observes, "it is winter. / Without journey. / Time passes." Near the end of *Waiting for Godot* Vladimir observes hopefully, "Well, that passed the time," to which Estragon replies sarcastically, "It would have passed anyway." And V's failure seems echoed in *Endgame*'s tale of the painter who, when Hamm meets him in the insane asylum, sees only "ashes" in a landscape that Hamm once described as "all that loveliness," filled with evidence of growth, "rising corn," and "sails of the herring fleet."

The failure of "he" (whether it be the fifth character we never see onstage, or the role into which Bam, Bem, Bim, and Bom fall when they, the interrogators, become the interrogated) has thereby been a foregone conclusion. The ultimate playwright and here perhaps an audience to his own surrogate imaged in the megaphone V and his onstage embodiment Bam, Beckett likewise knows the end of his play from the beginning. "He" cannot speak, he does not "lie," but rather tells the truth, that there is nothing to say, or that all we can determine is not *what* or *where* but that time passes. Rather than being merely ironic, V's repeated interjection "Good" reflects the playwright-director's (but not the character V's) sense of the play's honesty. It can deliver only itself, which is to say that absolute meaning is not to be found outside the confines of the theater. Similarly, despite any allegory we choose to place on *Waiting for Godot*, perhaps the only thing we can be sure of, the only truth, is that we, as audience, with our surrogates Vladimir and Estragon, wait. Vladimir says it for us, "that with Estragon my friend, at his place, until the fall of night, I waited for Godot" (I mercifully remove Vladimir's question mark). When he remarks, "Make sense who may," V, like P in *Catastrophe*, "fixes" us, the real, offstage audience that he has represented—a challenge, as I take it, not optimistic or pessimistic, but strangely and beautifully realistic.

7

The "four players" in *Quad* must share the billing in the text's opening line with "light and percussion," and this equity between humans and technology is symptomatic of the work's reluctance to accord the actor any uniqueness. "Some ballet training is desirable," Beckett indicates, yet the movements of the players take precision, rather than the skills of a dancer, let alone that of a gymnast.

Quad II, initially meant as a "variation" on *Quad I*, is a vastly shortened version. In the earlier work the four players are technologically, if not humanly, distinct. *Quad I* calls for each player to have a special colored gown, matching a special colored overhead light, and a separate percussive instrument during his or her ("sex indifferent") time onstage. In *Quad II*, however, there is to be "no colour, all four in identical white gowns, [and] no percussion, footsteps only sound, slow tempo, series 1 only." Even the four-color stage lighting of *Quad I*, abandoned as "impractical," is replaced by "constant neutral light throughout."

Martha Fehsenfeld speaks of Beckett here as distilling (not reducing) his work "to shadows of what *is* and is *to come*" in "a continuing beginning toward transparency."[8] The players, "short and slight for preference," appear more like nonplayers, or automatons, their faces covered by cowls, their steps regulated. Each enters the stage from one of the square's four corners yet traces the same pattern as it is distributed in a separate "course" assigned to each, with the four courses, once completed, themselves distributed over four series. *Quad I* ends with player 2 pacing alone, but any chance of individuality has been negated by the mathematical "parity" established by the completion of the four series.

Enoch Brater describes the stage picture here as having the "neutrality of a dehydrated image"[9] What spirit or life there is seems to come from the four percussionists (in *Quad I*) who, "barely visible in shadow on raised podium at back of set," provide a soruce of energy that is "seemingly gratuitous." If the players themselves move from the darkness surrounding the quad, their time onstage seems a mockery of life, their synchronized pacings almost comic, so much so that the mood becomes "hilariously frightening." In a review of the production for German television on 8 October 1981, S. E. Gontarski speaks of the crescendo and diminuendo of the movements as shattering "whatever comic possibilities were present initially."[10] *Quad II*, whose "tempo is monorhythmic," seems in the context established by *Quad I* to "dramatize the entropy of motion." Beckett's own response was that the even more minimal *Quad II* appears to take place

"100,000 years later."[11] Thus the cynical attitude toward the audience implied in the character of *Catastrophe*'s Director is here transferred to mankind generally, not only in the bare onstage life afforded the players but also in their own ironic movement out of the audience, that darkness surrounding the quad.

The real audience watches the televised production from the vantage point of a single stationary camera suspended at an oblique angle downstage. Hence, while players 1 and 2 make entrances and exits from upstage-right and upstage-left, players 3 and 4 emerge from the audience like spectators who, driven from the womblike security of the darkened house, wander by accident onstage. Here they become indistinguishable from the players, their compatriots, who enter from that upstage area generally off-limits to the audience. Yet the generic sameness of the four performers and the bare stage that is a perfect square erase any meaningful distinction between audience and actor. Indeed, the stage itself seems off-limits and threatening, for the center (E), supposedly "a danger zone," is avoided by the players. Gontarski speaks of this center as "Beckett's most vivid image of post-modern literary theory." If E is something of a black hole, a place of nonmeaning and hence nonexistence, its allegorical birth was itself the product of necessity. To avoid crowding the center, faced with the possibility that two or more actors approaching E might collide, Beckett established a "deviation" by which each player approaching the center makes a short right-hand turn, followed by a short-left-hand turn, as if there were a miniature raised stage in the middle of the quad, itself off-limits to the performers.

For me, the players resemble an audience that is carefully, symmetrically tracing an empty stage, one they enter almost hopefully, with an added touch of fanfare in *Quad I* from their percussive accompaniment. Yet the moment they take the stage, these escapees from the audience lose their humanity—Gontarski likens them to the damned of Dante's *Inferno*—and, what is more, find the very stage that initially seemed neutral in its barrenness now housing a stage within, like a play-within-a-play, that center E, the "danger zone" that at once retards and repels players. I am reminded of the audience member who, relaxed in the kindly darkness of the house, is brought onstage by some master of ceremonies and now stands before us, self-conscious, ill at ease in direct proportion to the actor's confidence onstage, and eager, desperately eager, to return to his or her seat. What had seemed his "big moment," a chance for a singular status onstage to replace his offstage anonymity, turns sour.

Beckett's four players seem ultimately one person, experiencing a comedy turned into comic nightmare, repeated from every possible corner of the stage, and seen from the double perspective of the upstage world of the actor and the downstage world of the audience. Neither actor nor audience can resist the stage, for the very notion of theater is ingrained in us, is part of our human makeup. We cannot avoid the need to play roles, the self-fashioning by which we consciously mold and adjust whatever basic personality has been handed us at birth. Yet such acting, our need to be on the stage of the *polis* (as the Greeks distinguished our public life from that of the home), only subjects us to the existential complexities and, at times, terrors of an audience. Fashioning our self, or playing a role, in turn subjects us to the critical eye, the stare, of a spectator who fashions us in turn. Like the Beckett characters in general, we are caught between our comfort in the idiosyncratic, womblike security of our inner self, and our human, communal need to express that self before others. We can speak effectively of our self only to others.

Afterword
"My" Theater and Its Audiences: Some Personal Experiences

I speak here about a few experiences, crude and sophisticated, planned and accidental, that I have had as a spectator in the house or as an actor and director aware of his audience. Such experiences have influenced this book and are "texts" that I now revisit in light of the previous chapters.

1

On a lovely May evening in a run-down theater in Urbana, Illinois, some 250 people had been confined for an hour in a stuffy, windowless lobby, waiting to see a play billed as *The Game Show.* I'm not sure if Pirandello would have approved of what was about to happen, but he certainly had inspired the evening's "experiment." In that lobby were real people, expecting to be an audience for the performance. But there were also actors pretending to be fellow audience members; and there was a young physicist and his wife—he was a real person, she, a member of the company, although he was unaware of the fact. I was was there as a fellow spectator, but with the difference that I had seen the script beforehand.

The lobby was now overheated, and the audience was irritated by the unexplained delay. When a rather surly theater manager, briefly poking his head through the house doors before locking them again, announced that we would have to wait thirty more minutes while some final, unspecified changes were made, the now angry audience, fanned by the actors pretending to be *us,* burst out sarcastically with "Well, of all the nerve" and "Who the hell do these theater people think they are anyway?" Its patience at low ebb, the audience was soon united in its common cause against the theater's management. One man courteously helped another (an actor in disguise) remove his jacket, and a woman (an actress in disguise) fanned two real-life companions with her program. When the doors finally opened, the audience, real and pretend, charged toward their seats, only to be irritated a second time when a rather oily master-of-ceremonies, resembling one of those bland television game-show hosts, took the stage and announced that the performance of *The Game Show* would have to be canceled because of wide-spread illness among the cast. Then, just as some especially enraged spectators were rising to leave, he pleaded with us: "But, ladies and gentlemen, let's not let this evening go to waste. As long as you're here, why don't we do something together? What about some audience participation games?" The request was greeted affirmatively, although cynically: "What the hell?—the night's shot anyway," or, "Oh, sure, just what I needed, an evening of fun and games!"

For the next hour we did just that—fun and games, reminiscent of that show from television's infancy, *Beat the Clock*. There was a steady parade of people to and from the stage, to compete in contests determining, say, who could most quickly push an egg with his or her nose across the stage, or who, blindfolded, could burst the most balloons with a pin. The offstage audience played a lively counterpart to the business onstage, rooting for their favorites, mocking the MC for his pathetic efforts to entertain us, or cursing the theater staff. In effect, we were an audience vocal and mobile, and one contradicting normal theater etiquette. I must confess that by this point in the evening I could no longer tell actor-spectator from real spectator.

At length the MC, looking concerned, spoke up: "I see, ladies and gentlemen, that you're tiring of our games." This observation was met, as you might imagine, with a volley of wisecracks: "What makes you think that?" or "No, I could take five more hours of this nonsense!" Unflapped, he continued, "I think we should bring this evening to a close, yet, before we do, may I suggest, ladies and gentlemen, that we play just one more game?" A man on my right—whether he was an actor or not I could not remember—shouted back, "If that will get us out of here, let's go for it!" The MC proposed, "I'd like to see just how far one of you would go, onstage, for money." With this last remark he brandished a wad of fresh, five-dollar bills as, according to script, eight ushers, large, brutish men looking like the front line of a football team, took the stage, four to a side. The physicist's wife, the actress pretending to be a spectator, volunteered and was asked to take the stage. After some perfunctory conversation—"And what's your name, little lady?" and "Mary, that's nice," and "Two children, how lovely!"—the MC introduced the game.

"Madam, I'd like to see, they [pointing to the audience] might like to see just how far you would go for money." Pulling a bill from his pocket, he asked, "Would you, for five dollars, allow me to kiss you lightly on the cheek?" Before she could answer, opinions shot forth from the crowd: "Watch out, you gotta be careful of these actors" or "Do it—it's only a game!" After a second's thought, she agreed, and once he had planted a discreet kiss and given her the five dollars, the MC went on. "Now, for ten dollars, would you allow me to kiss you more passionately?" The stakes had been raised, and the audience broke into a heated discussion. Half of them argued that she should say no, that to do what he wanted was "prostitution," that, "as everybody knows," actors have morals different from "the rest of us." The other half contended that whatever happened would take place before witnesses, that it was only make-believe, that we were "all adults," and after all it was "*only* the theater." A second time she agreed and, the passionate kiss delivered, the money paid, was now asked by the MC if he might put his arms around her, pulling her close to him and kissing her even more intimately. Again, she agreed, but to a louder accompaniment of very divided opinions from offstage—half the crowd apprehensive, the other half advising her to throw caution to the wind.

Finally, waving all the bills that were left, he asked with a leer, "Now, Mary, for fifty dollars would you take off your clothes onstage?" At this point the husband, normally a quiet fellow, rose from his seat and, although not an actor, called out with an intensity that would be an actor's envy, "For God's sake, Mary, stop this! Think of our kids . . . think of my reputation!" Looking down at him, anticipating the objection, she delivered a line straight from the script I had previewed: "Be quiet. Take your seat. I'm having too much fun!" Turning back to the MC, (the actress) Mary demanded that three conditions be met: she would appear naked for only ten seconds; she could try to cover herself with her hands as best she could; and she needed a screen behind which to change. When that screen appeared on cue upstage, I noticed that no one in the audience thought it odd that the company just happened to have the prop handy.

A second after Mary went behind that screen, an actor (playing a spectator) also rose on cue from the middle of the audience, crying out, "We've got to stop this! These theater people aren't like us. Don't you see what they're trying to do?" Leaping up on stage, before anyone could join him, he admonished the audience, "This is what happens when you give yourself too much to the theater." Fists flying, he charged toward the MC, who frantically gave a signal to the eight ushers. Backs to the audience and thereby blotting the "Intruder" (as he was called in the script) from our view, the ushers proceeded—or so it seemed—to beat him unconscious. Then, shocked by what they had done, they backed off toward the sides of the stage as the MC knelt over the body, feeling for the Intruder's pulse, pushing up an eyelid to check his condition.

Rising slowly and delivering the one sustained speech from the script, he announced that the Intruder was "probably dead," that he "couldn't detect any signs of life in him." Coming downstage, his face suddenly flushed with anger, the MC told an audience half stunned by what had happened, yet no less hesitant to trust his diagnosis, "You just watched a man being murdered onstage, and not one of you came forward to help. Why? Do you think that the theater is just fun and games, that we're children, that what we do has nothing to do with reality? How could you watch this happen and do nothing about it?" Signaling for his eight ushers to surround him in a semicircle, reminiscent of Pirandello's Henry IV and his courtiers at the end of that play, he equated the audience's immoral noninvolvement with the "Kitty Genovese case." You will recall the incident in New York City, where a man, in full view of some fifty apartment dwellers watching from their windows, brutally murdered a young girl in the street below, with none of the *audience* coming to her aid. The MC then announced, "Ladies and gentlemen, normally in the theater closing the curtains means the end of the performance, but this evening we're closing them because—quite frankly—the actors and I can't bear to look at you any longer. You don't take us, you don't take our theater seriously." Curtain. No applause. Feeling guilty, confused, indignant, defensive, and excited, the audience exited at intervals in small groups. The following day the Intruder (one of my students) miraculously appeared in class, and the hoax was exposed. Still, if it was soon forgotten, the experiment, albeit a crude one, has stayed in my memory.

Five years later, when I was teaching at Boston University, that experiment would be repeated—but with a significant difference. I was giving an evening course in modern drama for people who, working full-time during the day, tended to be older and more mature than my *day* students. Our class met in the lobby of the Psychology Department, an island of light and conviviality, fueled by generous supplies of coffee and doughnuts, in a building otherwise darkened since my colleagues had long since gone home. In this isolated, even romantic world my students and I became especially close. I established a rule from the outset: whenever anyone spoke, he or she had to link their remark with whatever had been said by the previous speaker. In fact, the speaker had to refer to their classmate by first name. My purpose here was to make sure that the students talked to each other rather than just playing to me—all this, you will understand, part of that *communal* mood of the 1960s to which I, among others, had fallen a happy victim.

The plan worked, in fact worked beyond my expectations. Within a few weeks, each speaker learned not only to make the required link with the remarks just delivered but to connect his or her comments with those made earlier in the evening, indeed sometimes two or three weeks before. Soon it became clear that what we said as an audience was a *text* no less important than that of the plays themselves; and because of this complex tapestry of audience response that we were mutually weaving, we took three or four weeks, instead of the one week assigned on the syllabus, to cover a single play. That audience response soon became a literal text when one of the students, a secretary, offered to take down what we said, and provide us at the next class meeting with a transcript. Another student, a manager of a television station, took this *publication* of our text one step further when he videotaped our classes. We could now *read* and *see* ourselves as an audience responding to the play: what *we* said quickly became the issue of the course. Across the Charles River, Norman Holland, now my colleague, was just beginning to define his own theory of reader response.

Once the numerous acting companies in the Boston area heard about us, we were besieged with actors wanting to do plays for the class, receiving as payment written and visual copies of this unique audience's reactions to the performance. One evening I introduced to my students two theater majors whom I had directed in Albee's *Zoo Story.* I had always thought of the relationship between Peter and Jerry as that of audience and actor, with those roles grotesquely reversed at the end when Peter stabs Jerry who, like an appreciative audience, slumps to the park bench, thanking this stranger for taking his performance so seriously that it has driven him to such violence. My actors were accomplished performers and it had been a special pleasure to work with them in rehearsals.

That evening I took a seat in the back as they began, but, three lines into the next, Jerry flubbed his line. When this happens in the theater, of course, the safest thing to do is to start over, although this option breaks the illusion. I assumed that my actors would take the more risky alternative of going on, trying to repair the missed line by improvising until they were back on-book. Instead, Jerry started from the top—"I've just been to the zoo." But, again, he missed the third line. He went once more from the top, and yet again—for whatever psychological quirk—the line was flubbed. Now I saw the panic on the actor's face, and as he looked toward me with a pained expression I tried to give him a comforting signal. "I've just been to the zoo," he said, but again he couldn't deliver that third line. Suddenly Jerry looked out at the audience and cried, "I can't do it! I can't do it!," before throwing at me a helpless "I'm sorry, Sid!" Grabbing his fellow actor, he made his way through the students, toward the door, apologizing just before both exited, "I'm sorry . . . I've . . . I've *broken the illusion!*"

My students, like the audience for *The Game Show,* were totally divided about what had just happened. Some thought it was *real,* that the actor had actually forgotten his line, had lost his cool, and embarrassed, had left—*naturally.* Yet an equal number argued that it was all a setup, that the two were enacting my own metadramatic interest in the thin line between reality and illusion, on- and offstage. As proof for their position several cited—revealingly—the line "I've broken the illusion" as something that could only come from a play, here a play about an actor failing in a play. As one student observed, "We don't say things in real life like 'I've broken the illusion,'" as if the vocabularies of the theater and reality were of different orders. I was neutral on the issue; in point of fact, I wasn't sure whether the event was real or staged.

The next day, "Jerry" came to my office to say he was sorry for not giving "the performance [I] had expected." Yet before he could tell me what *really* happened, I stopped him, saying, "No, don't tell me the truth. I think I can get more out of it by not resolving whether your 'I've broken the illusion' was heartfelt or scripted." I have cherished my self-imposed ignorance ever since.

2

Two years after I came to the University of Florida I had an experience with an audience, an experience initially unplanned and then carefully planned that had a radical influence on my thinking. In fact, it convinced me to put Shakespeare to the side for six years and plunge into directing and acting in all of Beckett's plays, with both professional and student actors. The warden of Florida State Prison, whose daughter was my student, called one evening to ask if I had a play I might perform for the inmates. Bacchus Productions, the company with which I worked, had staged Beckett's *Waiting for Godot* in theaters throughout the southeast, and so I volunteered this work, knowing nothing of its history. As you might recall, *Godot* premiered in this country at the Coconut Grove Playhouse in Miami, and after failing with the tourist audience—one of whom was heard to remark, "I paid good money for two acts and he gives me the same act twice!"—was taken to New York. There it had only a modest success with an intellectual audience who thought Beckett could not or would not deliver a philosophic *message* that one might then discuss. However, when the Actor's Workshop took the play to San Quentin—what would happen, the director speculated, if a play about men waiting were performed before men waiting?—it was a "howling success."

I did not know any of this as we approached the first of three guard towers of Florida State Prison, the majority of whose inhabitants were "lifers." We quickly put up our set (one rock and one leafless tree) at one end of the dining hall where, in ten minutes, some fifteen hundred inmates, half the prison's population, would soon gather. Precisely at eight our audience arrived. The warden's stern opening remarks—"You [so-and-sos] better behave and shut up! These visitors from Gainesville have been kind enough to come here and bring you slobs a little culture!"—struck me as the worst warm-up act I had ever heard. However, on this note we started. Now, we had performed *Godot* some fifty times for *straight* audiences and had learned to expect their reactions, just what line would fetch a laugh, and the mood of the spectators during this or that passage in the play. What happened this evening was beyond our imagination, our *wildest imagination* I am tempted to add.

Almost from the start, inmates began to rise up and address one or more of the "characters" onstage: "Why did you say that to him?"; or "You two guys, shut up and come down here [downstage] 'cause I've got something to say to you"; or "Now wait, what did you mean by that?" At first these interruptions threw us, yet we soon realized that the inmates were sincere, *serious*, that this prison audience, knowing nothing of that stultifying theater etiquette that often characterizes Broadway, were unable to, or perhaps refused to, make a distinction between their world offstage and ours onstage. For them, the "stage," properly, embraced both the "boards" and the house. Soon, we found the experience exhilarating. We were performing two plays, the one Beckett wrote and that larger play in which men were waiting no less than Vladimir and Estragon were waiting for their Godot, an alternate play whose audience insisted on being part of the scheduled production.

Because of this creative, profound, *additional* dialogue, the performance ran way overtime, and at the end the warden, angry with me for having fouled up the bed-check routine, ordered the men to line up and return to their cells. The company meanwhile was striking the set, disrobing, and packing the equipment for the return to Gainesville, when suddenly, unexpectedly, the inmates, ignoring the warden's order, broke rank and charged toward the stage. What were they going to do to us? Would we be attacked? Did I remember to leave my credit cards in the car? I panicked, a victim of my own ignorance. What the inmates *wanted* to do was to talk about the play, and about what was, to them, its most pressing question: who was Godot or, rather, who was their Godot? After some hurried negotations with the warden, we held a discussion, some two hours of the most eloquent conversations I have ever had with an audience, or with students, even with my graduate students.

I subsequently received a grant to take our production of *Godot* to Florida's other nine state prisons—men's and women's, maximum- and minimum-security institutions. In every instance the experience was exactly the same: the inmates refused to be an audience in the conventional sense, insisting instead on breaking into the script, talking with characters as if they were real, as if Vladimir, Estragon, Pozzo, and Lucky were fellow prisoners. This time I took along students and colleagues for the discussion so that after the performance we could divide into more manageable groups.

I remember one night most of all. Our last performance was at Cross City on Florida's Gulf Coast, where the prison, a former army base, was more like a college campus than the single fortresslike building of Florida State. We had our usual actor-audience performance, some three hours long, followed by a prearranged two-hour conversation with the inmates, and then, after they had returned to their cells, an hour's conversation with the warden and his staff. At two in the morning we were being led to the gates by the guards, who were a bit nervous, I should add, because there had been sporadic riots at Cross City earlier in the month. We could see only the dark outlines of the dormitory-style cell building at the opposite end of the yard, where—everyone supposed—the inmates were now asleep.

However, just as we neared the gates we heard windows (barred, to be sure) being pushed up from the prisoners' side. The guards fingered their weapons, expecting the worst, and then, from across the blackened prison yard, we heard the inmates. They had been waiting up to say goodnight to us! Nothing more threatening than that! Soon all of us began shouting out accompanying goodnights to an audience we could only hear. In the midst of these goodbyes I heard a familiar voice, the Brooklyn accent of one "John," an inmate who had been particular troublesome in the Florida system and, as a result, had been transferred among four prisons. Since he had seen four productions of our *Godot,* the actors and I had fondly called him our "resident Beckett scholar." "Sid," he shouted out, "that Beckett fellow, he wrote another play called *Endgame,* didn't he?" Thrilled that my friend knew not one but two plays of this most cryptic playwright, I replied eagerly, "Yes, John, *yes* he did!" John's simple, seemingly illogical response taught me as much about audiences as I am ever liable to know: "Well, look, buddy, why don't you all bring *Endgame* here tomorrow and do it for us!"

As we drove back to Gainesville, I thought to myself: doesn't he know that plays take rehearsals? But wait! For him, for this precious, articulate audience of one, a play is as natural, as much a part of life as conversation. In a way he's right. *Endgame* doesn't need rehearsals. It's something that transpires between actor and audience, the way a conversation, unplanned, unrehearsed, takes place between two friends. When we speak we are the actor, and when we listen we become an audience. I merely repeat here the anecdote from the preface to my *Beckett's Theaters: Interpretations for Performance*. In a very real sense, that book, and the present one, are collaborations with my inmate friend.

3

If experiences such as these influence my writing about the theater, they no less affect my work as a director. Here I have always sided with Blanche Dubois in preferring "magic" to realism, and, for me, this means doing everything possible during a production to alert the audience to the coequal significance of the *world* of the play (or what the performance is *about*, in the sense of issues, or its mirror image of reality) and the craft of the actor (what the onstage performers are *about* as they make a patent illusion seem real).

For me, this in turn parallels a duality between actor and audience, as the latter is made no less conscious of its role during the performance. Allow me in this study of twentieth-century playwrights to use, as illustration, three personal examples from that eternally modern playwright, Shakespeare.

In a recent production of *The Comedy of Errors*, for instance, I established an "aside spot" downstage-left, near the first row of seats, just at the entrance to the "vom" (or vomitory) leading out of the house. When actors had an aside—Antipholus of Syracuse, in particular, has several in this early comedy—they would go to this area and be lit by a special overhead spot, while the other onstage actors, now seen in greatly reduced light, would freeze in position. Turning his back on the stage, the actor delivering the aside would address the audience directly.

In *Errors*, of course, there is a tremendous disparity between the audience's knowledge and that of the characters: we know that the one-day's tragic or mad misunderstandings are actually the ground for a family reunion, since both sets of twins, along with their parents and twin servants, occupy the same space in Ephesus. We hold, in effect, an answer to their dilemma, a fact I stressed during act 3, scene 3, when Antipholus of Ephesus finds the doors of his house locked and his own identity denied, while inside his twin Syracusian brother, mistaken for him, dines in his place. For this scene we established stage-left as the interior and stage-right as the exterior, with a single, mobile door dividing the two sides. That door was made of see-through plexiglass, so that while the spectators sitting on audience-right and audience-left could see both Antopholi and the two Dromios simultaneously, for the characters themselves the door was opaque. At this point in the plot the reunion of the brothers, while actual for us, did not occur for them. The actors behind the characters, of course, knew that the audience could see both groups, and this situation led to a decision to have them, increasingly, address the audience directly, breaking the stage's illusory fourth wall by appealing to them, the omniscient spectators, for help, for understanding.

I also took the liberty of inserting a preshow mime in which the audience saw Aemilia and Egeon before their separation at sea, after which the two actors *dropped* their characters and became fellow performers wishing each other luck before Shakespeare's play, proper, began. I tried, that is, to establish a special bond between actor and audience—we know as well as the actors that Aemilia will appear at some point during the evening—in a play where, until the final moments, there is a marked division between what the audience and the characters know. My silent but involved audience sat, therefore, like some implacable god, unwilling to disclose the secret that would convert a seeming tragedy to a comedy, waiting for time itself, and the now-anticipated appearance of the mother, Aemilia, to resolve the problem. The abbey door upstage-center, flanked by those of the brothel and the Phoenix, stayed closed, remained unused, until the final minutes, yet my audience, having seen Aemilia in that preshow mime, knew that this middle door held the key, was the means of converting Egeon's potential tragedy to a comedy of nothing but coincidental errors.

A few months later, in a production of *A Midsummer Night's Dream*, I used this same audience involvement to surmount an unexpected, last-minute technical problem. In my own reading of that play, I envisioned a single world, stretching from Athens to Oberon's forest, a unity that Theseus would deny in his rigid separation of reason from imagination. However, the actor playing Theseus doubled as Oberon, and thus the character Theseus had an *other*, an imaginative dimension to his personality that his conscious self would deny. In fact, we did the play with just eight actors, and while Bottom alone did not double (except to play Pyramus), every other actor did; for instance, one actor played Lysander, Flute, Mustardseed, and, of course, Thisby. We did little to conceal such doubling—and tripling—from the audience. Quite the contrary, I was asking my audience to entertain a reading of the play that defined man as simultaneously rational and imaginative, as a creature of both court and forest, as possessing a multiple identity dependent upon the eye of the perceiver and, no less, upon his or her own self-fashioning.

Before we moved from the rehearsal hall to the theater for a scant two days on the main stage before opening night, I had planned for the final scene to put Theseus and his audience stage-right and then, just before the inner-play, *Pyramus and Thisby,* started, to darken that area. That would leave just Hippolyta (who doubled only as Titania) and Egeus (who doubled only as Puck) to handle the dialogue of the onstage aristocratic audience, while the other five actors (the actor doubling as Oberon and the two pairs of lovers) crossed backstage, changed quickly, and reassembled stage-left as Bottom's theatrical company now playing before the court. When we moved to the main stage, however, I discovered that the lighting, unchanged since the days when the theater had housed vaudeville acts, was too primitive: we would not be able to darken one-half of the stage. I was in a state of panic!

Then I thought to myself: if I've asked the audience to accept the convention of doubling, if by this time in the evening they are well acquainted with the metadramatic concept of the performance, then can't I ask them to come to our aid to pretend that Theseus, Hippolyta, the four lovers, and Egeus are still watching the play from stage-right, despite the fact that this audience has been reduced from seven to two and has metamorphosed stage-left as Quince (doubling as Demeterius, by the way) and the players? Do the actors even need to cross backstage behind the curtain to change into the *Pyramus and Thisby* costumes in the wings before reentering? A simple "no" to this rhetorical questions led to having the four lovers, plus Theseus (playing Snout), cross in full view of the audience, change onstage, and join Bottom (as Pyramus) for the inner-play. By the way, they returned just as obviously stage-right to resume their roles as aristocrats during those closing moments when Theseus thanks the actors, before leading the couples offstage to consummate the marriages. I was asking my audience for help, as collaborators, as *actors* in the broadest sense of that term, who would aid in the deception practiced on these characters who were unaware that their identity is not singular, that the play's three seemingly distinct groups—the supernaturals, the aristocrats, and the laborers—are one. Without their consent, this involved audience thereby solved what had first seemed like an insurmountable problem with the stage lights.

A year later I received an invitation to go the People's Republic of China to teach at Jilin University and to direct there two companies, the Jilin Art College Players and the Changchun Modern Drama Theater, in a production of *The Comedy of Errors*. But two months before I departed, I received a letter from the actors asking if I would direct, instead, *The Merry Wives of Windsor*. Why this change of heart? I speculated that perhaps this middle-class comedy, with its rural setting, might have had a special appeal for the Chinese audience, since the notion of a community initially threatened by a decadent aristocrat like Falstaff and then dealing with him outside the law paralleled China's own system of informal, provincial justice.

I had heard that, by our standards, Chinese audiences were "noisy," but after attending several performances in Changchun City, ranging from Marxist dramas to traditional opera, I realized that these audiences, in their own way, were as productive as my prison audiences, or those audiences I had tried to encourage in my own productions. In the Chinese theater the audience is clearly engaged, commenting during the performance, even moving down the aisle to chat with friends about this or that issue being raised onstage. For the production of *The Merry Wives of Windsor* I decided, therefore, to blend my own notion about the audience's role with the traditions of their theater. Hence, in "our"[1] *Wives*, actors initially made their entrances from upstage; but as both actors and audience here experienced more of the play, entrances were increasingly made from downstage, with the actors emerging from the audiences as if they were fellow citizens taking the stage to represent those remaining in their seats.

Furthermore, the actors often played to the audience, acknowledging its presence. In act 3, scene 3, for instance, when Ford rushes back onstage after failing to find Falstaff in his house, I had him deliver directly to the audience his line, "I cannot fathom him. May be the knave bragged of that he could not compass," as if he needed to share with them the possibility that Falstaff lacked courage to enter the house, and that his wife, if only through the fat knight's cowardice, was still faithful. Through this remark, delivered to the spectators surrounding the stage, Ford pleaded that someone in the house would comfort him that his doubts about himself, as manifest through this projection in Falstaff, were groundless.

I was also influenced by the Chinese concern that plays focus on the individual's obligation to the community. *Wives*, for me, involves a community initially divided by the defensive postures of its inadequate men and, in this weakened condition, becoming easy prey to this intruder from court who misreads the virtues of Mistresses Page and Ford. Yet, at the part when the citizens of Windsor, male and female, come together to punish and reform Falstaff, I decided to ask the audience to assist us in a major onstage set change in the final act, where the scene moved from the single indoor/outdoor set that had served so far, to the forest. Upstage were three frames that had suggested front doors for outside scenes, or interior doors for when the action moved, say, to the living room of Ford's house. However, in act 5, scene 2, I had Page, Shallow, and Slender, while delivering their dialogue, bring in and drape over those three upstage frames a green hanging, thereby obscuring the frames and suggesting a grassy knoll. When Mistress Page, Mistress Ford, and Caius entered in the following scene, they would carry on the oak tree, centering it on the down side of an upstage platform, while making sure that the hanging was firmly in place and relatively free of folds. My thought here was that by this stage in the plot, characters (with the exception of Falstaff, to be sure) and audience would be at the same level of awareness. We were thus watching actors playing characters staging a play to trap Falstaff; thematics and metadramatics overlapped here. By simultaneously being in character and functioning as stage hands, so as to break the illusion, the reconciled Windsor community could thereby draw even closer to the audience otherwise *unknown* to them. By raising the house lights for curtain calls before the characters made their final exits, I allowed both halves of the performance, actor-characters and the audience, to be seen by and to see each other: the now solid Windsor community paralleled that united community of performer and audience who together had sustained the stage's illusory world.

4

In baseball the fans, that game's audience, are often spoken of as "the tenth man," complementing the nine players on the field. The label here acknowledges more than such inspiration as the home crowd gives to its team. Rather, the players depend on that tenth man—for revenue, of course, but also for that judgment, negative or positive, that in part determines how well they perform during the game. In the seven playwrights considered here, the audience also plays that role of tenth man—or, rather, the tenth person.

In Ionesco's *The Chairs* the spectator fills up the physical vacuum left by the invisible onstage guests, while in Pinter's *The Birthday Party* the playwright engages us by a paucity of facts in a script whose profundity we sense but cannot make manifest. In Genet's *The Balcony* our pleasure in the theatrical illusion, in the "other," unites us with the clients of Irma's brothel, or house of illusions, and in Brecht's *Galileo* the issue of the scientist's social responsibility is reexpressed in our own task, assigned by the playwright, to think about, instead of merely empathizing with, the onstage drama. In Stoppard's *Rosencrantz and Guildenstern* the pair would prefer a reductive definition of *audience* as noninvolved, as voyeurs, yet they are pulled relentlessly into *Hamlet*'s world, first as actors and then as apprentice playwrights. In Williams's *A Streetcar Named Desire* Blanche's "magic," her preference for fiction over reality, for a life as imagined rather than as merely "given," is at once exhilarating and fragile. Ultimately fraudulent, this theatrical perspective is still as meaningful to Blanche as is our experience in assessing her character. In Beckett's most recent works, the playwright, in staging himself or watching projections of himself, by definition shows us an image of our own role as spectator during the production.

This concern with the audience, I believe, is a salient feature of our modern drama. The play is, properly, an imaginative collaboration among all those present, a union of seeming opposites acknowledging that what unites reality and the theater is the principle that identity is an ongoing process between perceiver and the perceived, that *reality* itself is not an exclusive term. Our theater tells us, in effect, that we are no longer just images of some offstage, godlike playwright, but rather actors who—to the degree depending on where one situates mankind along the gamut from optimism to pessimism, humanism to determinism—fashion themselves or, at very least, attempt to influence the *look* or *stare* of their audience, of the other.

The role of the audience is central to contemporary criticism, whether it takes the form of deconstructing the text or of reader-response theories. If "the word" begins with the author, the author still might not have the last word; critics as diverse as Northrop Frye and Jacques Derrida would question even the subjunctive clause at the front of this sentence. Norman Holland comments on this coequal role of the critic, one that in turn suggests the role of the audience, when he observes that in post-modern art "for the critic as for the artist, the work of art exists in a relation to audience, readers, critics, author, other works of art, and [that] the business of the critic is to enter into that relationship, deepening and complicating it."[2] Philip McGuire, a performance critic, makes a similar equation between playwright and actor-director or reader-student when each is "called upon to endow the play with details that Shakespeare's words establish are crucial but do not themselves furnish. . . . [E]ach time actors and directors do, they in effect bring to fulfillment a process of creation that Shakespeare initiated but did not himself complete."[3]

This role for the audience is of course not new. When, early in *The Taming of the Shrew,* Christopher Sly disappears from his vantage point as audience to the story of Kate and Petruchio, not to return as he does in the anonymous play *The Taming of a Shrew,* we must assume the place vacated by him. At the end of *A Midsummer Night's Dream* we watch Oberon watch Theseus watch Bottom and his actors perform. If each circle of audience is, from our perspective, a mere fiction, if we think of ourselves as the ultimate or real spectator, thereby separating ourselves from "them," Puck challenges this assumption in his epilogue: perhaps we ourselves have been asleep, are no more than fellow dreamers, caught up in this "dream" or gross vision—this play. When Shakespeare first offers a mime version of *The Murder of Gonzago* before adding dialogue, is it not possible that his purpose is to acquaint the audience with the play so that, when it is repeated with dialogue, they can give more attention to the real issue—watching Hamlet, as onstage audience, watch his fellow spectator, Claudius, watch a play designed to catch his conscience? One can trace this concern for the audience even further back. What would be the effect of townspeople's seeing their fellow workers as actor-characters in the mystery or morality plays of the 1570s? In the Greek theater, the chorus, voicing the concerns, the fears, and the ongoing *reading* of the offstage audience, occupied a place intermediary between spectator and actor.

In his book *Of English Poetrie* (1597) William Webbe speaks of the playwright's task as being to "bring men together, create good fellowship."[4] He refers here, I think, not just to the obligation to please the audience, or to provide it with a good time; Webbe speaks, instead, of a certain ethical dimension of the theater. It *is* a bringing together, a joining of two groups, one onstage, the other offstage, one required to give up the self to enact a fictive character, the other asked to entertain a larger, more imaginative notion of reality than it would have outside the theater, or if the very concept of theater did not exist. As I tell my own theater majors, going to the theater is an act of love, one that involves two consenting parties. For actors performing before an empty house are not, properly, in a play but only in rehearsal, and a crowd staring at an empty stage is not really an audience with the informing purpose of an audience, but just a crowd. Performance brings the two together, for Webbe's "fellowship," and together they accomplish what they could not do singly.

When I was young, just starting out in the theater, I complained one day to a veteran actor about the "quality" of the audiences coming to our playhouse located in a well-heeled community north of Philadelphia. They came, I declared, only because it was "the thing to do." They thought of the theater as little more than "entertainment" after a hard day in the office, or as a mere excuse for a preshow cocktail party. "I hate them," I confided to him, "I wish we had a better audience." My actor-friend, my *teacher,* grabbed me roughly by the shoulders, admonishing me with, "Listen, you amateur, they're your audience. You have an obligation to them. You need to work with them—and *for* them. Whether they're smart or stupid, sober or drunk—that's another matter. First things first. Without them, buddy, you're nothing." This book, I like to fancy, is a way, feeble but my own, of atoning for such youthful indiscretion.

Notes

Chapter 1. Ionesco, *The Chairs*

1. Eugene Ionesco, *Fragments of a Journal,* trans. Jean Stewart (New York: Grove Press, 1968), p. 61. My text for *The Chairs* is that published in *Four Plays by Eugene Ionesco,* trans. Donald M. Allen (New York: Grove Press, 1958). On this notion of detachment see also: Enoch Brater, "Beckett, Ionesco, and the Traditions of Tragicomedy," *College Literature* 1 (1974): 119–20; Charles I. Glicksberg, *The Literature of Nihilism* (Lewisburg, Pa.: Bucknell University Press, 1975), p. 227; David I. Grossvogel, *The Blasphemers: The Theater of Brecht, Ionesco, Beckett, Genet* (Ithaca: Cornell University Press, 1962), p. 68. I should point out here that I found invaluable, as always, the work of Richard N. Coe, *Eugene Ionesco* (New York: Grove Press, 1961). And the several studies of Alfred Cismaru: "Ionesco on His Theater: L'homme en question," *Claudel Studies* 9 (1982): 47–52; "Ionesco's Latest: *Jeux de Massacre,*" *University of Windsor Review* 10 (1975): 5–10; "Ionesco's L'Homme aux Valises: The Absurdist Turned Classic," *French Review* 50 (1977): 732–36; "Ionesco's Rhino Pronouncements," *Antigonish Review* 40 (1980): 87–94.

2. Eugene Ionesco, *Notes and Counter Notes: Writings on the Theater* (New York: Grove Press, 1964), p. 121.

3. Eugene Ionesco, *Present/Past/Past/Present,* trans. Helen R. Lane (New York: Grove Press, 1971), pp. 51–52. In *Angels of Darkness: Dramatic Effect in Samuel Beckett, with Special Reference to Eugene Ionesco* (London: George Allen and Unwin, 1972), Colin Duckworth, speaking of "the participation mystique," says that "we must allow [the play] to shape us as it shaped the creator" (p. 89).

4. Ionesco, *Present/Past,* p. 173.

5. I paraphrase the keen observation by Richard Schechner, "The Enactment of the 'Not' in *Les Chaises* of Eugene Ionesco," *Yale French Studies* 29 (1963): 65–72.

6. I cite here the review of Ionesco's canon in Ronald Hayman's *Eugene Ionesco* (New York: Frederick Ungar, 1976).

7. Eugene Ionesco, *A Hell of a Mess,* trans. Helen Gary Bishop (New York: Grove Press, 1975), p. 152.

8. Ionesco in Claude Bonnefoy, *Conversations with Eugene Ionesco,* trans. Jan Dawson (New York: Holt, Rhinehart and Winston, 1966), p. 72.

9. In *Notes* Ionesco insists that the world is a creation "of *our own* minds, yes, not of *my* mind" (p. 192). Patrick Roberts speaks of how the "empty chairs . . . do of themselves suggest a theater," in *The Psychology of Tragic Drama* (London: Routledge and Kegan Paul, 1975), p. 116. Schechner in "The Enactment" remarks that without the projected consciousness of the old couple the chairs would radically change in meaning and hence in significance (p. 71). David Mendelson notes that as the Invisible Lady takes a chair once held by the Old Man, the imaginary perforce becomes real, in "Science and Fiction in Ionesco's 'Experimental' Theater," in *Ionesco: A Collection of Critical Essays,* ed. Rosette C. Lamont (Englewood Cliffs, N.J.: Prentice-Hall, 1973), p. 81.

10. Mendelson, "Science and Fiction," p. 78.

11. Hayman makes a parallel observation in *Eugene Ionesco,* p. 59–60.
12. Ionesco, *Notes,* p. 149.
13. Ibid., p. 192.
14. Ionesco, *Fragments,* p. 64.
15. Ibid., p. 89.
16. Allan Lewis, *Ionesco* (New York: Twayne Publishers, 1972), p. 42.
17. Ionesco, *Notes,* p. 192.
18. This sense of our participation as audience has been expressed in various ways. Albert Bermel sees the playwright as attempting "to transfer" the feelings of the old couple to us, in "Ionesco: Anything But Absurd," *Twentieth Century Literature* 21 (1975): 415. Grossvogel in *Blasphemers* says that in recognizing oneself in "the absurd world of the stage" Ionesco allows himself and his audience to experience through laughter "the release of his frustrations" (p. 68). Emmanuel Jacquart argues that our identification is on the level of the Jungian unconscious, or of dreams, in "Interview/ Eugene Ionesco," *Diacritics* 3 (1973): 47. In "The Absurd Professor in the Theater of the Absurd," *Modern Drama* 21 (1978), Alexander Fischler reminds us that professors especially "understand the fear generated by the lack or the presence of an audience" (p. 150).
19. Gloria Feman Orenstein comments on this parody in *The Theater of the Marvelous: Surrealism and the Contemporary Stage* (New York: New York University Press, 1975), p. 166.
20. Bonnefoy, *Conversations,* p. 72, 83; and Ionesco, *Notes,* p. 192.
21. Schechner, "Enactment," pp. 65–72.
22. Anne D. Cordero expresses this valuing of process over end with the term *waiting*. "Waiting, an Ambivalent Mood, in Beckett and Ionesco," *Studies in the Twentieth Century* 13 (1974): 51–63.
23. Ionesco, *Notes,* p. 192.
24. Mendelson, "Science and Fiction," p. 97. Bermel says in "Anything but Absurd" that at the end we see "life departed," that our response here is "the spirit of final consciousness" (p. 418).
25. On this issue of doubling, parallels, and the uniting of seemingly distinct entities, see: Richard M. Eastman, "Experiment and Vision in Ionesco's Plays," *Modern Drama* 4 (1961): 3–19; Edith Kern, "Ionesco and Shakespeare: *Macbeth* on the Modern Stage," *South Atlantic Bulletin* 39 (1974): 3–16; Moshe Lazar, "The Psychodramatic Stage: Ionesco and His Doubles," in *The Dream and the Play: Ionesco's Theatrical Quest,* ed. Moshe Lazar (Malibu, Calif.: Undena, 1982), pp. 135–59; Linda Davis Kyle, "The Grotesque in *Amedee, or How to Get Rid of It,*" *Modern Drama* 19 (1976): 281–90; and Mendelson, "Science and Fiction," p. 98.
26. Ionesco, *Fragments,* p. 41.
27. This sense of theatrical presence has been observed by: J. S. Doubrovsky, "Ionesco and the Comedy of Absurdity," *Yale French Studies* 23 (1959): 5–6; Grossvogel, *Blasphemers,* p. 51; Ronald Hayman, *Theater and Anti-Theater: New Movements Since Beckett* (New York: Oxford University Press, 1979), pp. 59–60; Rosette Lamont, "The Metaphysical Farce: Beckett and Ionesco," *French Review* 32 (1959): 323; Alfred Schwartz, *From Buchner to Beckett: Dramatic Theory and the Modes of Tragic Drama* (Athens, Oh.: Ohio University Press, 1978), p. 342; and Richard N. Coe, "On Being Very, *Very* Surprised: Eugene Ionesco and the Vision of Childhood," in *The Dream and the Play,* ed. Lazar, pp. 1–19. Jacques Guicharnaud, with Jane Beckeleman, in *Modern French Theater—Giraudoux to Beckett* (New Haven: Yale University Press, 1961), likens this atmosphere of presence to that of the "end-of-the-world" (p. 185).

28. On this interaction between the child and the adult see Coe, "On Being Very, *Very* Surprised," pp. 1–19.

29. Ionesco, *Fragments,* p. 134.

30. Sidney Homan, *Beckett's Theaters: Interpretations for Performance* (Lewisburg, Pa.: Bucknell University Press, 1984), p. 52.

31. M. S. Barranger, in "Death as Initiation in *Exit the King,*" *Educational Theater Journal* 27 (1975): 504–7, finds Ionesco using death in the Eastern sense of rebirth. And see Ruby Cohn, "Berrenger, Protagonist of an Anti-Playwright," *Modern Drama* 8 (1965), where she speaks of the character's "consciousness of death" (p. 133). On the inner life, and whether or not it surfaces in Ionesco, see: Martin Esslin, "Ionesco and the Creative Dilemma," *Tulane Drama Review* 7 (1963): 175; Bermel, "Anything But Absurd," p. 417; and Roberts, *Tragic Drama,* p. 116.

32. Ionesco, *Notes,* p. 116.

33. Robert Champigny, "Designations and Gestures in *The Chairs,*" in *The Two Faces of Ionesco,* ed. Rosette C. Lamont and Melvin J. Friedman (Troy, N.Y.: Whiston Publishing, 1978), pp. 155–74.

34. In the original production the blackboard was not used; the curtain fell on the mumblings of the deaf mute.

35. In *Notes* Ionesco comments, "It is in our solitude that we can all be reunited. And this is why true society transcends our social machinery" (p. 108). In "Beyond Realism: Ionesco's Theory of the Drama," in *Dream and the Play,* ed. Lazar, George E. Wellwarth speaks of "the instinctive congruence of his vision with his audience's subconsciously apprehended truths" (p. 38).

36. In "Science and Fiction" Mendelson observes, "With the stage transformed into an auditorium, the audience is now invited to take part in the 'experiment' " (p. 90).

37. Champigny, in "Designations," describes the Orator's failure as "simply one more example of the neutralization of designative meaning" (p. 165), while Leonard Cabell Pronko defines the character as a "mechanized imprint," or as a "theatrical experience of nothingness," in *Eugene Ionesco,* Columbia Essays on Modern Writers (New York: Columbia University Press, 1965), pp. 16, 18.

38. See the comments on Ionesco's distrust of systems and saviors in Josephine Jacobsen and William R. Mueller, *Ionesco and Genet: Playwrights of Silence* (New York: Hill and Wang, 1968), p. 62.

39. I expand here on my analysis of the play in *When the Theater Turns to Itself: The Aesthetic Metaphor in Shakespeare* (Lewisburg, Pa.: Bucknell University Press, 1981), pp. 79–103.

40. I am reminded of the stage direction in Ionesco's *The Lesson,* where the Maid "*takes out an armband with an insignia, perhaps the Nazi swastika*" and then puts it around the Professor's arm. In Ionesco, *Four Plays,* pp. 77–78.

41. Ionesco, *Notes,* p. 108.

42. Ibid., p. 116.

43. Judith D. Suther, "Ionesco's Symbiotic Pair: *Le Solitaire* and *A Formidable Bordello!,*" *French Review* 49 (1976): 699. She effectively contrasts the states of solitude and collectivism in the playwright.

44. See commentary on the early critical reaction to Ionesco in Donald Watson, *Ionesco and His Early Critics,* vol. 10 of the *Collected Works* (London: Calder, 1976), pp. 115–34.

45. Ionesco, *Notes,* pp. 189–91.

46. Champigny, "Designations," p. 171.

47. Doubrovsky, "Comedy of Absurdity," p. 10.

48. Ionesco, *Notes*, p. 192.
49. Marian Toplin, "Eugene Ionesco's *The Chairs* and the Theater of the Absurd," *American Imago* 25 (1968): 131–32.
50. Lamont, "Metaphysical Farce," p. 183.
51. Schechner, "Enactment," p. 72.

Chapter 2. Pinter, *The Birthday Party*

1. Guido Almansi and Simon Henderson, *Harold Pinter* (London: Methuen, 1983), p. 39. John Russell Brown sees the playwright as "protecting himself" by disclosing as little as possible, in *Theatre Language: A Study of Arden, Osborne, Pinter, and Wesker* (New York: Taplinger, 1972), p. 24. My text for *The Birthday Party* is *The Birthday Party and The Room: 2 Plays by Harold Pinter* (New York: Grove Press, 1977).
2. Richard Schechner, "Puzzling Pinter," *Tulane Drama Review* 11 (1966): 177.
3. R. F. Storch, "Harold Pinter's Happy Failures," *Massachusetts Review* 8 (1967): 145.
4. John Russell Taylor, *Anger, and After: A Guide to the New British Drama* (London: Methuen, 1969), p. 120. And see Lorraine H. Burghardt, "Game Playing in Three by Pinter," *Modern Drama* 17 (1974): 387.
5. James T. Boulton speaks of the audience as "faced with a world of Kafka-like uncertainty," in "Harold Pinter: *The Caretaker* and Other Plays," *Modern Drama* 6 (1963): 103. After offering several very different interpretations of the play, Martin Esslin finds "no contradiction" among them. *Pinter: A Study of His Plays* (New York: W. W. Norton and Company, 1976), pp. 75–86. For complementarious responses to *The Birthday Party* and its playwright see also Arthur Ganz, "Introduction" to his edition of *Pinter: A Collection of Critical Essays* (Englewood Cliffs, N.J.: Prentice-Hall, 1972), p. 7; and James R. Hollis, *Harold Pinter: The Poetics of Silence*, Crosscurrents/Modern Critiques Series (Carbondale: Southern Illinois University Press, 1970), p. 41.
6. Bert O. States, *Great Reckonings in Little Rooms: On the Phenomenology of Theater* (Berkeley: University of California Press, 1985).
7. Bernard Dukore's contention in *Harold Pinter* (New York: Grove Press, 1982), p. 29.
8. See Katharine H. Burkman's comments on Petey as an audience in *The Dramatic World of Harold Pinter: Its Basis in Ritual* (Columbus: Ohio State University Press, 1971), p. 36.
9. I find illustrative here Valerie Minogue's observations on the relation between the audience and the Tramp in "Taking Care of the Caretaker," *Twentieth Century* 168 (1960): 76.
10. Michael W. Kaufman has a particularly insightful essay on the "birthday party" sequence. "Actions That a Man Might Play: Pinter's *The Birthday Party*," *Modern Drama* 16 (1973): 167–78.
11. Charles A. Carpenter, "'What Have I Seen, the Scum or the Essence?': Symbolic Fallout in Pinter's *The Birthday Party*," *Modern Drama* 17 (1974): 389–402.
12. I combine here, in order, the views of: Burkman, *Dramatic World*, p. 35; Lois G. Gordon, *Stratagems to Uncover Nakedness: The Drama of Harold Pinter* (Columbia: University of Missouri Press, 1968), pp. 21–29; Jacqueline Hoefer, "Pinter and Whiting: Two Attitudes Towards the Alienated Artist," *Modern Drama* 4 (1962): 403; Lucina Paquet Gabbard, *The Dream Structure of Pinter's Plays* (East

Rutherford, N.J.: Fairleigh Dickinson University Press, 1976), p. 47; John Ditsky, *The Onstage Christ: Studies in the Persistence of a Theme* (Totowa, N.J.: Barnes and Noble, 1980), p. 136; Peter Thornton, "Blindness and Confrontation with Death: Three Plays by Harold Pinter," *Die Neuren Spracken* 18 (1968): 217; E. T. Kirby, "The Paranoid Pseudo-Community in Pinter's *The Birthday Party,*" *Educational Theater Journal* 30 (1978): 161; and Esslin, *Pinter,* pp. 82–86.

13. Samar Attar, *The Intruder in Modern Drama* (Frankfurt: Peter D. Lang, 1981), p. 187.

14. Hollis, *Poetics of Silence,* p. 41.

15. Austin E. Quigley, *The Pinter Problem* (Princeton: Princeton University Press, 1975), p. 276.

16. Thomas F. Van Laan, "*The Dumb Waiter:* Pinter's Play with the Audience," *Modern Drama* 24 (1981): 498–501.

17. Harold Pinter, "Harold Pinter: An Interview," from *Writers at Work,* ed. George Plimpton, in Ganz, *A Collection,* p. 20.

18. See Augusta Walker, "Messages from Pinter," *Modern Drama* 10 (1967), where she speaks of Pinter's characters as "clutching outwardly instead of building inwardly" (p. 10).

19. Bert O. States, "Pinter's *Homecoming:* The Shock of Nonrecognition," *The Hudson Review* 21 (1968): 151.

20. A. R. Braunmuller, "Harold Pinter: The Metamorphosis of Memory," in Hedwig Bock and Albert Wertheim, eds., *Essays on Contemporary British Drama* (Munich: Max Hueber, 1981), p. 160.

21. Ibid., pp. 159–60.

22. In a parallel way, Elin Diamond effectively links the playwright's own metaphysics and his use of comic dramatic conventions in *Pinter's Comic Play* (Lewisburg, Pa.: Bucknell University Press, 1985).

23. Barbara Kreps, "Time and Harold Pinter's Possible Realities: Art as Life, and Vice Versa," *Modern Drama* 22 (1979): 56.

24. Esslin, *Pinter,* pp. 75–86.

25. Simon Trussler, *The Plays of Harold Pinter: An Assessment* (London: Gollancz, 1973), p. 47.

26. Boulton, "*The Caretaker,*" p. 103.

27. See the detailed analysis of this eye imagery in Michael Anderson, *Anger and Detachment: A Study of Arden, Osborne, and Pinter* (London: Pitman, 1976), pp. 89–96.

28. On the link with Oedipus see Michael Cleary, "Opposing Images in Pinter's 'Plays of Menace': The Room as Sanctuary and Nightmare," *Theatre Annual* 35 (1980): 51.

29. See States's intriguing commentary on the phenomenology of the curtain call in *Great Reckonings,* pp. 197–206.

30. For this reading see Gordon, *Stratagems,* p. 21.

31. Harriet and Irving Deer observe that the "blackout functions to place the audience in the same state of confusion that Stanley feels," in "Pinter's *The Birthday Party:* The Film and the Play," *South Atlantic Bulletin* 45 (1980): 29.

32. I echo here the distinction made by Murray Krieger in *A Window to Criticism: Shakespeare's Sonnets and Modern Poetics* (Princeton: Princeton University Press, 1964)—one of my favorite books.

Chapter 3. Genet, *The Balcony*

1. I am especially indebted to the masterful analysis of Genet by Richard N. Coe, *The Vison of Jean Genet* (London: Peter Owen, 1968). For a psychological and

mythical study see Lewis T. Cetta, *Profane Play, Ritual, and Jean Genet* (University: University of Alabama Press, 1973). For detailed commentary on production see Richard Schechner, "Genet's *The Balcony:* A 1981 Perspective on a 1979/1980 Production," *Modern Drama* 25 (1982): 82–104; and Peter Zadek, "Acts of Violence," *New Statesman* 53 (4 May 1957): 568–70. Jerry L. Curtis observes that unlike Genet, Sartre doesn't believe that others' looks paralyze or that we can free ourselves from play, in "The World Is a Stage: Sartre versus Genet," *Modern Drama* 17 (1974): 33–41. On Irma, Gisela Feal suggests that the female embodies the unconscious, the male the conscious, and yet the revolutionaries replace a male-reality with a myth dominated by negation that is at one with the matriarchal cult, in "*Le Balcon* de Genet ou le Culte Matriarchal, une Interpretation Mythique," *French Review* (1948): 897–907. My texts for Genet's plays are those published by Grove Press, New York, and translated by Bernard Frechtman: *The Maids* (1954), *Deathwatch* (1954), *The Balcony* (1966), *The Blacks* (1960), and the *The Screens* (1962).

2. In "The Psychological Universe of Jean Genet," *Drama Survey* 3 (1964): 386–92, Thomas B. Markus comments that "all the individual sees is a reflection of himself" (p. 387), and yet if we see ourselves as others see us, we become "schizophrenic" (p. 390).

3. See, particularly, the chapters "Heads down, Feet up" (pp. 31–65) and "Murder and Metaphysics" (pp. 170–209) in Coe, *Vision*.

4. W. F. Sohlich, "Genet's Drama: Rites of Passage of the Anti-Hero: From Alienated Existence to Artistic Alienation," *Modern Language Notes* 89 (1974): 641–53.

5. Jean Genet, *Reflections on the Theater, and Other Writings,* trans. Richard Seaver (London: Faber and Faber, 1972), p. 79.

6. David K. Jeffrey, in "Genet and Gelber: Studies in Addiction," *Modern Drama* 11 (1968): 151–56, argues that the spontaneous characters in Genet "improvise rebellion from the rituals" and thereby "rebel against the 'addicts,'" with the result that they become "moral" (p. 156). In "The Image and the Revolutionary: Sartrean Relationships in the Work of Jean Genet," *Southern Review* (Adelaide) 11 (1978): 57–71, L. A. C. Dobrez sees the playwright finding himself in this maze of mirrors (p. 64). But for J. M. Svendsen, Genet is too much his own audience, "captivated by his own creation: hedonistically, punitively, or curatively" (p. 105).

7. Jean-Paul Sartre, *Saint-Genet Comedien et Martyr* (Paris: Gallimard, 1952).

8. See Sartre's "Introduction" to *The Maids and Deathwatch,* pp. 7–31, extracted from his *Comedien et Martyr.*

9. Harry E. Stewart, "Jean Genet's Mirror Image in *Le Balcon,*" *Modern Drama* 12 (1969): 197–203. Stewart calls the mirror "an agent of unification" (p. 198). Also, see Thomas P. Adler, "The Mirror as Stage Prop in Modern Drama," *Comparative Drama* 14 (1980): 355–73; and Y. Went-Daoust, "Objets et Lieux dans *Le Balcon* de Jean Genet," *Neophilologus* 63 (1979): 23–43.

10. Coe, *Vision,* pp. 9–10.

11. In *Holy Theater: Ritual and the Avant Garde* (Cambridge: At the University Press, 1981), Christopher Innes argues that in Genet truth comes from the negation of the false self as defined by reality and is thereby linked with death, that "absolute negation of reality" (pp. 144–47).

12. Again, see Sohlich, "Rites of Passage," for an especially insightful analysis of this man/beggar/slave: at the end the "cop . . . copies the gesture of a prostitute who pleases a timid client who fulfills his destiny as a poet" (pp. 651–52).

13. On the political and sociological implications in Genet see Lucien Goldman, "The Theater of Jean Genet: A Sociological Study," trans. Pat Dreyfus, *The Drama Review* 38 (1968): 51–61.

14. For the Renaissance equivalent to this questioning of the audience's reality, see Anne Barton (née Righter) in *Shakespeare and the Idea of the Play* (London: Chatto and Windus, 1964).

15. Genet, *Reflections*, p. 11.

16. Ronald Hayman speaks of the play as making "a metaphysical assault on the audience," in *Artaud and After* (London: Cambridge University Press, 1977), p. 153. And Rima Drell Reck observes that in blurring the lines between reality and illusion the play establishes a complicity between the stage and the audience, in "Appearance and Reality in Genet's *Le Balcon*," *Yale French Studies* 29 (1962): 20–25.

17. Murray Krieger, *A Window to Criticism: Shakespeare's Sonnets and Modern Poetics* (Princeton: Princeton University Press, 1964).

18. In *Contradictory Characters: An Interpretation of the Modern Theater* (New York: E. P. Dutton, 1973), Albert Bermel comments that a "play is a dream filled out, a schematic arrangment of a dream" (p. 8).

19. Speaking of *The Blacks*, although surely the same observation is relevant for the present play, Jacques Ehrmann argues that Genet establishes "illusions on both sides of the footlights" (p. 41), in "Genet's Dramatic Metamorphosis: From Appearance to Freedom," *Yale French Studies* 29 (1962): 33–42.

20. Tom F. Driver, *Romantic Quest and Modern Query: A History of the Modern Theater* (New York: Delacorte Press, 1970), p. 454. And see Jonas A. Barish, "The Veritable Saint Genet," *Wisconsin Studies in Comparative Literature* 6 (1965): 285.

21. Contrasting Peter Weiss and Genet himself, Norman A. Rasulis argues that whereas in Weiss the issue is what is to be done, in Genet it is one of questioning identity, in "Identity and Action in the Revolutionary Worlds of *The Balcony* and *Marat/Sade*," *Theatre Annual* 30 (1974): 60–72.

22. The last line in Virginia Woolf's *To the Lighthouse* (New York: Harcourt, Brace, and World, 1955): "I have had my vision."

23. In *Theater of Protest and Paradox: Development in the Avant-Garde Drama* (New York: New York University Press, 1964), George Wellwarth calls us all prisoners of illusions, all inauthentic; when all layers of illusion are stripped away, the audience stares at an empty stage, at nothingness (pp. 113–33). This is how Genet disturbs our conventional suspension of belief in the stage illusion, as Michèle Piemme notes in "Espace Scenique et Illusion Dramatique dans *Le Balcon*," *Obliques* 2 (1972): 23–31.

24. Loren Kruger, "Ritual into Myth—Ceremony and Communication in *The Blacks*," *Critical Arts* 1 (1980): 63.

25. See the commentary on Chantal as an image and a reflection by Harry E. Stewart, "Jean Genet's Saintly Preoccupation in *Le Balcon*," *Drama Survey* 7 (1967): 24–30.

26. Charles Marowitz defines Genet's goal as "to reach that realm of psychic myth and instinctual poetry which is the only alternative to a debilitating, mind-dwarfing, sense-dulling, repulsively predictable naturalistic theater," in "The Revenge of Jean Genet," *Encore* 33 (1961): 24. Without the theater as defined by Genet, without its meaningful presence, life itself is incomplete, its inhabitants less than human. John Elsom argues that in Genet "no man can resign himself to being human," in "Genet and the Sadistic Society," *The London Magazine* 3 (1963): 61–67.

27. In "*The Balcony* and Parisian Existentialism," *Tulane Drama Review* 7 (1963): 60–79, Benjamin Nelson suggests that in Genet the alternatives are incoherent existence or a lifeless image controlled by the social hierarchy, or what he calls "the coincidence of contraries" (p. 61).

28. Jean-Luc Dejean, *Le Théâtre français d'aujourd'hui* (Paris: Nathan, 1971), pp. 92–95.

29. Josephine Jacobsen and William R. Mueller, *Ionesco and Genet: Playwrights of Silence* (New York: Hill and Wang, 1968), p. 155.

30. Joseph H. McMahon, *The Imagination of Jean Genet* (New Haven: Yale University Press, 1963), p. 174.

31. Lionel Abel, "Metatheatre," *Partisan Review* 27 (1960); 239.

32. Martin A. Bertman, "A Metaphysical Analysis of Genet's *Le Balcon*," *Argora* 4 (1979–1980): 82; and Christina Howell, *Sartre's Theory of Literature* (London: Modern Humanities Research Association, 1979), p. 85.

33. I adjust the term "complementarity" as used by Norman Rabkin in *Shakespeare and the Common Understanding* (New York: The Free Press, 1964).

34. Bernard Dort, "Le Jeu de Genet," *Temps Modernes* 171 (1969): 1875–84.

35. Alfred Simon, "La Metaphore Primordiale," *Espirit* 338 (1965): 837–44.

36. Jacques Petit, "Structures Dramatiques dans *Le Balcon* et *Les Negres* de Genet," *L'Onirisme et L'insolite dans le Theatre Francasis Contemporain,* ed. Paul Vernois (Paris: Klincksieck, 1974), pp. 231–51.

37. George G. Strem, "The Theatre of Jean Genet: Facets of Illusion—the Anti-Christ and the Underdog," *Minnesota Review* 4 (1964) 226–36.

38. Tom Driver, *Jean Genet* (New York: Columbia University Press, 1966), p. 37.

39. Leslie Epstein, "Beyond the Baroque, the Role of the Audience in the Modern Theater," *Triquarterly* 12 (1968): 213–34.

40. F. H. Mares, "Jean Genet's *The Balcony*," *Meanjin* 24 (1965): 354–56.

41. Thomas R. Whitaker, *Fields of Play in Modern Drama* (Princeton: Princeton University Press, 1977), p. 113. David I. Grossvogel offers a brilliant analysis of Genet, and particularly of his virtues and limitations as a playwright, in *The Blasphemers: The Theater of Brecht, Ionesco, Beckett, Genet* (Ithaca: Cornell University Press, 1962), pp. 135–74, although I would disagree with his final assessment that Genet's theater is magnificent inside, on its own terms, but weakens once it is applied to the world outside the stage (p. 174). Along with Coe's, one of the most insightful and balanced analyses of Genet is Robert Brustein's seminal *The Theater of Revolt: An Approach to Modern Drama* (New York: Little, Brown, 1964), pp. 361–411.

42. Jonas Barish, *The Antitheatrical Prejudice* (Berkeley: University of California Press, 1981), p. 477.

43. Ruby Cohn observes in *Currents in Contemporary Drama* (Bloomington: Indiana University Press, 1969) that in *Deathwatch* hell is solitude, not other people (p. 65).

44. In *The Worm of Consciousness and Other Essays,* ed. Mary Miriam (New York: Harcourt Brace Jovanovich, 1976), Nicola Chiaromonte defines this audience as judges who are judged (p. 168). For a good analysis of *The Blacks,* with a special focus on its multiple audiences, see Susan Taubes, "The White Mask Falls," *Tulane Drama Review* 7 (1963): 85–92.

45. In "Sculpture into Drama: Giacometti's Influence on Genet," *Drama Survey* 3 (1964): 378–85, Robert Nugent observes that the audience of *The Blacks* "have undergone suffering, terror, solitude; the experience is total and therefore has such purity" (p. 384).

46. For an insightful structural analysis of *The Maids* see Oreste F. Pucciani, "Tragedy, Genet, and *The Maids*," *Tulane Drama Review* 7 (1963): 42–59.

47. John Cruickshank speaks of the "utter futility" of the audience in *The Blacks.* "Jean Genet: The Aesthetics of Crime," *Critical Quarterly* 6 (1964): 202–10.

48. In *The Imagination,* McMahon puts it more bluntly: Genet's failure is in thinking that art can stimulate rather than reflect feelings (p. 259).

49. See Edith Melcher, "The Pirandellism of Jean Genet," *French Review* 36

(1962): 32–36; and R. B. Parker, "The Theory and Theatre of the Absurd," *Queen's Quarterly* 73 (1966): 421–41.

Chapter 4. Brecht, *Galileo*

1. See Frederick Ewen, *Bertolt Brecht: His Life, His Art and His Times* (New York: Citadel Press, 1967), p. 339. My text for *Galileo* is that translated by Charles Laughton and edited by Eric Bentley (New York: Grove Press, Inc., 1966). In the original version of this chapter I had used the text in the edition by Ralph Manheim and John Willett, published by Vintage Books. While there are *losses* to be confronted in the Laughton translation—Mrs. Sarti, for instance, is much more prominent in the Vintage edition—my judgment as a director was that the Laughton text was more viable for actors—and was *tighter.*

Productions notes on *Galileo*. Presented at the Acrosstown Repertory Theater, Gainesville, Florida, 13 January–14 February, 1988. *Director,* Sidney Homan; *Assistant Director,* Stuart Horowitz; *Set Design,* Dan Hughes, Jim Evangelist (mural), Sidney Homan; *Lighting,* Douglas Hornbeck, Elayne Shields; *Music,* John Kitts; *Costume Accessories,* Michael Rogers. CAST: *Andrea Sarti,* John Lennon; *Boy,* Donovan Panone; *Cardinal Barberini* (later, Pope Urban VIII), Kurt Orwick; *Cardinal Bellarmin,* Mathew Marko; *Cardinal Inquisitor,* David Preuss; *Chaperon,* Amanda Fry; *Children,* Daniel Gordon, Daniel Homan, David Homan, Sky Muncaster, Tara Muncaster, Joshua Wood; *Christopher Clavius,* John Lennon; *Customs Official,* Kurt Orwick; *First Ballad Singer,* Kurt Orwick; *First Senator,* Mathew Marko; *Fulganzio* (Monk), Mathew Marko; *Galileo Galilei,* Andrew Gordon; *Lord Chamberlain,* Kevin Main; *Loud Voice,* Amanda Fry; *Ludovico Marsili,* Kevin Main; *Mathematician,* Mathew Marko; *Matti,* Bob Freeman; *Messenger* (Assistant, Scribe), Stuart Horowitz; *Mrs. Sarti,* Marcia Brown; *Narrator,* Marcia Brown; *Newsboy,* David Preuss; *Old Cardinal,* Kevin Main; *Philosopher,* Kurt Orwick; *Prince Cosimo De'Medici,* Donovan Panone; *Pruili* (Curator), David Preuss; *Sagredo,* Stuart Horowitz; *Second Ballad Singer,* Mathew Marko; *Second Senator,* Kurt Orwick; *Virginia Galilei,* Amanda Fry.

2. Ronald Speirs, "Brecht and the German Democratic Republic," in *Brecht in Perspective,* ed. Graham Bartram and Antony Waine (London: Longman, 1982), p. 185.

3. Denis Huston makes this point in "The Shakespearean Scholar and Teacher on Stage: Double Identity or Personality?" *CEA Critic* 51 (1988).

4. Ronald Taylor, *Literature and Society in Germany 1918–1945* (Totowa, N.J.: Barnes and Noble, 1980), p. 304.

5. David I. Grossvogel, *The Blasphemers: The Theater of Brecht, Ionesco, Beckett, Genet* (Ithaca: Cornell University Press, 1962), pp. 43–44.

6. Heinz Politzer, "How Epic Is Brecht's Epic Theater?" *Modern Language Quarterly* 23 (1962): 114.

7. Ewen, *Bertolt Brecht,* p. 345.

8. Ronald Speirs, *Brecht's Early Plays* (London: The Macmillan Press, 1982), p. 184.

Note: I drew much more directly, indeed, cited more frequently other scholars and critics in the original version of this chapter. These writers have, with a few exceptions, "disappeared" in the present version, but I acknowledge them here (and, when relevant, refer to the specific pages cited in the original chapter) since they shaped my approach to the play as its director:

Walter Benjamin, *Understanding Brecht* (London: NLB, 1977).

Eric Bentley, *The Brecht Commentaries* (New York: Grove Press, 1981).
Frank K. Borchardt, "Marx, Engels and Brecht's *Galileo*," *Brecht Heute/Brecht Today* 2 (1972): 161.
Oscar Budel, "Contemporary Theater and Aesthetic Distance," in *Brecht: A Collection of Critical Essays*, ed. Peter Demetz (Englewood Cliffs, N.J.: Prentice-Hall, 1965), p. 85.
Bruce Cook, *Brecht in Exile* (New York: Holt, Rinehart and Winston, 1982), pp. 179–80.
Keith Dickson, *Toward Utopia: A Study of Brecht* (Oxford: Clarendon Press, 1978).
Martin Esslin, *Brecht: The Man and His Work* (Garden City, N.J.: Doubleday, 1960).
John Fuegi, *The Essential Brecht*, University of Southern California Studies in Comparative Literature, Vol. 4 (Los Angeles: Hennessey and Ingalls, Inc. 1972), p. 166.
Ronald Gray, *Brecht the Dramatist* (Cambridge: At the University Press, 1978).
Werner Hecht, "The Development of Brecht's Theory of Epic Theater: 1918–1933," *Tulane Drama Review* 6 (1961): 94–96.
Jim Hinley, *Theatre at Work: The Story of the National Theatre's Production of Brecht's "Galileo"* (London: Routledge and Kegan Paul, 1981).
James K. Lyon, *Bertolt Brecht's American Cicerone* (Bonn: Bouvier, 1978), pp. 114–15.
Charles R. Lyons, "*The Life of Galileo:* The Focus of Ambiguity in the Villain Hero," *Germanic Review* 41 (1966): 57–71.
John Milfull, *From Baal to Keuner: The "Second Optimism" of Bertolt Brecht* (Bern: Lang, 1974), pp. 127–28.
Jan R. Needle and Peter Thompson, *Brecht* (Chicago: University of Chicago Press, 1981).
Ernst Schumacher, *Drama und Geschichte. Bertolt Brechts "Leben des Galilei" und Andere Stucke* (Berlin: Henschelverlag, 1968); and *Die Dramatischen Versuche Bertolt Brechts, 1918–1933* (Berlin: Rutten and Loening, 1955).
Walter H. Sokel, "Brecht's Concept of Character," *Comparative Drama* 3 (1971): 177–92.
Otto M. Sorensen, "Brecht's *Galileo:* Its Development from Ideational into Ideological Theater," *Modern Drama* 11 (1969): 422.
W. A. J. Steer, "Brecht's Epic Theater: Theory and Practice," *Modern Language Review* 63 (1968): 637.
Walter Weideli, *The Art of Bertolt Brecht*, trans. David Russell (New York: New York University Press, 1963).
Alfred D. White, *Bertolt Brecht's Great Plays* (New York: Barnes and Noble, 1978).
Timothy J. Wiles, *The Theater Event: Modern Theater and Performance* (Chicago: University of Chicago Press, 1980), pp. 80–81.
John Willett, *The Theatre of Bertolt Brecht: A Study from Eight Aspects* (London: Methuen, 1960).
Jilian H. Wulbern, *Brecht and Ionesco: Commitment in Context* (Urbana: University of Illinois Press, 1971).

Chapter 5. Stoppard, *Rosencrantz and Guildenstern Are Dead*

1. My text for Stoppard's *Rosencrantz and Guildenstern Are Dead* is that published by Grove Press (New York, 1968). The line in the chapter's subtitle is Rosencrantz's;

and he continues, "Dear God, is it too much to expect a little sustained action?!" (p. 118). In the random world of our century and our theater, the issue, as I see it, is not the action made meaningful in a cosmos ruled by some divine plan, but rather incidents that we, as playwright, actor, and audience, can deliver from such randomness, or absurdity, by our own imaginative, collaborative effort.

2. In *Tom Stoppard's Plays* (New York: Grove Press, 1982), Jim Hunter speaks of these would-be audiences, those characters whose only task, they wrongly assume, is to serve and wait as spectators, as afflicted with a kind of "Moon-ishness" (p. 138).

3. "Farcical bomb" is the judgment of Gabrielle Scott Robinson in "Plays Without Plot: The Theater of Tom Stoppard," *Educational Theatre Journal* 29 (1977): 48. The more serious reading, that Stoppard's plays suggest a human stage world surrounded by an inhuman cosmos, comes from Clive James, "Count Zero Splits the Infinite: Tom Stoppard's Plays," *Encounter* 45 (1975): 75.

4. Ronald Hayman explores this "visual riddle" in *Tom Stoppard* (London: Heinemann Education, 1979), p. 86.

5. Ibid., p. 41. Hayman argues that "Stoppard translates the Brechtian need for a witness into a professional need for an audience."

6. Norman Berlin, "Death: Hamlet and Rosencrantz and Guildenstern," in *The Secret Cause: A Discussion of Tragedy* (Amherst: University of Massachusetts Press, 1981), p. 81.

7. Robert Brustein's well-known and—as I hope to show—hasty judgment in "Waiting for Hamlet," *New Republic* 157 (4 Nov. 1967): 25.

8. Richard Corballis speaks of the two as a downstage extension of ourselves, in "Extending the Audience: The Structure of *Rosencrantz and Guildenstern Are Dead*," *Ariel* 11 (1980): 68. And see the discussion of this opening event in Douglas Colby, *As the Curtain Rises: On Contemporary British Drama 1966–1976* (Rutherford, N.J.: Fairleigh Dickinson University Press, 1978), pp. 35–43.

9. In "The Strategy of *Rosencrantz and Guildenstern Are Dead*," *Educational Theatre Journal* 27 (1975), Helen Keyssar-Franke comments on how this addition of the Tragedians' audience makes the onstage events appear less bizarre to us (p. 91).

10. Robert Egan offers a splendid analysis of the Player's role in "A thin beam of light: The Purpose of Playing in *Rosencrantz and Guildenstern Are Dead*," *Theatre Journal* 31 (1979): 59–69—an article that has very much influenced my reading.

11. Phyllis Ruskin and John H. Lutterbie pit this sense of play or theatricality against the play's otherwise rigid, abstract concepts, in "Balancing the Equation," *Modern Drama* 26 (1983): 547.

12. Rodney Simard speaks of how "the individual has the capacity to accept what he experiences, or does not experience, as his own reality," in "The Logic of Unicorns: Beyond Absurdism in Stoppard," *Arizona Quarterly* 38 (1982): 40.

13. William Babula, "The Play-Life Metaphor in Shakespeare and Stoppard," *Modern Drama* 15 (1972): 279.

14. On the play's language as dramatic device, see Jill L. Levenson, "*Hamlet* Andante/*Hamlet* Allegro: Tom Stoppard's Two Versions," *Shakespeare Survey* 36 (1983): 21–28, where she finds Stoppard manipulating both language and philosophy. See also Robert Wilcher, "Tom Stoppard and the Art of Communication," *Journal of Beckett Studies* 8 (1982): 105–23, where he argues that the playwright is preoccupied with language because it is the "value-system of our society" (p. 107).

15. In his excellent book, *Tom Stoppard* (New York: Grove Press, 1983), Thomas R. Whitaker observes that the play's "own full meaning therefore inheres in our acting and witnessing of a contradictory pseudo-representation that acknowledges our presence in the theatre" (p. 40).

16. Robert Wilcher, "The Museum of Tragedy: *Endgame* and *Rosencrantz and Guildenstern Are Dead*," *Journal of Beckett Studies* 4 (1979): 50.
17. Stoppard speaks of this movement as "ambushes" in "Ambushes for the Audience: Towards a High Comedy of Ideas," *Theatre Quarterly* 4 (1971): 6.
18. Keyssar-Franke, "The Strategy," pp. 92–93.
19. James L. Calderwood, *To Be and Not To Be: Negation and Metadrama in "Hamlet"* (New York: Columbia University Press, 1983), pp. 140–43.
20. I condense my argument here in *Shakespeare's Theater of Presence: Language, Spectacle, and the Audience* (Lewisburg, Pa.: Bucknell University Press, 1986), pp. 31–45.
21. In *Beyond Absurdity: The Plays of Tom Stoppard* (Rutherford, N.J.: Fairleigh Dickinson University Press, 1979), Victor L. Cahn defines the characters' dilemma as the binary fears of being caught in Hamlet's world and of being separated from that same world (p. 57).
22. In "Museum of Tragedy" Wilcher suggests that what unites audiences on- and offstage is the fact that Shakespeare's play serves as "a substitute for a cultural consensus about the nature and the meaning of the universe," and that *Hamlet* is "a formal equivalent for the agreement between dramatist and audience on which tragedy depends" (p. 51).
23. Whitaker, *Stoppard*, p. 48.
24. Gillan Farish calls the audience "a character in the play" in "Into the Looking-Glass Bowl: An Instance of Grateful Terror," *University of Windsor Review* 10 (1975): 14.
25. In *The Stoppard Plays* (Troy, N.Y.: Whiston Publishing, 1982), Lucina P. Gabbard links Stoppard's characters with the audience in their wish to know or to escape uncertainty (pp. 12–13), while Julian Gitzen, in "Tom Stoppard: Chaos in Perspective," *Southern Humanities Review* 10 (1976): 143–52, contends that neither Rosencrantz nor Guildenstern, nor the audience, can control the situation (p. 149).
26. Joan Fitspatrick Dean argues that in insisting on his own reality Guildenstern denies his role as a spectator and hence denies the application of *The Murder of Gonzago* to his own situation, in *Tom Stoppard: Comedy as a Moral Matrix* (Columbia: University of Missouri Press, 1981), pp. 38–39.
27. In "Extending the Audience," Corballis sets the "real world" of Rosencrantz and Guildenstern against the stage world of *Hamlet* (pp. 72–76); my argument will go in just the opposite direction, toward a merging of would-be real spectators and seemingly unreal characters preset from Shakespeare.
28. I stress the word *seemingly* here. Philip Roberts holds the opposite view in "Tom Stoppard: Serious Artist or Siren," *Critical Quarterly* 20 (1978): 84–92, suggesting that Stoppard professes a "refusal to believe in the efficacy, in any sense, of theatre to affect anything, including an audience" (p. 85).
29. Stoppard, "Ambushes," p. 6.
30. Berlin, *Secret Cause*, p. 84.
31. William E. Gruber, "Wheels within wheels, etcetera: Artistic Design in *Rosencrantz and Guildenstern Are Dead*," *Comparative Drama* 15 (1981–1982): 299–300. He refashions the question: "Is mimesis the only way toward real understanding, or, pursued too far, is it merely empty theatricality?" Confronted with the same pervasive theatricality in this play, Andrew K. Kennedy finds Stoppard thinking too much about the theater, with the result that his parody lacks a "centre of gravity," in *Dramatic Dialogue: The Dialogue of Personal Encounter* (Cambridge: At the University Press, 1983), p. 233.

32. In "A thin beam of light," Egan opposes the Player's "miracle of art" to Guildenstern's "philosophy of non-existence" (pp. 68–69).

33. For C. J. Gianakaris the two hold "dual positions as both actor in a story and spectator of a fable (or life?)," in "Absurdism Altered: *Rosencrantz and Guildenstern Are Dead*," *Drama Survey* 7 (1968–1969): 56.

34. In Oleg Kennedy's words, "The uncertainty in the plays mirrors life." *The New British Drama: Fourteen Playwrights Since Osborne and Pinter* (New York: Taplinger, 1977), p. 152.

35. Hersh Zeifman, in "Comedy of Ambush: Tom Stoppard's *The Real Thing*," *Modern Drama* 26 (1983), observes that in Stoppard "just when we think we have latched on to 'the real thing,' the reality alters" (p. 141). Jill Levenson reads the play differently, finding the disappearance of the two "inconsequential." "Views from a Revolving Door: Tom Stoppard's Canon to Date," *Queen's Quarterly* 78 (1971): 438.

36. C. W. E. Bigsby describes the audience as "collaborating in the establishment of contingent truths," in *Tom Stoppard* (Burt Mills: Longman, 1979), pp. 13–14.

37. Ruby Cohn speaks of the two, in both Shakespeare and Stoppard, as "Everymen." *Modern Shakespeare Offshoots* (Princeton: Princeton University Press, 1976), p. 216.

38. Along with Gianakaris, "Absurdism Altered," p. 57, Leslee Lenoff finds the two developing some self-awareness as the play ends, in "Life Within Limits: Stoppard on the HMS *Hamlet*," *Arizona Quarterly* 38 (1982): 45–61.

39. In *Fields of Play in Modern Drama* (Princeton: Princeton University Press, 1977), Thomas Whitaker comments that in Stoppard life is art, "and we are its impotent masters" (p. 15).

40. I am obviously miles apart from Felicia Hardison Londre who concludes, simply, that "the play pleases its audiences primarily because it is funny." *Tom Stoppard* (New York: Frederick Ungar, 1981), p. 44.

41. Whitaker, *Stoppard*, p. 63; and I find especially appealing his remarks on the play's "celebration of theatrical presence."

42. Keyssar-Franke, "The Strategy," p. 85.

43. Again, I am close here to the readings, particularly, of Gianakaris, "Absurdism Altered," p. 57, and Lenoff, "Life Within Limits," pp. 45–61. John M. Perlette addresses the issue of whether the theater can successfully enact death, in his fine essay "Theatre at the Limit: *Rosencrantz and Guildenstern Are Dead*," *Modern Drama* 28 (1985): 659–69.

44. Again, the impressive argument of Whitaker, in *Stoppard*, pp. 63–67, especially.

45. On the parallels between Stoppard and Shakespeare see Walter D. Asmus, "*Rosencrantz and Guildenstern Are Dead*," *Shakespeare-Jahrbuch* (Heidelberg) 106 (1970): 118–31.

46. I borrow and then adjust slightly the phrases here of Egan, in "Light," pp. 68–69. See also Dennis Huston's insightful essay, "'Misreading' *Hamlet:* Problems of Perspective in *Rosencrantz and Guildenstern Are Dead*," in *Tom Stoppard: A Casebook*, ed. John Harty (New York: Garland Publishing, 1988), pp. 47–66.

Chapter 6. Williams, *A Streetcar Named Desire*

1. In "Tennessee Williams Enters Dragon Country," *Modern Drama* 16 (1973): 61–67, Albert E. Kalson observes that perhaps Williams has gone too far "into the solitary country of the sterile, the lost and unloved" (p. 67). My text for *Streetcar* is that published by New Directions (New York, 1980).

I will be arguing for an open-ended *Streetcar,* a play asking us to assess the conflicting claims of Stanley and Blanche, without passing judgment. Other critics have felt more confident in making such judgments. Blanche has been seen, variously, as the heroine, a portrait of the artist, a guilt-ridden "gay," a woman torn between her cultured and primitive instincts, a schizophrenic alternating between private illusions and public reality, an intruder threatening the healthy physicality of Stanley's house, and a villain. Depending on the interpretation of Blanche, Stanley is the fated revenger of her homosexual husband, an American primitive defending his home, the half of Blanche that she desires yet cannot sustain, a brute, and a villain whose narrow mentality destroys what it cannot comprehend. See Esther Merle Jackson, *The Broken World of Tennessee Williams* (Madison: University of Wisconsin Press, 1965), pp. 49, 58, 81; Joseph N. Riddel, "*A Streetcar Named Desire*—Nietzsche Descending," *Modern Drama* 5 (1963): 421–39; J. L. Styan, *The Dark Comedy: The Development of Modern Comic Tragedy* (Cambridge: At the University Press, 1968), pp. 214–16; Alan Ehrlich, "*A Streetcar Named Desire* and *Desire Under the Elms,*" in *Tennessee Williams: A Tribute,* ed. Jac Tharpe (Jackson: Mississippi University Press, 1977), pp. 126–36; Arthur Ganz, "Tennessee Williams: Desperate Morality," in *Tennessee Williams: A Collection of Critical Essays,* ed. Stephen S. Stanton (Englewood Cliffs, N.J.: Prentice-Hall, 1977), pp. 123–37. Others argue that Blanche is a surrogate for her playwright, or, conversely, that the stage set demonstrates Williams's partiality to Stanley: see Gerald M. Berkowitz, "Williams' 'Other Places'—A Theatrical Metaphor in the Plays," in Tharpe, *Tribute,* pp. 712–19; Nancy M. Tischler, "The Distorted Mirror: Tennessee Williams' Self-Portraits," *Mississippi Quarterly* 25 (1972): 389–403; Constance Drake, "Blanche Dubois: A Re-evaluation," *Theater Annual* 24 (1969): 58–69. Robert Heilman, however, warns against finding an "unqualified monopathic structure" in Williams's characterization, in *The Iceman, the Arsonist, and the Troubled Agent: Tragedy and Melodrama on the Modern Stage* (Seattle: University of Washington Press, 1973), p. 118.

Thematic studies cast a similarly wide net: Williams himself is said to be imprisoned by his perverse view; the play is a tragicomedy where life goes on at an absurd level; the playwright offers a secular world searching in vain for a god or some ordering scheme; the clash is between idealism and vitalism, or harsh reality and the ego, or poetry and the truth. See Harry Taylor, "The Dilemma of Tennessee Williams," *Masses and Mainstream* 1 (1948): 51–55; John M. Roderick, "From 'Tarantula Arms' to 'Della Robbia Blue': The Tennessee Williams Tragicomic Transit Authority," in Tharpe, *Tribute,* pp. 116–25; Francis L. Kunkle, "Tennessee Williams: God, Sex, and Death," in *Passion and the Passion* (Philadelphia, Pa.: Westminister Press, 1975), pp. 99–107; Thomas P. Adler, "The Search for God in the Plays of Tennessee Williams," *Renascence* 26 (1973): 48–56; Roger Asselineau, *The Transcendentalist Constant in American Literature* (New York: New York University Press, 1980), pp. 153–62; Mary A. Corrigan, "Realism and Theatricalism in *A Streetcar Named Desire,*" *Modern Drama* 19 (1976): 385–96; Foster Hirsch, *A Portrait of the Artist: The Plays of Tennessee Williams* (Port Washington, N.Y.: Kennikat Press, 1979), pp. 30–34.

I should also mention here accounts of the play's stage history, particularly those of: Signi Falk, *Tennessee Williams* (Boston: Twayne Publishers, 1978), pp. 55–71; and Felicia H. Londre, *Tennessee Williams* (New York: Frederick Ungar, 1979). And, of course, Elia Kazan's "Notebook for *A Streetcar Named Desire*" in *Directors on Directing: A Source Book for Modern Theater,* ed. Toby Cole and Helen Krich Chinoy (Indianapolis: Bobbs-Merrill, 1963), pp. 364–79. Britton J. Harwood offers a negative assessment of the play's theatrical dimension in "Tragedy as Habit: *A Streetcar Named Desire,*" in Tharpe, *Tribute,* pp. 104–15. I have been particularly impressed by the more positive reading of Norman Berlin, in "Complementarity in *A Streetcar Named Desire*," in Tharpe, *Tribute*, pp. 97–103.

2. Ehrlich in "Study of Dramatic Space" calls Blanche the intruder entering this constricted environment (p. 133).

3. See the clever argument by John J. Mood that the six blocks from Cemetaries to Elysian Fields corresponds to the climactic scene 6 where Blanche experiences her one moment of tenderness with Mitch, in "The Structure of *A Streetcar Named Desire*," *Ball State University Forum* 14 (1973): 9–10.

4. See n. 25.

5. Henry Popkin speaks of Stanley's world as being presided over by an Adonis, who in the course of the play meets Blanche, or the Gargoyle, in "The Plays of Tennessee Williams," *Tulane Drama Review* 4 (1960): 45.

6. For Maurice Yacowar this provincial world is at one with "the compression of the play." *Tennessee Williams and Film* (New York: Frederick Ungar, 1977), p. 17.

7. See commentary on such shifts in the audience's sympathies in Hirsch, *Portrait*, p. 34.

8. Leonard Quirino speaks of Blanche's timeless world as taking precedence over the realistic nature of Stanley's, in "The Cards Indicate a Voyage on *A Streetcar Named Desire*," in Tharpe, *Tribute*, pp. 77–96. Thomas E. Porter argues that Stanley's is "a society of the actual, the present," in *Myth and the Modern American Drama* (Detroit: Wayne State University Press, 1969), p. 165.

9. Asselineau, *Transcendentalist Constant*, p. 160.

10. In "God, Sex, and Death," Kunkle has a very negative view of the playwright's theological dimensions: "Williams's inability to grasp the possibility of the world being grounded in a transcendent Presence and his reliance on secular values as a source of moral action and religious belief probably explain, in part at least, why his literature is a literature of exhausted romanticism" (p. 103).

11. Donald P. Costello calls this artistic vision a "path to escape," in "Tennessee Williams' Fugitive Kind," *Modern Drama* 15 (1972): 39.

12. Dan Vogel finds Blanche building "bulwarks" against truth and reality, in *The Three Masks of American Tragedy* (Baton Rouge: Louisiana State University Press, 1974), p. 87. On her artistry see also Yacowar, *Williams and Film*, p. 19; and Hirsch, *Portrait*, p. 32.

13. Costello contrasts the fugitive and earth-bound in the characters of Blanche and Stanley, in "Fugitive Kind," p. 36.

14. On Blanche's role playing see Ruby Cohn, "The Garrulous Grotesques of Tennessee Williams," in *Critical Essays*, ed. Stanton, pp. 45–60.

15. See Williams's comments on the origin of this line in *Where I Live: Selected Essays*, ed. Christine R. Day and Bob Woods (New York: New Directions, 1978), p. 124.

16. Riddel, "Nietzsche Descending," p. 430.

17. Harwood, "Habit," pp. 114–15.

18. See Gene D. Phillips, *The Films of Tennessee Williams* (Philadelphia: Arts Alliance Press, 1979), p. 75; and Edward Murray, *The Cinematic Imagination: Writers and the Motion Pictures* (New York: Frederick Ungar, 1972), p. 58.

19. Vogel, *Three Masks*, p. 87.

20. On the sources of this line see the very fine article by Vivienne Dickson, "*A Streetcar Named Desire:* Its Development through the Manuscripts," in Tharpe, *Tribute*, p. 171.

21. Quirino speaks of Blanche's exit with the Doctor as her second voyage, in "Cards Indicate," in Tharpe, *Tribute*, p. 96. Henry Schivey argues that at the end she

experiences a "heroic transcendence," alongside her "tragic destruction," in "Madonna at the Poker Night: Pictorial Elements in Tennessee Williams' *A Streetcar Named Desire*," in *From Cooper to Philip Roth: Essays on American Literature*, ed. J. Bakker and D. R. M. Wilkinson (Amsterdam: Rodopi, 1980), p. 75.

22. This is the view of Joseph Golden in *The Death of Tinker Bell: The American Theatre in the 20th Century* (Syracuse, N.Y.: Syracuse University Press, 1967), p. 128.

23. W. David Sievers observes that "Although Blanche closes her mind to any awareness as she escapes to psychosis, the insight happens to the audience," in *Freud on Broadway: A History of Psychoanalysis and the American Drama* (New York: Heritage House, 1955), p. 380.

24. Edward A. Napieralski suggests that the playwright "uses the drama itself to intensify the illusion of virtual life," in "Tennessee Williams' *The Glass Menagerie:* The Dramatic Metaphor," *Southern Quarterly* 16 (1977): 12. And see the similar argument by Robert Skloot in "Submitting Self to Flame: The Artist's Quest in Tennessee Williams, 1934–1954," *Educational Theater Journal* 25 (1973): 200. There is a good discussion of the productive use of theatrical conventions in Williams and elsewhere in Harvey M. Powers, Jr., "Theatrical Conventions: The Conditions of Acceptability," *Bucknell Review* 7 (1957): 20–26.

25. Roderick calls this ambivalence the play's "keynote," in "Tragicomic Transit," p. 122. See also Robert Emmet Jones, "Sexual Roles in the Works of Tennessee Williams," in Tharpe, *Tribute*, pp. 545–57; and Nancy M. Tischler, *Tennessee Williams: Rebellious Puritan* (New York: Citadel Press, 1961). And see Ellen Dowling and Nancy Pride, "Three Approaches to Directing *A Streetcar Named Desire*," *Tennessee Williams Newsletter* 2 (1980): 16–20, where they offer several ways of dealing with the play's "delicate balance of ambiguity" (p. 10).

26. Styan, *Dark Comedy*, p. 216.

27. Thomas P. Adler, "Theatre Looking at Theatre: A Self-image of the Post World War II American Drama, *Claudel Studies* 9 (1982): 31–42.

28. After I had written the first draft of this chapter, I came upon a fine article by Kathleen Hulley, "The Fate of the Symbolic in *A Streetcar Named Desire*," in *Drama and Symbolism, Themes in Drama* 4 (Cambridge: At the University Press, 1981), pp. 89–99. Hulley has a series of keen observations about the play's "system of signs" (p. 88), how Blanche tries to rearrange Stanley's "scene" (p. 94), the conflict between law (Stanley) and desire (Blanche), and how the reality of the set is undercut by its transparency and by Blanche's presence. Most interesting is Hulley's argument that at the end Stella is the onstage audience (p. 97) forced to take a position (by sending her sister to the asylum) in a play that has until then offered not a balance but a "*discourse*" on reality and illusion (p. 94). I should also mention an equally impressive essay by Anca Vlasopolos, "Authorizing History: Victimization in *A Streetcar Named Desire*," *Theatre Journal* 38 (1986): 322–38. In a reading that has many parallels with the Hulley essay, Vlasopolos *rescues* the play, I think, from the pervasive critical focus on its ethical or generic aspects, concentrating, instead, on the antithetical claims made on the audience by Blanche and Stanley, as the "control" of the play moves from one character to the other. In a limited sense, Stanley "wins" in what Vlasopolos calls their "struggle over history," but the victory represents force only, male dominance. As we participate in Blanche's imaginative "mental life," Williams asks us, in effect, to assess two claims, in a "problem play" designed "to disquiet us so that perhaps we might hear, if not speak for, those whom history has silenced" (p. 338).

Chapter 7. Beckett, *Nacht und Träume, Catastrophe, What Where,* and *Quad*

1. Since the first three sections of this chapter represent a distillation of the comments in my *Beckett's Theaters: Interpretations for Performance* (Lewisburg, Pa.: Bucknell University Press, 1984), I do not give page references for citations from Beckett's various plays, but, instead, refer the reader to the book itself. My text for these four plays is *The Collected Shorter Plays of Samuel Beckett*, published by Grove Press (New York, 1984).

2. Norman Holland, "Afterword," *Shakespeare and the Triple Play: From Study to Stage to Classroom,* ed. Sidney Homan (Lewisburg, Pa.: Bucknell University Press, 1988), p. 227.

3. Sidney Homan, *Shakespeare's Theater of Presence: Language, Spectacle, and the Audience* (Lewisburg, Pa.: Bucknell University Press, 1986).

4. Barbara S. Becket and Charles R. Lyons, "Directing/Acting Beckett," *Comparative Drama* 19 (1985–1986): 289–304.

5. Homan, *Beckett's Theaters,* pp. 198–200.

6. Enoch Brater, "Towards a Poetics of Television Technology: Beckett's *Nacht und Träume* and *Quad,*" *Modern Drama* 28 (1985): 48–51. I am also indebted to Brater's *Beyond Minimalism: Beckett's Late Style in the Theater* (New York: Oxford University Press, 1987), which I read in manuscript while writing the present study.

7. Antonio Libera, "Beckett's *Catastrophe,*" *Modern Drama* 28 (1985): 341–47.

8. Martha Fehsenfeld, "Beckett's Late Work: An Appraisal," *Modern Drama* 25 (1982): 361.

9. Brater, "Television Technology," pp. 51–54.

10. S. E. Gontarski, "Review: *Quad I* and *II:* Beckett's Sinister Mime(s)," *Journal of Beckett Studies* 9 (1984): 137–38.

11. Samuel Beckett, quoted in Brater, "Television Technology," p. 52.

Afterword. "My" Theater and Its Audiences

1. I say "our" production since my schedule was so tight during my summer in China that I did not have enough rehearsal time to see the actors through opening night. Rather, I got them into rehearsals, outlined my concept of the production for the directors of the two companies, and, once I returned to the United States, sent them detailed director's notes. I discuss my involvement in this production in much greater detail in "*The Merry Wives of Windsor* in the People's Republic of China: A Director's Notebook," in my edition of *Shakespeare and the Triple Play,* pp. 116–37.

2. Norman Holland, "Afterwood," in *Shakespeare and the Triple Play: From Study to Stage to Classroom,* ed. Sidney Homan (Lewisburg, Pa.: Bucknell University Press, 1987), p. 227.

3. Philip C. McGuire, "Intention, Options, and Greatness: An Example from *A Midsummer Night's Dream,*" in Homan, *Triple Play,* p. 183.

4. William Webbe, *Of English Poesie,* in *Elizabethan Critical Essays,* ed. G. G. Smith (London: Oxford University Press, 1904), 1: p. 234.

Select Bibliography

Abel, Lionel. "Metatheatre." *Partisan Review* 27 (1960): 324–30.

Adler, Thomas P. "The Mirror as Stage Prop in Modern Drama." *Comparative Drama* 14 (1980): 355–73.

———. "The Search for God in the Plays of Tennessee Williams." *Renascence* 26 (1973): 48–56.

———. "Theater Looking at Theater: A Self-Image of the Post World War II American Drama." *Claudel Studies* 9 (1982): 31–42.

Almansi, Guido, and Simon Henderson. *Harold Pinter.* London: Methuen, 1983.

Anderson, Michael. *Anger and Detachment: A Study of Arden, Osborne, and Pinter.* London: Pitman, 1976.

Asmus, Walter D. "*Rosencrantz and Guildenstern Are Dead.*" *Shakespeare-Jahrbuch* 106 (1970): 118–31.

Asselineau, Roger. *The Transcendentalist Constant in American Literature.* New York: New York University Press, 1980.

Babula, William. "The Play-Life Metaphor in Shakespeare and Stoppard," *Modern Drama* 15 (1972): 279–81.

Barish, Jonas A. *The Antitheatrical Prejudice.* Berkeley: University of California Press, 1981.

———. "The Veritable Saint Genet." *Wisconsin Studies in Comparative Literature* 6 (1965): 267–85.

Becket, Barbara S., and Charles R. Lyons. "Directing/Acting Beckett." *Comparative Drama* 19 (1985–86): 289–304.

Beckett, Samuel. *The Collected Shorter Plays of Samuel Beckett.* New York: Grove Press, 1984.

Benjamin, Walter. *Understanding Brecht.* London: NLB, 1977.

Bentley, Eric. *The Brecht Commentaries.* New York: Grove Press, 1981.

Berkowitz, Gerald M. "Williams' 'Other Places'—A Theatrical Metaphor in the Plays." In *Tennessee Williams: A Tribute,* edited by Jac Tharpe. Jackson: Mississippi University Press, 1977.

Berlin, Norman. "Complementarity in *A Streetcar Named Desire.*" In *Tennessee Williams: A Tribute,* edited by Jac Tharpe. Jackson: Mississippi University Press, 1977.

Bermel, Albert. *Contradictory Characters: An Interpretation of the Modern Theater.* New York: E. P. Dutton, 1973.

———. "Ionesco: Anything But Absurd." *Twentieth Century Literature* 21 (1975): 411–20.

Bigsby, C. W. E. *Tom Stoppard.* Burt Mills: Longman, 1979.

Bonnefoy, Claude. *Conversations with Eugene Ionesco,* translated by Jan Dawson. New York: Holt, Rhinehart and Winston, 1966.

Braunmuller, A. R. "Harold Pinter: The Metamorphosis of Memory." In *Essays on Contemporary British Drama*, edited by Hedwig Block and Albert Wertheim. Munich: Max Hueber, 1981.

Brecht, Bertolt. *Galileo*, translated by Charles Laughton, edited by Eric Bentley. New York: Grove Press, 1966.

Brown, John Russell. *Theatre Language: A Study of Arden, Osborne, Pinter, and Wesker*. New York: Taplinger, 1972.

Brustein, Robert. *The Theater of Revolt: An Approach to Modern Drama*. New York: Little, Brown, 1964.

Budel, Oscar. "Contemporary Theater and Aesthetic Distance." In *Brecht: A Collection of Critical Essays*, edited by Peter Demetz. Englewood Cliffs, N.J.: Prentice-Hall, 1985.

Cahn, Victor L. *Beyond Absurdity: The Plays of Tom Stoppard*. Rutherford, N.J.: Farleigh Dickinson University Press, 1979.

Calderwood, James L. *To Be and Not To Be: Negation and Metadrama in "Hamlet"*. New York: Columbia University Press, 1983.

Carpenter, Charles A. "'What Have I Seen, the Scum or the Essence?': Symbolic Fallout in Pinter's *The Birthday Party*." *Modern Drama* 17 (1974): 389–402.

Cetta, Lewis T. *Profane Play, Ritual, and Jean Genet*. University: University of Alabama Press, 1973.

Champigny, Robert. "Designations and Gestures in *The Chairs*." In *The Two Faces of Ionesco*, edited by Rosette C. Lamonte and Melvin J. Friedman. Troy, N.Y.: Whiston Publishing, 1978.

Chiaromonte, Nicola. *The Worm of Consciousness and Other Essays*, edited by Mary Miriam. New York: Harcourt Brace Jovanovich, 1976.

Cismaru, Alfred. "Ionesco on His Theater: L'Homme en question." *Claudel Studies* 9 (1982): 47–52.

———. "Ionesco's *L'Homme aux Valises:* The Absurdist Turned Classic." *French Review* 50 (1977): 732–36.

———. "Ionesco's Rhino Pronouncements." *Antigonish Review* 40 (1980): 87–94.

Coe, Richard N. *Eugene Ionesco*. New York: Grove Press, 1961.

———. "On Being Very, *Very* Surprised: Eugene Ionesco and the Vision of Childhood." In *The Dream and the Play: Ionesco's Theatrical Quest*, edited by Moshe Lazar. Malibu, Calif.: Undena, 1982.

———. *The Vision of Jean Genet*. London: Peter Owen, 1968.

Cohn, Ruby. *Currents in Contemporary Drama*. Bloomington: Indiana University Press, 1969.

———. "The Garrulous Grotesques of Tennessee Williams." In *Tennessee Williams: A Collection of Critical Essays*, edited by Stephen S. Stanton. Englewood Cliffs, N.J.: Prentice-Hall, 1977.

———. *Modern Shakespeare Offshoots*. Princeton, N.J.: Princeton University Press, 1976.

Colby, Douglas. *As the Curtain Rises: On Contemporary British Drama*. Rutherford, N.J.: Fairleigh Dickinson University Press, 1978.

Cook, Bruce. *Brecht in Exile*. New York: Holt, Rinehart and Winston, 1982.

Corballis, Richard. "Extending the Audience: The Structure of *Rosencrantz and Guildenstern Are Dead*." *Ariel* 11 (1980): 65–79.

Cordero, Anne D. "Waiting, an Ambivalent Mood, in Beckett and Ionesco." *Studies in the Twentieth Century* 13 (1974): 51–63.

Costello, Doanld P. "Tennessee Williams' Fugitive Kind." *Modern Drama* 15 (1972): 26–43.

Cruickshank, John. "Jean Genet: The Aesthetics of Crime." *Critical Quarterly* 6 (1964): 202–10.

Curtis, Jerry L. "The World Is a Stage: Sartre versus Genet." *Modern Drama* 17 (1974): 33–41.

Dean, Joan Fitspatrick. *Tom Stoppard: Comedy as a Moral Matrix*. Columbia: University of Missouri Press, 1981.

Diamond, Elin. *Pinter's Comic Play*. Lewisburg, Pa: Bucknell University Press, 1985.

Dickson, Keith A. *Toward Utopia: A Study of Brecht*. Oxford: Clarendon Press, 1978.

Dickson, Vivienne. "*A Streetcar Named Desire:* Its Development through the Manuscripts." In *Tennessee Williams: A Tribute*, edited by Jac Tharpe. Jackson: Mississippi University Press, 1977.

Dobrez, L. A. C. "The Image of the Revolutionary: Sartrean Relationships in the Work of Jean Genet." *Southern Review* 11 (1978): 51–71.

Doubrovsky, J. S. "Ionesco and the Comedy of Absurdity." *Yale French Studies* 23 (1959): 3–10.

Drake, Constance. "Blanche Dubois: A Re-evaluation. *Theater Annual* 24 (1969): 58–69.

Driver, Tom F. *Jean Genet*. New York: Columbia University Press, 1966.

———. *Romantic Quest and Modern Query: A History of the Modern Theater*. New York: Delacorte Press, 1970.

Duckworth, Colin. *Angels of Darkness: Dramatic Effect in Samuel Beckett, with Special Reference to Eugene Ionesco*. London: George Allen and Unwin, 1972.

Dukore, Bernard. *Harold Pinter*. New York: Grove Press, 1982.

———. *Money and Politics in Ibsen, Shaw, and Brecht*. Columbia: University of Missouri Press, 1980.

Eastman, Richard M. "Experiment and Vision in Ionesco's Plays." *Modern Drama* 4 (1961): 3–19.

Egan, Robert. "A thin beam of light: The Purpose of Playing in *Rosencrantz and Guildenstern Are Dead*." *Theater Journal* 31 (1979): 59–69.

Ehrlich, Alan. "A Streetcar Named Desire Under the Elms: A Study of Dramatic Space in *A Streetcar Named Desire* and *Desire Under the Elms*." In *Tennessee Williams: A Tribute*, edited by Jac Tharpe. Jackson: Mississippi University Press, 1977.

Ehrmann, Jacques, "Genet's Dramatic Metamorphosis: From Appearance to Freedom." *Yale French Studies* 29 (1962): 33–42.

Elsom, John. "Genet and the Sadistic Society." *The London Magazine* 3 (1963): 61–67.

Epstein, Leslie. "Beyond the Baroque: the Role of the Audience in the Modern Theater." *Triquarterly* 12 (1968): 213–34.

Esslin, Martin. *Brecht: The Man and His Work*. Garden City, N.J.: Doubleday, 1960.

———. "Ionesco and the Creative Dilemma." *Tulane Drama Review 7 (1963): 169–79.*

———. *Pinter: A Study of His Plays*. New York: W. W. Norton and Company, 1976.

Ewen, Frederic. *Bertolt Brecht: His Life, His Art and His Times*. New York: Citadel Press, 1967.

Falk, Signi. *Tennessee Williams*. Boston: Twayne Publishers, 1978.

Farish, Gillan. "Into the Looking-Glass Bowl: An Instance of Grateful Terror." *University of Windsor Review* 10 (1975): 14–29.

Feal, Gisela. "*Le Balcon* de Genet ou le Culte Matriarchal, une Interpretation Mythique." *French Review* (1948): 897–907.

Fehn, Ann Clark. "Vision and Blindness in Brecht's *Leben Des Galilei*." *Germanic Review* 53 (1978): 27–34.

Fehsenfeld, Martha. "Beckett's Late Work: An Appraisal." *Modern Drama* 25 (1982): 361.

Fischer, Alexander. "The Absurd Professor in the Theater of the Absurd." *Modern Drama* 21 (1978): 137–52.

Fuegi, John. *The Essential Brecht*. Los Angeles: Hennessey and Ingalls, 1972.

Gabbard, Lucina Paquet. *The Dream Structure of Pinter's Plays*. East Rutherford, N.J.: Fairleigh Dickinson University Press, 1976.

———. *The Stoppard Plays*. Troy, N.Y.: Whiston Publishing, 1982.

Ganz, Arthur. "Introduction" to *Pinter: A Collection of Critical Essays*. Englewood Cliffs, N.J.: Prentice-Hall, 1972.

———. "Tennessee Williams: Desperate Morality." In *Tennessee Williams: A Collection of Critical Essays*, edited by Stephen S. Stanton. Englewood Cliffs, N.J.: Prentice-Hall, 1977.

Genet, Jean. *The Balcony*, translated by Bernard Frechtman. New York: Grove Press, 1966.

———. *The Blacks*, translated by Bernard Frechtman. New York: Grove Press, 1960.

———. *The Maids and Deathwatch*, translated by Bernard Frechtman. New York: Grove Press, 1954.

———. *Reflections on the Theater and Other Writings*, translated by Richard Sever. London: Faber and Faber, 1972.

———. *The Screens*, translated by Bernard Frechtman. New York: Grove Press, 1962.

Gianakaris, C. J. "Absurdism *Altered: Rosencrantz and Guildenstern Are Dead*." *Drama Survey* 7 (1968–69): 32–58.

Gitzen, Julian. "Tom Stoppard: Chaos in Perspective." *Southern Humanities Review* 10 (1976): 143–52.

Golden, Joseph. *The Death of Tinker Bell: The American Theater in the 20th Century.* Syracuse: Syracuse University Press, 1967.

Goldman, Lucien. "The Theater of Jean Genet: A Sociological Study," translated by Pat Dreyfus, *The Drama Review* 38 (1968): 51–61.

Gontarski, S. E. "Review: *Quad I* and *II:* Beckett's Sinister Mime(s)." *Journal of Beckett Studies* 9 (1984): 137–38.

Gray, Ronald. *Brecht the Dramatist*. Cambridge: At the University Press, 1978.

Grossvogel, David I. *The Blasphemers: The Theater of Brecht, Ionesco, Beckett, Genet.* Ithaca: Cornell University Press, 1962.

Gruber, William E. "Wheels Within Wheels, Etcetera: Artistic Design in *Rosencrantz and Guildenstern Are Dead*." *Comparative Drama* 15 (1981–82): 291–309.

Guicharnaud, Jacques, with Jane Beckleman. *Modern French Theater—Giraudoux to Beckett*. New Haven: Yale University Press, 1961.

Harwood, Britton J. "Tragedy as Habit: *A Streetcar Named Desire*." In *Tennessee Williams: A Tribute*, edited by Jac Tharpe. Jackson: Mississippi University Press, 1977.

Hayman, Ronald, *Artaud and After*. London: Cambridge University Press, 1977.

———. *Eugene Ionesco*. New York: Frederick Ungar, 1976.

Heilman, Robert. *The Iceman, the Arsonist, and the Troubled Agent: Tragedy and Melodrama on the Modern Stage*. Seattle: University of Washington Press, 1973.

Hiley, Jim. *Theatre at Work: The Story of the National Theatre's Production of Brecht's "Galileo."* London: Routledge and Kegan Paul, 1981.

Hirsch, Foster. *A Portrait of the Artist: The Plays of Tennessee Williams*. Port Washington, N.Y.: Kennikat Press, 1979.

Holland, Norman. "Afterward," *Shakespeare and the Triple Play: From Study to Stage to Classroom*, edited by Sidney Homan. Lewisburg, Pa.: Bucknell University Press, 1988.

Hollis, James R. *Harold Pinter: The Poetics of Silence*. Carbondale: Southern Illinois University Press, 1970.

Homan, Sidney. *Beckett's Theaters: Interpretations for Performance*. Lewisburg, Pa.: Bucknell University Press, 1984.

———. *Shakespeare's Theater of Presence: Language, Spectacle, and the Audience*. Lewisburg, Pa.: Bucknell University Press, 1986.

———. *When the Theatre Turns to Itself: The Aesthetic Metaphor in Shakespeare*. Lewisburg, Pa.: Bucknell University Press, 1981.

Howell, Christina, *Sartre's Theory of Literature*. London: Modern Humanities Research Association, 1979.

Hulley, Kathleen. "The Fate of the Symbolic in *A Streetcar Named Desire*." In *Drama and Symbolism, Themes in Drama*. Cambridge: At the University Press, 1981.

Hunter, Jim. *Tom Stoppard's Plays*. New York: Grove Press, 1982.

Huston, J. Dennis. "'Misreading' *Hamlet:* Problems of Perspective in *Rosencrantz and Guildenstern Are Dead*." in *Tom Stoppard: a Casebook*, edited by John Harty. New York: Garland Publishing, 1988.

Innes, Christopher. *Holy Theater: Ritual and the Avant Garde*. Cambridge: At the University Press, 1981.

Ionesco, Eugene. *Four Plays by Eugene Ionesco*, translated by Donald M. Allen. New York: Grove Press, 1958.

———. *A Hell of a Mess*, translated by Helen Gray Bishop. New York: Grove Press, 1975.

———. *Notes and Counter Notes: Writings on the Theater*. New York: Grove Press, 1971.

———. *Present/Past/Past/Present*, translated by Helen R. Lane. New York: Grove Press, 1971.

Jackson, Esther Merle. *The Broken World of Tennessee Williams*. Madison: University of Wisconsin Press, 1965.

Jacobsen, Josephine, and William R. Mueller. *Ionesco and Genet: Playwrights of Silence*. New York: Hill and Wang, 1981.

Jacquart, Emmanuel. "Interview/Eugene Ionesco." *Diacritics* 3 (1973): 47.

James, Clive. "Count Zero Splits the Infinite: Tom Stoppard's Plays." *Encounter* 45 (1975): 68–75.

Jeffrey, David K. "Genet and Gelber: Studies in Addiction." *Modern Drama* 11 (1968): 151–56.

Jones, Robert Emmet. "Sexual Roles in the Works of Tennessee Williams." In *Tennessee Williams: A Tribute*, edited by Jac Tharpe. Jackson: Mississippi University Press, 1977.

Kalson, Albert E. "Tennessee Williams Enters Dragon Country." *Modern Drama* 16 (1973): 61–67.

Kaufman, Michael W. "Actions That a Man Might Play: Pinter's *The Birthday Party*." *Modern Drama* 16 (1973): 167–78.

Kazan, Elia. "Notebook for *A Streetcar Named Desire*." In *Directors on Directing: A Source Book for Modern Theater*, edited by Toby Cole and Helen Krich Chinoy. Indianapolis: Bobbs-Merrill Company, 1963.

Kennedy, Andrew K. *Dramatic Dialogue: The Dialogue of Personal Encounter*. Cambridge: At the University Press, 1983.

Kennedy, Oleg. *The New British Drama: Fourteen Playwrights Since Osborne and Pinter*. New York: Taplinger, 1977.

Keyssar-Franke, Helene. "The Strategy of *Rosencrantz and Guildenstern Are Dead*." *Educational Theater Journal* 27 (1975): 85–97.

Kirby, E. T. "The Paranoid Pseudo-Community in Pinter's *The Birthday Party*." *Educational Theater Journal* 30 (1978): 157–64.

Kreps, Barbara. "Time and Harold Pinter's Possible Realities: Art as Life, and Vice Versa." *Modern Drama* 22 (1979): 47–60.

Krieger, Murray. *A Window to Criticism: Shakespeare's Sonnets and Modern Poetics*. Princeton: Princeton University Press, 1964.

Kunkle, Francis L. "Tennessee Williams: God, Sex, and Death." In *Passion and the Passion*. Philadelphia: Westminster Press, 1975.

Lamont, Rosette. "The Metaphysical Farce: Beckett and Ionesco." *French Review* 32 (1959): 319–28.

Lazar, Moshe. "The Psychodramatic Stage: Ionesco and His Doubles." In *The Dream and the Play: Ionesco's Theatrical Quest*, edited by Moshe Lazar. Malibu, Calif.: Undena, 1982.

Lenoff, Leslee. "Life Within Limits: Stoppard on the HMS *Hamlet*." *Arizona Quarterly* 38 (1982): 45–61.

Levenson, Jill L. "*Hamlet* Andante/*Hamlet* Allegro: Tom Stoppard's Two Versions." *Shakespeare Survey* 36 (1983): 21–28.

———. "Views from a Revolving Door: Tom Stoppard's Canon to Date." *Queen's Quarterly* 78 (1971): 431–42.

Levy, Ralph. *Brecht as Thinker: Studies in Literary Marxism and Existentialism*. Normal, Ill.: Applied Literature Press, 1979.

Lewis, Allan. *Ionesco*. New York: Twayne Publishers, 1972.

Libera, Antonio. "Beckett's *Catastrophe*." *Modern Drama* 28 (1985): 341–47.

Londre, Felicia Hardison. *Tennessee Williams*. New York: Frederick Ungar, 1979.

———. *Tom Stoppard*. New York: Frederick Ungar, 1981.

Lyon, James K. *Bertolt Brecht's American Cicerone*. Bonn: Bouvier, 1978.

Lyons, Charles R. *Bertolt Brecht: The Despair and the Polemic*. Carbondale: Southern Illinois University Press, 1968.

———. "*The Life of Galileo:* The Focus of Ambiguity in the Villain Hero." *Germanic Review* 41 (1966): 57–71.

Mares, F. H. "Jean Genet's *The Balcony*." *Meanjin* 24 (1965): 354–56.

Markus, Thomas B. "The Psychological Universe of Jean Genet." *Drama Survey* 3 (1964): 386–92.

Marowitz, Charles. "The Revenge of Jean Genet." *Encore* 33 (1961): 17–24.

McGraft, John. *A Good Night Out: Popular Theater, Audience, Class and Form*. Bonn: Bouvier, 1978.

McGuire, Philip C. "Intention, Options, and Greatness: An Example from *A Midsummer Night's Dream*." In *Shakespeare and the Triple Play: From Study to Stage to Classroom,* edited by Sidney Homan. Lewisburg, Pa.: Bucknell University Press, 1988.

McLean, Sammy K. *The Bankelsang and the Work of Bertolt Brecht*. The Hague: Mouton, 1972.

McMahon, Joseph H. *The Imagination of Jean Genet*. New Haven: Yale University Press, 1963.

Melcher, Edith. "The Pirandellism of Jean Genet." *French Review* 36 (1962): 32–36.

Mendelson, David. "Science and Fiction in Ionesco's 'Experimental' Theater." In *Ionesco: A Collection of Critical Essays,* edited by Rosette C. Lament. Englewood Cliffs, N.J.: Prentice-Hall, 1973.

Milfull, John. *From Baal to Keuner: The "Second Optimism" of Bertolt Brecht*. Bern: Lang, 1974.

Mood, John J. "The Structure of *A Streetcar Named Desire*." *Ball State University Forum* 14 (1973): 9–10.

Needle, Jan R., and Peter Thompson. *Brecht*. Chicago: University of Chicago Press, 1981.

Nelson, Benjamin. "*The Balcony* and Parisian Existentialism." *Tulane Drama Review* 7 (1963): 61–67.

Nugent, Robert. "Sculpture into Drama: Giacometti's Influence on Benet." *Drama Survey* 3 (1964): 378–85.

Orenstein, Gloria Feman. *The Theater of the Marvelous: Surrealism and the Contemporary Stage*. New York: New York University Press, 1975.

Parker, R. B. "The Theory and the Theater of the Absurd." *Queen's Quarterly* 73 (1966): 421–41.

Perlette, John M. "Theater at the Limit: *Rosencrantz and Guildenstern Are Dead*." *Modern Drama* 28 (1985): 659–69.

Petit, Jacques. "Structures Dramatiques dans *Le Balcon* et *Les Negres* de Genet." *L'Onirisme et L'insolite dans le Theatre Francais Contemporain,* edited by Paul Vernois. Paris: Klincksieck, 1974.

Phillips, Gene D. *The Films of Tennessee Williams*. Philadelphia: Arts Alliance Press, 1979.

Piemme, Michèle. "Escape Scenique et Illusion Dramatique dans *Le Balcon*." *Obliques* 2 (1972): 23–31.

Pinter, Harold. *The Birthday Party and The Room: 2 Plays by Harold Pinter.* New York: Grove Press, 1977.

———. "Harold Pinter: An Interview." From *Writers at Work,* edited by George Plimpton. New York: Viking Press, 1981.

Politzer, Heinz. "How Epic is Brecht's Epic Theater?" *Modern Language Quarterly* 23 (1962): 99–128.

Popkin, Henry. "The Plays of Tennessee Williams." *Tulane Drama Review* 4 (1960): 45–65.

Porter, Thomas E. *Myth and the Modern American Drama.* Detroit, Mich.: Wayne State University Press, 1969.

Powers, Harvey M. "Theatrical Conventions: The Conditions of Acceptability." *Bucknell Review* 7 (1957): 20–26.

Pucciani, Oreste F. "Tragedy, Genet, and *The Maids.*" *Tulane Drama Review* 7 (1963): 85–92.

Quigley, Austin E. *The Pinter Problem.* Princeton: Princeton University Press, 1975.

Quirino, Leonard. "The Cards Indicate a Voyage on *A Streetcar Named Desire.*" In *Tennessee Williams: A Tribute,* edited by Jac Tharpe. Jackson: Mississippi University Press, 1977.

Rabkin, Norman. *Shakespeare and the Common Understanding.* New York: The Free Press, 1964.

Rasulis, Norman. "Identity and Action in the Revolutionary Worlds of *The Balcony* and *Marat/Sade.*" *Theatre Annual* 30 (1974): 60–72.

Reck, Rima Drell. "Appearance and Reality in Genet's *Le Balcon.*" *Yale French Studies* 29 (1962): 20–25.

Riddel, Joseph N. "*A Streetcar Named Desire*—Nietzsche Descending." *Modern Drama* 5 (1963): 421–39.

Roberts, Patrick. *The Psychology of Tragic Drama.* London: Routledge and Kegan Paul, 1975.

Roberts, Philip. "Tom Stoppard: Serious Artist or Siren." *Critical Quarterly* 20 (1978): 84–92.

Robinson, Gabrielle Scott. "Plays Without Plot: The Theater of Tom Stoppard." *Educational Theater Journal* 29 (1977): 37–48.

Roderick, John M. "From 'Tarantula Arms' to 'Della Robbia Blue': The Tennessee Williams Tragicomic Transit Authority." In *Tennessee Williams: A Tribute,* edited by Jac Tharpe. Jackson: Mississippi University Press, 1977.

Ruskin, Phylllis, and John H. Lutterbie. "Balancing the Equation." *Modern Drama* 26 (1983): 543–53.

Sartre, Jean-Paul. *Saint-Genet Comedien et Martyr.* Paris: Gallimard, 1952.

Schechner, Richard. "The Enactment of the 'Not" in *Les Chaises* of Eugene Ionesco." *Yale French Studies* 29 (1963): 65–72.

———. "Puzzling Pinter." *Tulane Drama Review* 11 (1966): 176–84.

Schivey, Henry. "Madonna at the Poker Night: Pictorial Elements in Tennessee Williams' *A Streetcar Named Desire.*" In *From Cooper to Philip Roth: Essays on American Literature,* edited by J. Bakker and D. R. M. Wilkinson. Amsterdam: Rodopi, 1980.

Schumacher, Ernst. *Die Dramatischen Versuche Bertolt Brechts, 1918–1933.* Berlin: Rutten and Loening, 1955.

———. *Drama und Geschichte. Bertolt Brechts "Leben des Galilei" und Andere Stucke*. Berlin: Henschelverlag, 1968.

Schwartz, Alfred. *From Buchner to Beckett: Dramatic Theory and the Modes of Tragic Drama*. Athens: Ohio University Press, 1978.

Sievers, W. David. *Freud on Broadway: A History of Psychoanalysis and the American Drama*. New York: Heritage House, 1955.

Simard, Rodney. "The Logic of Unicorns: Beyond Absurdism in Stoppard." *Arizona Quarterly* 38 (1982): 37–44.

Simon, Alfred. "La Metaphore Primordiale." *Espirit* 338 (1965): 837–44.

Skloot, Robert. "Submitting Self to Flame: The Artist's Quest in Tennessee Williams, 1934–1954." *Educational Theater Journal* 25 (1973): 199–206.

Sohlich, W. F. "Genet's Drama: Rites of Passage of the Anti-Hero: From Alienated Existence to Artistic Alienation." *Modern Language Notes* 89 (1974): 641–53.

Sokel, Walter H. "Brecht's Concept of Character." *Comparative Drama* 3 (1971): 177–92.

Sorensen, Otto M. "Brecht's *Galileo*: Its Development from Ideational into Ideological Theater." *Modern Drama* 11 (1969): 410–22.

States, Bert O. *Great Reckonings in Little Rooms: On the Phenomenology of Theater*. Berkeley: University of California Press, 1985.

———. "Pinter's *Homecoming:* The Shock of Nonrecognition." *The Hudson Review* 21 (1968): 474–86.

Steer, W. A. J. "Brecht's Epic Theater: Theory and Practice." *Modern Language Review* 63 (1968): 636–49.

Stewart, Harry E. "Jean Genet's Mirror Image in *Le Balcon*." *Modern Drama* 12 (1969): 197–203.

———. "Jean Genet's Preoccupation in *Le Balcon*." *Drama Survey* 7 (1967): 24–30.

Storch, R. F. "Harold Pinter's Happy Failures." *Massachusetts Review* 8 (1967): 703–12.

Strem, George G. "The Theater of Jean Genet: Facets of Illusion—the Anti-Christ and the Underdog." *Minnesota Review* 4 (1964): 226–36.

Styan, J. L. *The Dark Comedy: The Development of Modern Comic Tragedy*. Cambridge: At the University Press, 1968.

Taubes, Susan. "The White Mask Falls." *Tulane Drama Review* 7 (1963): 85–92.

Taylor, Harry. "The Dilemma of Tennessee Williams." *Masses and Mainstreams* 1 (1948): 51–55.

Taylor, John Russell. *Anger, and After: A Guide to the New British Drama*. London: Methuen, 1969.

Taylor, Ronald. *Literature and Society in Germany 1918–1945*. Totowa, N. J.: Barnes and Noble, 1980.

Tischler, Nancy. "The Distorted Mirror: Tennessee Williams' Self-Portraits." *Mississippi Quarterly* 25 (1972): 389–403.

———. *Tennessee Williams: Rebellious Puritan*. New York: Citadel Press, 1961.

Trussler, Simon. *The Plays of Harold Pinter: An Assessment*. London: Gollancz, 1973.

Van Laan, Thomas, "*The Dumb Waiter:* Pinter's Play with the Audience." *Modern Drama* 24 (1981): 498–501.

Vlasopolos, Anca. "Authorizing History: Victimization in *A Streetcar Named Desire*." *Theater Journal* 38 (1986): 322–38.

Vogel, Dan. *The Three Masks of American Tragedy.* Baton Rouge: Louisiana State University Press, 1974.

Walker, Augusta. "Messages From Pinter." *Modern Drama* 10 (1967): 1–10.

Watson, Donald. *Ionesco and His Early Critics.* London: Calder, 1976.

Webbe, William. *Of English Poesie.* In *Elizabethan Critical Essays,* edited by G. G. Smith. London: Oxford University Press, 1904.

Weideli, Walter. *The Art of Bertolt Brecht,* translated by David Russell. New York: New York University Press, 1963.

Wellwarth, George E. "Beyond Realism: Ionesco's Theory of the Drama." In *The Dream and the Play: Ionesco's Theatrical Quest,* edited by Moshe Lazar. Malibu, Calif.: Undena, 1982.

Whitaker, Thomas R. *Fields of Play in Modern Drama.* Princeton: Princeton University Press, 1977.

White, Alfred D. *Bertolt Brecht's Great Plays.* New York: Barnes and Noble, 1978.

Wilcher, Robert. "The Museum of Tragedy: *Endgame* and *Rosencrantz and Guildenstern are Dead.*" *Journal of Beckett Studies* 4 (1979): 43–54.

———. "Tom Stoppard and the Art of Communication." *Journal of Beckett Studies* 8 (1982): 105–23.

Wiles, Timothy J. *The Theater Event: Modern Theater and Performance.* Chicago: University of Chicago Press, 1980.

Willett, John. *The Theatre of Bertolt Brecht: A Study from Eight Aspects.* London: Methuen, 1960.

Williams, Tennessee. *A Streetcar Named Desire.* New York: New Directions, 1947.

———. *Where I Live: Selected Essays,* edited by Christine Day and Bob Woods. New York: New Directions, 1978.

Wulbern, Jilian H. *Brecht and Ionesco: Commitment in Context.* Urbana: University of Illinois Press, 1971.

Yacowar, Maurice. *Tennessee Williams and Film.* New York: Frederick Ungar, 1977.

Zadek, Peter. "Acts of Violence." *New Statesman* 53 (1957): 658–70.

Zeifman, Hersh. "Comedy of Ambush: Tom Stoppard's *The Real Thing.*" *Modern Drama* 26 (1983): 139–49.

Index